[redacted]

PITTSBURGH SPORTS

PITTSBURGH SPORTS

STORIES FROM THE STEEL CITY

EDITED BY **RANDY ROBERTS**

UNIVERSITY OF PITTSBURGH PRESS

Published by the University of Pittsburgh Press, Pittsburgh, Pa., 15260

Manufactured in the United States of America
Printed on acid-free paper
10 9 8 7 6 5 4 3 2 1

ISBN 0-8229-5773-6

CONTENTS

INTRODUCTION

RANDY ROBERTS

THERE ARE TWO sides to every story, but if you ask me, Pittsburgh was on the side of the angels. Of course, Philadelphia thought otherwise. The controversy was a direct result of the muddled nature of professional baseball in the late nineteenth century. In 1890 the players, tired of grumbling over their low salaries and the imperious attitudes of the owners, formed their own league. The Players League, owned and run by both players and investors, was something new in professional sports and American industry. For many it seemed like a workers' paradise, and players abandoned their old teams to join the new organization. But their paradise was soon lost in a jumble of scheduling problems, outside competition, internal disputes, and a nagging lack of money. After one season the league folded.

The question was what to do about the renegade players. Were they "hot-headed anarchists" banned from organized baseball, or were they protocapitalists at liberty to negotiate as free agents? The owners pondered the question, and then decided that there were simply too many outlaw players to banish them all but that their treasonable actions should not in any way work to their benefit. The solution the owners decided upon was simple: Each club retained the rights to the players who had competed for them before the revolt. All they had to do was to send to the National Board a list of reserve players and surplus players. The reserve players would be theirs; the surplus players would be redistributed to other teams.

Philadelphia of the American Association sent in their list, which inexplicably did not include Louis Bierbauer, who had been a star player for the 1889 Athletics squad before jumping to the Players League in 1890. Seeing an opportunity, the management of the National League Pittsburgh Nationals seized it, signing second-baseman Bierbauer to a contract. The howls in Philadelphia were heard across the Appalachians at the other end of the state. Athletics fans dubbed Nationals owner J. Palmer O'Neill "J. Pirate O'Neill," and the signing caused quite a row between the National League and the American Association, leading directly to a trade war between the two organizations.

But that's another story. For Pittsburgh, the episode resulted only in a new name for its baseball team and a reputation. To the rest of baseball, it was a city of pirates, a town so obsessed with the bottom line that anything was acceptable. And so it seemed with Pittsburgh itself—a city run by pirates for the benefit of pirates. How else could one explain the physical landscape of the town?

In the late nineteenth century and much of the first half of the twentieth century, Pittsburgh's leaders seemed so devoted to the production of steel and the accumulation of wealth—to the bottom line and their own pockets—that they allowed their city to develop willy-nilly, a maze of crooked streets sneaking over and around hills, rivers, and factories. Day and night, those same factories, temples to American industrialism, belched fire, smoke, and ash, covering the city in an unforgettable blanket of filth. It was appalling. Journalists compared Pittsburgh to "hell" or some terrible cavity in Dante's *Inferno*. Pittsburgh was "filthy," they said; Pittsburgh was "ugly" and "squalid" and "oppressive." And more, it was a symbol, argued historian Roy Lubove, "synonymous with the spectacular advance of American industry, and the byproducts: labor unrest, poverty, assimilation of a heterogeneous immigrant labor force, and disruption of community cohesion."

But the men bred in those factories were special. They made steel, steel to fill millions of railroad cars, steel to build the infrastructure of a nation. They were in a double sense *steel men,* because in the process of making steel they remade themselves. The heat, back-breaking physical labor, and danger of the factories demanded tough, hard men. If a man wasn't tough, he didn't last, and if he lasted, he became even tougher. He became like what he produced—steel. Even the men who did not work in the factories copped the "steeler" attitude. One longtime resident of the city described it perfectly: "Back in the thirties, forties, fifties you could walk into a bar and maybe not see one smiling face. Maybe not one. I'll tell you what would raise a few smiles, though. If some new punk swaggered into a bar full of himself, men would look at him with a 'who-the-hell-are-you' smile. Then someone would say something and then, Bam! it was go time."

Steel men demanded steel heroes, and the greatest Pittsburgh athletes and teams conformed to the temper of the city. Even the names of the players were steel hard—Bill Mazeroski, Harry Greb, Mike Ditka, and Fritzie Zivic. The names carried freight—steel names, railroad names, coal names. That toughness, that steel-worker, no-nonsense fatalism became the dominating characteristic of Pittsburgh sports. Pittsburghers young and old followed the exploits of their best athletes, measuring their toughness against the grit of their heroes. Real old-timers recalled Big Poison and Little Poison—Paul and Lloyd Waner—who took the Pirates to the World Series in 1927, only to be swept by the New York Yankees of Babe Ruth and Lou Gehrig. Revenge came in 1960 when Bill Mazeroski's seventh-game, ninth-inning homer stuck a knife in the heart of the Eastern Establishment Yankees in their Wall Street pinstripes.

Over the last century the city's teams occasionally enjoyed spectacular success. Barney Dreyfuss's Pirates won three straight pennants early in the century, then in the second half of the century the Pirates claimed World Series championships in 1960, 1971, and 1979. Before Jackie Robinson broke the "color line" in baseball, the Homestead Grays and Pittsburgh Crawfords were two of the finest teams in the Negro Leagues. Art Rooney's Steelers, after decades of frustration, built one of football's greatest dynasties under coach Chuck Noll and won Super Bowl championships in 1974, 1975, 1978, and 1979. The Penguins, latecomers on the Pittsburgh sports scene, blossomed in the 1980s and 1990s; led by the brilliant play of Mario Lemieux they won Stanley Cup championships in 1991 and 1992.

And some of the greatest athletes of the century played in Pittsburgh uniforms, players whose names will outlive their deeds—James "Cool Papa" Bell, Josh Gibson, and Satchel Paige; Roberto Clemente, Willie Stargell, and Barry Bonds; Joe Greene, Franco Harris, and Terry Bradshaw. Johnny Unitas, Joe Namath, Jim Kelly, Joe Montana, and Dan Marino passed through Western Pennsylvania high schools on their way to NFL glory. Mike Ditka, Tony Dorsett, Cookie Gilchrist, and hundreds of others also left trails of bloody noses and broken bones. Maurice Stokes, Jack Twyman, Maurice Lucas, Norm Van Lier, and Pete Maravich played hoops in the area. Arnold Palmer, Billy Conn, Harry Greb—they were men who helped to define their sports and times.

But for all the success, following Pittsburgh teams has more often than not meant living with frustration and the realization that things probably would not be any better the next year. The pre-Renaissance Steelers, the hapless Bucs, the Pitt teams that played patsy for Notre Dame and Penn State—these, too, are part of the Pittsburgh sports tradition, perhaps even the most important part. They taught steel workers and immigrants and other Pittsburghers about losing and life and fighting the good fight, the good fight against long odds and almost certain defeat. Harvey Haddix pitched twelve innings of perfect baseball against the Milwaukee Braves on May 26, 1959, only to lose the game in the thirteenth on a Joe Adcock home run. But Haddix never looked back with regret. "It's because I lost that makes it interesting," he said. It's because, in the end, he—and the others who played in the sun and rain and snow, under dim gym lights and the white lights of modern auditoriums—is like the rest of us because we care.

Pittsburgh Sports is about those players and those teams, about the champions and the championships as well as the losers and the failures. But it is not a laundry list of victories won and opportunities squandered. Nor is it a history of sports in Pittsburgh. Instead, it is a collection of essays, all grounded firmly in history, several anchored in personal experience as well. Together they suggest that sport is both impersonal and personal, objective and subjective. When we, the Pittsburgh faithful, watch a Steeler game on television, we see generally the same thing. Announcers and instant replay almost guarantee a uniform viewing experience. But when we try to describe why we love the Steelers or Pirates or Penguins—or a high school team or a boxer or any area athlete—we dip into our memories and ladle out something highly personal. Then it's not about what is on television, but what is in our hearts. And that is what makes it interesting.

The goal of *Pittsburgh Sports* is to give a sense of the history, range, and emotional impact of the city's sporting experience. Each piece can be read independent of the others, but each also adds to the whole. Some are more personal: Frank Lambert describes his years as a punter for the pre-Renaissance Steelers; Harold Tinker discusses with Rob Ruck his life in Pittsburgh's African American community and career in the Negro Leagues; Randy Roberts details how his father instructed him in the history and lore of Pittsburgh boxers Fritzie Zivic, Harry Greb, and Billy Conn; Richard Peterson exposes his misspent—or wisely spent—youth sneaking into Pittsburgh sporting events and following the city's teams; Laurie Graham meditates on her lifelong love of the Pirates; and Brooks Simpson traces how he became a fan of the Penguins.

Other of the essays are firmly grounded in history and narrative: Paul Zbiek explores the history of western Pennsylvania high school football; Thomas Schott revisits the careers of the Waner brothers and the early century successes of the Pirates; Aram Goudsouzian examines the legacy and meaning of the Pirates of Roberto Clemente, Willie Stargell, Dock Ellis, and Dave Parker; Rob Ruck recounts the life and world of Art Rooney; and Chris Elzey traces the short, glorious history of the Pittsburgh Pipers of the American Basketball Association. Taken together, the stories reflect some of the triumphs and defeats of Pittsburgh teams and players, but more than that they suggest what it is about the city's sports that commands our passion—why what happens at a ballpark, stadium, gym, rink, or locker room has the power to make us laugh, swear, and cry. Why, in the end, it has the pull to make us care.

1

BETWEEN THE WHALE AND DEATH

RANDY ROBERTS

NOT LONG AGO I heard the familiar opening of the Gillette Cavalcade of Sports song, and it took me back to Friday and Saturday nights when I used to sit close to my dad watching boxers on a black-and-white TV and listening to his tales of Fritzie Zivic. He—my dad—was overweight and bent by rheumatism and something called Marie-Strumpell disease. He walked with a cane and slept sitting upright on a mammoth pillow, and I think he lived in constant pain. But it didn't touch his eyes, which were blue and pleasant, particularly when he told stories about Fritzie, Pittsburgh, and Josie the Whale.

The first tales I remember were about the whale. He told them at dusk after fine, long summer days as shadows lengthened into night. He told them to my two brothers and me, and no Homer ever had a more rapt audience. We listened to every word, imagining the world of Josie and believing everything he told us. We just assumed that he knew what he was talking about, not only because he was our dad but because he had been a lifeguard before World War II and had served as an underwater welder during the war. Dressed in one of those Jules Verne outfits with the bubbled, windowed headgear, he had descended far beneath the surface of the ocean and did something with torches to sunken ships. Now exactly how one could light a torch underwater was as mysterious to me then as it is now. I have never tried to discover anything about the process, content to allow it to remain as a symbolic reminder that there are limits to human knowledge. Anyway, it seemed to my younger brother and me—and we discussed it in our bedroom long after we were tucked in and the light was turned out—that any man who had been a lifeguard *and* served in the Navy was fully conversant with things nautical, a category that included whales and such.

I really should say something more about my dad. He lived then, as he still does, in a mythical world, one consisting entirely of vague memories, stories, rumors, and wild speculations. The lining of his heart must have been about as thick as tissue paper, rendering him hopelessly prone to heart attacks. And back in the days before heart transplants, bypass surgery, artificial hearts, angioplasty, and whatever else they can do today, there was not much a father could do about a bad ticker, except, I guess, stop smoking and lose weight, two palliatives that my dad failed at miserably. The point of this medical aside is that when I was seven or eight his heart began to fail. He had a series of heart attacks—maybe six or seven—and spent considerable time in the hospital. Toward the end he couldn't work or even negotiate steps very well; in fact, he vacated his second-floor bedroom and spent all his time on a hospital bed in the living room. I think he probably did this so he could remain in the center of the family and watch TV with us at night. When I was twelve and my brother was ten, he died—died in the hospital in the early morning of Saturday, November 16, 1963.

That morning when my mom told me he died was sad. It is still sort of a blur, but I think I remember that aunts and uncles materialized out of thin air and there was plenty of food to eat. He was buried on Wednesday, and I think I went back to school on Thursday, though I don't really remember. But I do remember Friday, or at least a few minutes of Friday afternoon. I was in seventh grade, and the senior high had a rehearsal for a play scheduled to open that night for long-suffering parents and patient relatives. We, the junior highers, were given the choice of attending the rehearsal or going to our regular classes. No-brainer, right? I went and did what I expect every other male seventh-grader did—talk with friends, throw spitballs, check out the eighth- and ninth-grade girls, and generally make a lout of myself.

Then—and this is the moment I remember clearly—a teacher came on stage and said the president had been shot. Everyone laughed, suspecting it was the subplot of the drama that none of us was paying the slightest attention to. The teacher said it again, and we laughed again. Slowly, though, he impressed upon our smiling faces that what he was saying was not part of the play and that John Kennedy really had been shot. With that the show went on, at least until the same teacher walked on stage again and told us that the president was dead. Then I'm not sure the play did go on. I'm not sure what I thought or what I did next or how I got home. I just know that I didn't go back to school for almost a week, and that the same aunts and uncles and cousins again mysteriously reappeared around the house. And I still have trouble separating in my mind my own personal loss with the larger national loss. It was almost as if watching Kennedy's funeral on TV I was watching my own dad's funeral.

But the fact that my dad had his first heart attack at thirty-five and died at forty doesn't really tell much about him, except to a cardiologist. If his death became confused during our national tragedy, his life is also shrouded. He was born in Pittsburgh, but for some reason at some point he got himself deported to New Kensington, a factory town slightly to the northeast of the 'Burgh. I don't know why or when, and neither does my mother. Perhaps he absconded with the church funds; maybe he ran off with a senator's wife; I hope he didn't kill a man. I'm fairly confident that he didn't move to New Kensington for the waters of the Allegheny River, which as I recall were Coke-bottle green except for the areas right around the factories. There the waters were a thick, sluggish gray. I do know that before the war he played football for New Kensington, lifeguarded, and then worked in a factory. He probably thought his life was pretty well set. But the war changed all that. After it ended he spent time in a veterans' hospital, and there was no chance that he would ever lifeguard or work in a factory again. But he was smart, and aided by the GI Bill he went through the University of Pittsburgh in a flash and became an accountant.

But nobody my dad knew in Pittsburgh and New Kensington was ever just one thing. It seemed to me growing up that by definition a man was a person who could do many things, and any male who just did one thing was incomplete. My uncles, for example, could drive trucks, repair engines, build houses, and fix just about anything. My dad's friends—men with names like Eddie George and Nick Eddie, and nicknames like Sailor and Marine Ed—did many vaguely defined things. My mother used to tell me that this or that one worked in the big Alcoa mill, but they never seemed to go to work, and their nondescript homes were filled with all sorts of good things to eat and games to enjoy. They luxuriated in a universe of unemployed abundance, laughed a lot, and really seemed to enjoy life, though occasionally they would leave their homes and families for a few years.

Exactly what these men had to do with my dad I am not quite sure. The thought never crossed my mind when I was young. I've got a few hunches now. What I know with some degree of certainty is that my dad—Pitt grad with "almost" a master's in economics—ended up in Democratic politics. He ended up there, I think, shortly after I was born. And because he ended up there we ended up in Camp Hill, just across the Susquehanna River from the state capitol in Harrisburg. At the age of five I was an exile, separated from all save my nuclear family, cast adrift in a sea of Republican Penn State, Philadelphia Phillies, and Philadelphia Eagles fans, people who called pop "soda," John L. Sullivan "John L. Sul-li-vin," duntun "downtown," gumbands "rubberbands," and insisted upon extracting the *r* from "warsh" and "Warshington." They didn't even have a plural of "you," and cocked their heads a bit when I said, "Watch yunz guys doin'?" Odd WASPish people, really. They were friendly, but in a colder way, never laughing from the belly like Sailor and Marine Ed.

It was not so much that I thought I was out of place in Camp Hill; I *knew* I was out of place. The teams I pulled for—and just assumed everyone else in America pulled for as well—were the Pitt Panthers, Pittsburgh Steelers, and Pittsburgh Pirates. Conversations with new friends proved my innocent assumption groundless. Added to this was the fact that my dad was a Democratic politician in a town that went 87 percent for Goldwater in 1964 and most likely 100 percent for Eisenhower in 1952 and 1956. The notion that "Everybody Likes Ike" undoubtedly originated in Camp Hill. Why this was so, I don't know. Perhaps it was because the army of Robert E. Lee was in Camp Hill when it swung south toward Gettysburg, a sort of we-were-that-close-to-being-sacked-by-them-damn-Confederate-Democrats-and-saved-only-by-the-Party-of-Lincoln. Or maybe it was because wealthy Camp Hill residents nursed grudges against Roosevelt for the 1935 "Soak the Rich" revenue act. But whatever the reason, except for my friend Bobby Chrencik whose father worked with his hands, everyone I knew was a Republican. This first hit me in 1960 when a straw poll in my third-grade class at Lincoln Elementary School—a name, incidentally, that supports my Civil War thesis (the other two elementary schools named after presidents in Camp Hill were Hoover and Eisenhower; not even a bone thrown to a Democrat)—went two for Kennedy, everyone else for Nixon. Bobby and I just shook our heads, feeling a bit sad, I guess, for Mr. Kennedy and his lovely wife.

My dad tried to compensate for my family's otherness by giving my brothers and me life lessons in the guise of stories. He was one of the world's great storytellers, at least that's how I have preserved him in my memory. The earliest tales I remember were of Josie the Whale. Now as my dad told it, Josie was a most extraordinary whale who could be counted on when a sailor "got into a pinch." And thinking about the stories, I can only conclude that my dad must have been a singularly maladroit sailor who spent most of his career in the Navy getting into and out of pinches. Every story began with him getting into a pinch. Perhaps he was watching a sunset and forgot to "go below" when his submarine dived beneath the sea, or was concentrating on a poker game and fell overboard when his destroyer hit a Pacific wave "as big as the Empire State Building," or was repairing a battleship "one hundred miles under the sea" when a shark bit through his "hundred-mile air hose." Whatever the case, it was always dire.

At this point when the three Roberts boys were so afraid that he might not survive that we allowed our ice cream to drip onto our hands, his stories became interactive. "So I thought to myself," he would muse with a contemplative air, "should I call Josie or shouldn't I call Josie?" And we, his Greek chorus, would shout, "Call Josie! Call Josie!" only to be cut short with a stern "Who's telling this story, you or me?" That would shut us up, and we would draw our knees and arms together in suspenseful and eager anticipation.

Now why not call Josie, you might ask? That's where the life lesson came in. It seems to me now that he was telling us that in this world there are no free rides, no fairy godmothers, and nobody gets nothin' for nothin'. Maybe he was talking about his life, maybe about his political universe. But one thing was as certain as taxes: Josie was nobody's dupe. Oh sure, he could get my dad out of his pinch, but there was always the bill. Josie, evidently, was the Earl Long of whales, functioning by a strict "You goose me and I'll goose you" code.

My brothers and I loved Josie's bill. My dad had a weakness for large quantities of food, and he could eat more than any person I knew, but even he was not in the same league as Josie. That whale's appetite was gargantuan; it was Homeric. When my dad called Josie, the whale would be on the spot instantaneously, but the mere act of that superwhale response seemed to light his gastronomic fires. "Sure, I can get you out of your pinch," he invariably whined, "but I'm awfully hungry." Then it started, a string of demands that would have strained the powers of Hercules. Fifty dumptrucks of French fries, seventy boxcars of cheeseburgers, ninety barges of hot dogs, a hundred sixteen-wheelers of ice cream—just chocolate and vanilla, for no self-respecting whale would eat strawberry. Then, when we had reached the limits of our culinary knowledge, my dad would add, "And Josie was just getting started."

My dad's pinch varied from story to story, but Josie's demands remained remarkably constant, though I suspect the numbers changed. If my dad left any of the basic food groups—cheeseburgers, hot dogs, French fries, and ice cream—unmentioned, his chorus would immediately chime, "What about the hot dogs?" or "What about the ice cream?" only to be stopped dead with "Who's telling this story, you or me?" Only the boldest cricket would make a sound after that withering admonition.

As my brothers and I grew older, my father began to tell us about Pittsburgh—I suspect to remind us that our roots were not embedded in the Republican soil of Camp Hill. His father, I think, was a Welsh coal miner—or son of a Welsh coal miner—who died very young. That was really all I ever remember hearing about my paternal granddad, until after my dad's only sister died and the family papers, meager as they were, were sent to me. I surmise that my relatives thought that as a historian and writer I might be interested in them. They were right. From the few documents I gathered that my granddad's name was Charles, that he was born in 1897 and died in 1929, and that on three separate occasions he had enlisted in and been honorably discharged from the U.S. Army. From his discharge papers I learned that he had served with Gen. John "Black Jack" Pershing during the Mexican Border campaign, with the American Expeditionary Force on the Western Front during the Great War, and with the joint American–Western European force that landed in Murmansk and Archangel in an effort to "influence" the Russian Revolution—altogether an interesting trifecta. But since he died when my dad was only five, he played no part in my father's dramas and I don't know what he did, saw, or thought about any of the places he visited in uniform.

Pittsburgh seemed more interesting to my dad than the circumstances of his own family, and he passed on a greater sense of place than personal history. Camp Hill lives in a perpetual summer sunshine of perfect lawns and the smell of freshly mowed grass. It is an old, small town with a quaint main street, agreeable parks, and pleasant homes. During the time I served there local Blue Laws prohibited bars and the sale of alcohol, and the main duty of policemen seemed to be finding dogs who had wandered away from their homes and corraling teenagers who were out past curfew. It was a town without locked doors, where nobody lived more than a short bicycle ride from anybody else, and realtors did not sell to Jews and blacks.

The Pittsburgh of my dad's memory was a dark, strange dreamscape. Since he was fatherless at a young age, I entertained some vague impression that Pittsburgh adopted and raised him, nurturing him in a placenta of soot. I now know that for some seventy-five years Pittsburgh shocked and appalled visitors, most of whom insisted upon informing the rest of humankind that the city should be shunned. "It looked like hell, literally," said the American communist journalist Lincoln Steffens, echoing an earlier description of Pittsburgh as "Hell with the lid taken off" by writer James Parton, who may or may not have been a communist. To English novelist Anthony Trollope it was "the blackest . . . place I ever saw." To writer H. L. Mencken it was a landscape "so dreadfully hideous, so intolerably bleak and forlorn, that it reduced the whole aspiration of men to a macabre and depressing joke." It was a city of smokestacks and mills, a steel, coke, and ugly town.

To hear my dad talk, though, it was a land fully magical, filled with shadows and streetlights that had to be turned on at noon. His Pittsburgh was not a wretched place at all; if anything, it was recherché. When I later read about Sherlock Holmes's fog-drenched London or looked at misty Carot landscapes, my thoughts eased toward his description of Pittsburgh. Somehow I never connected the city's peculiar lighting with the pollution that its factories belched. I recall him saying that it was a "land of silhouettes," and imagined it as a place where nothing was ever seen distinctly, where people moved by each other invisibly, and buildings always appeared incomplete, some with bases that ended abruptly after a few stories, others with tops that seemed to sprout out of clouds. Occasionally a person might spy the top of a bridge, but mostly the rivers seemed flooded by a lighter river of fog. And, of course, all sounds were appropriately disjointed—streetcars bumping along muffled tracks, the novocained peal of church bells, voices that never got nearer, only faded away. My dad could not have described a place more unlike sunny Camp Hill, or more apt to transfix my imagination. I date my love of low, overcast skies and foggy days to his tales.

I coveted that singular image of Pittsburgh until some time during my junior year in college. Then I happened across a history of Pittsburgh with hundreds of photographs and text by a number of noted historians. The text portion was about what one would expect from such books, a sort of onward-and-upward saga of a great city, where dedicated leaders solved problems and progress triumphed. The soul of the work, however, was the pictures and the marvelous captions written by editor Stefan Lorant. The chapter that caught my attention focused on Pittsburgh between the wars, the magical period of my dad's youth. And there it was, everything he had said—a photograph of Wood Street at 3 P.M. with streetlights burning into the fog and looking eerily like 3 A.M.; a noon street scene where the smog has transformed everyone into silhouettes; a postcard called HIGH NOON where everything is black except the whites of a few people's eyes. Everything considered, the photographs were enough to make me wonder if somewhere in the blue Pacific there was a hamburg-eating whale.

Lorant's captions captured the mood of the images. Under one congested street scene he noted,

> The city grew into a jungle. The skies were dark. Traffic was in a snarl. The days seemed like nights. White shirts turned into black in minutes. There was smoke and smog and grime.

In another photograph that is so misty I initially thought a row house was an old Mississippi steamboat and a street was the edge of a river, Lorant commented,

> There was an eternal mist, and everlasting fog in the air. The silhouettes of the buildings and those of boats were soft, at times hardly visible, more felt than seen. The figures of humans as they walk through the streets seemed unreal, like a fairyland. The world was quiet, one could hardly hear the steps of the men who emerged from the fog, coming out of nowhere and disappearing into nowhere. The city had about it a dreamlike quality—a fantastic and romantic paradise for photographers and painters.

The captions read like one of my dad's tales, though how he forgot the white shirt detail is somewhat mysterious.[1]

Maybe he didn't mention anything about shirts—white or black—because Pittsburgh's peculiar conditions were not an end in themselves; rather, they added atmospheric details that served a grander narrative. You had to know something about Pittsburgh to understand the sort of men that it produced, and you had to understand the sort of men that it produced before you could understand the handful of Pittsburgh men who became gods and champions—or champions and gods, they were really the same thing in my dad's eyes. They were boxers, these gods, with names like Harry Greb, Billy Conn, and Fritzie Zivic. I don't know where my dad developed his love of boxing, and I don't know whether he passed it on to me or just told me stories about Pittsburgh fighters because he noticed that I was fascinated by the sport. And, quite frankly, I don't care which—chicken or egg—came first. I'm content with the memory of sitting close to him watching the *Friday Night Fights,* which provided the perfect context for his Pittsburgh narratives.

As I said, I don't know how or why he came to boxing. He must have fought some before the war because I recall him telling me about boxing in the Navy. In one fight he battled a "real fighter," smaller and lighter than himself, who put him in such a pinch that not even Josie could help him. "He kept his chin tucked behind his shoulder and never looked at my head or hands," I clearly remember him saying. "Just watched my feet and knew from them everything I was trying to do." The idea that a fighter could watch another fighter's feet and know when he was going to throw a right or a left, a jab or a roundhouse, appealed to me enormously. I hadn't the slightest notion of the physics of the process—nor, I suspect, had my dad—but I had no doubt that such mapping was possible. Maybe that was why the sport was dubbed "the sweet science." I often thought about how it was done, and tried it several times with painful results during my own youthful pugilistic career.

One thing that made me certain that it was possible was the stories my dad told me about Harry Greb. Born in the Garfield section of the city, Greb was the perfect prototype of a Pittsburgh fighter—tough, smart, dirty, odd, and . . . well, real tough. He started fighting professionally in 1913 and stopped when he died in 1926. *The Ring Record Book and Boxing Encyclopedia* lists 294 fights for Greb, but like most boxers of his era he probably fought many more. And he battled and defeated most of the best middleweights and light-heavyweights of his day—such men as George Chip, Jack Dillon, Frank Klaus, Battling Levinsky, Gunboat Smith, Tommy Gibbons, Tommy Loughran, Tiger Flowers, Mickey Walker, and the great Gene Tunney, the man who took the heavyweight crown from Jack Dempsey himself. He fought in a style that bordered on savage, an all-out attack that involved the offensive use of his fists, elbows, knees, thumbs, head, and teeth. If he could have figured out a way to clobber his opponent with his Adam's apple I'm sure he would have used that part of his anatomy as well. As Greb—nicknamed the "Human Windmill" or the "Pittsburgh Windmill"—liked to say, "Prize fighting ain't the noblest of arts, and I ain't its noblest artist."[2]

My dad gave me the general outlines of Greb's career, but I searched for confirmation in books and magazines about fighters. If sixteenth-century Protestants learned to read so that they could interpret the Bible, I mastered the mystery of words so that I could study the history of boxing. In Tunney's autobiography—one of the very few boxer autobiographies that was probably written by the fighter himself—Greb received high praise. "Few human beings have fought each other more savagely or more often than Harry Greb and I. We punched and cut and bruised each other in a series of bouts, five of them."

Writing more than a decade after he retired, Tunney said that the memory of his first fight with Greb remained "terrifying." Tunney climbed into the ring that night with hands that had been fractured and "imperfectly mended." A trainer shot the sore and swollen hands full of Novocain just to allow Tunney to compete. To make matters worse, a sparring partner had cut Tunney's left eye during a training session, and it too had healed imperfectly, forcing the same needle-happy trainer to inject it with adrenaline chloride to prevent it from "bleeding too much if reopened by Greb's punches." Unfit but numbed, Tunney answered the opening bell and stepped into a nightmare.

"In the first exchange of the fight, I sustained a double fracture of the nose which bled continually until the finish," Tunney noted factually, robbing Greb of all agency by his shameful use of the passive voice. "Toward the end of the first round, my left eyebrow was laid open four inches. I am convinced that the adrenaline solution that had been injected so softened the tissue that the first blow or butt I received cut the flesh right to the bone. In the third round another cut over the right eye left me looking through a red film. For the better part of twelve rounds I saw a red phantomlike form dancing before me."[3]

Greb won the first fight, and the American Light-Heavyweight title with it. Tunney did better in their next four bouts. In their last match Tunney had Greb in trouble, and during a clinch Harry mumbled, "Gene, don't knock me out."

"Pain and punches meant nothing to him—the cruel mauling, the bruising punishment," Tunney commented. "But Harry, hopelessly beaten, didn't want the folks back home to read that he had been knocked out. I was never paid a higher tribute. Here was one of the gamest and greatest fighters of all time laying down on his shield, admitting defeat and knowing that I would not expose him."

Between my dad and Tunney I obtained a pretty complete portrait of Greb. My dad knew somebody who knew somebody who had kind of known Greb, and what filtered down to him was that Harry had been as mean as a hornet. "Would fight anybody at any time for money or just to fight" was the way I heard it.

Tunney also suggested that Greb was inclined toward moodiness, adding that he was "oddly vain" as well. "He was concerned about his looks. Strange that anyone so careful of his face should have selected prizefighting for a profession." But that was Greb, and before each fight he carefully slicked down and combed his hair, then powdered his face with a powder puff. In his own unique style, Tunney commented, "this was one of the strangest eccentricities I ever observed in the realm where fists thud into the human visage."

Tunney and my dad disagreed about the end of Harry Greb. The great fighter said that vanity did in Harry: Greb was so sensitive about his flat fighter's nose that two months after he retired, "like an aging society beauty, he resorted to plastic surgery." The operation killed him. My dad said that the operation that killed Harry Greb involved his eyes. "By the time he retired, Harry Greb couldn't see anything out of one eye and hardly anything out of the other," my dad said. I imagined that Greb—not unlike the foot-watcher my dad fought in the Navy—was so good that he had some sixth sense, that he just knew when to duck and when to swing, that like the blind pinball player in the musical *Tommy* he boxed by a sense of touch. All that the *Ring Record Book* says for the end of Greb is "Died, October 22, 1926, Atlantic City, N.J., following an operation."

I never got a chance to raise this point with my dad, and I still have no doubt that Greb did fight practically blind, but I suspect that Tunney was right about the operation. For one thing Tunney knew Greb; my dad was only three years old when Greb died. But even more convincingly, I can't imagine why anyone would go to Atlantic City for an eye operation. To New York City or Boston, sure. But Atlantic City? A guy goes there for a vacation, and perhaps after a day on the beach, an evening gambling, a night with a woman, and a few too many drinks, a nose job sounds like a good idea. I think that even Harry Greb would have put more thought into an operation to restore his sight. (In fairness to Atlantic City, the fate of Tiger Flowers should be noted. Flowers was a fine middleweight who in 1926 took the title from Greb. He was the last person Greb fought. The next year, however, he too needed an operation and had it performed in New York City, with the same results as Greb's. So maybe the moral for the 1920s was that middleweights should avoid operations.)

Oddly, I remember my dad talking more about Greb, a fighter of his dad's generation, than Billy Conn, the darling of Pittsburgh boxing in the 1930s and 1940s. Of course, he discussed the night of June 18, 1941, when Conn fought Joe Louis for the heavyweight title. Nobody gave Conn a chance. He was only a light-heavyweight, matched against the most lethal heavyweight in the history of the sport. But for that one night Conn was almost perfect, as far into the zone as an athlete is likely to get. For most of the match he stuck and moved, making Louis look slow and vulnerable. At the end of the twelve rounds, Conn was even on one scorecard and ahead on the other two. All he had to do to become the new heavyweight champion was to win one round and not get knocked out.

Conn knew this. The secret to boxing Louis was not getting hit, he later suggested.

> That's the game. Get out of the way. I knew that you had to keep moving from side to side and keep him off balance and never let him get a good shot at you because he was a real dangerous man. Keep away from him. Just move in and out. Feint him out of position and whack him and just keep going. Left hook and a right cross, a left hook to the body and a left hook to the chin—all in the same combination, bing, bang, boom! Real fast, like a machine gun, then get the hell out of the way. . . . But every time that you lead with one hand you have to know to keep the other one up so you don't get hit. You can't let him get set to get a clear, good shot.[4]

In the thirteenth round he forgot. In the previous round he had hurt Louis and the idea of winning by a knockout had invaded his imagination like a Mongol horde. Between rounds he told his cornermen, "I'm going to knock this son of a bitch out. Don't worry about it." Then in the thirteenth he landed a few more good shots. But Louis wasn't hurt nearly as much as Conn suspected. "He was waiting for me. He'd have never hit me in the ass if I didn't make a mistake and try to knock him out." Overconfident, Conn gave Louis an opening, and Joe snatched it. "He hit me about twenty-five real good shots." With two seconds left in the round the referee stopped the fight.

How he almost beat the great Joe Louis became the central tale of Conn's life.

> Of all the times to be a wise guy, I had to pick it against him to be a wise guy. Serves me right. He should have killed me. What a bastard I was. . . . I was twenty-three years old. I didn't have any sense. He was knocking everybody out, see? Here I come along, I'm a middleweight, and I almost kicked his ass for him.

Conn sometimes pondered what defeating Louis would have meant to his life. Maybe he would have held the title for six months or a few years. Maybe he would have been the champion during the war. But Louis tended to discount Conn's ideas. "How was you gonna keep the title for six months when you couldn't keep it for 12 rounds?"

If the Louis-Conn fight was the climax to most stories about Pittsburgh boxers, it was only a prelude to the hero of my dad's grand narrative. "Conn was a great boxer," he would venture. "Should have beaten Joe Louis. Did you know he fought Fritzie Zivic?" That was the name all his fight stories meandered toward. Fritzie Zivic, son of a Croatian immigrant. Fritzie Zivic, whose nose the great sportswriter Red Smith compared to a mine cave-in. Fritzie Zivic, unquestionably the dirtiest fighter ever to scrape his laces across another fighter's cut eye.

The way my dad talked about Fritzie gave me the impression that he knew him personally, but I don't know that for sure. Perhaps he had met Fritzie's father, who owned a saloon in the Lawrenceville section of Pittsburgh. Maybe he knew one of Fritzie's older brothers. Besides Fritzie, there was Pete, Jack, Eddie, and Joe, and all save Joe fought professionally. The two older boys, Pete and Jack, represented the United States in the 1920 Olympics in Antwerp, though neither won a medal. Pete placed fifth in flyweight competition and Jack placed fourth in the featherweight classification. But none of the other Zivic boys went very far as professionals.

"Fritzie Zivic was a Depression fighter," my dad once said. That meant two things. First, he fought often because hard times had shrunken the purses. Zivic began his career in 1931 under the reign of Herbert Hoover, and by 1933, when Franklin Roosevelt took Hoover's title, Fritzie was fighting once or twice a month. Most of his fights took place in Pittsburgh, but as he got better he started to roam, battling in smaller towns such as Holyoke, Kent, Johnstown, Canton, and Steubenville, as well as such fight cities as Chicago, Los Angeles, St. Louis, and New York City. I loved reading the names of his early opponents, names that seemed exotic and wonderful, names of fighters I had never heard of and whose biographies I could invent. Just in 1933 alone he fought U. S. Carpentier, Patsy Henningan, Don Asto, Joe Pimenthal, Gus Vagas, Homer Foster, Vincent Martinez, and Rudy Ayon. That was before he traded blows with Louis Carranza, Perfecto Lopez, Young Joe Firpo, Laddie Tonelli, Johnny Jadick, Kayo Castillo, Dom Mancini, Freddy Chenowyth, Jackie McFarland, Gene Buffalo, Tony Falco, Cleto Locatelli, Gaston LeCadre, and, of course, Eddie Cool. How could I have resisted the sport? In all of Camp Hill, there was not one Carpentier—though there was a "Diamond Jack" Carpenter—to say nothing of a Perfecto Lopez or an Eddie Cool.

Being a Depression fighter also entailed knowing one's craft. Twenty or so matches a year taught boxers how to fight and fighters how to box, and if it didn't, their careers usually ended abruptly in a hospital. Boxing was not without its home-court advantages. When Fritzie was away from Pittsburgh he faced angry spectators, hostile referees, and blind officials, as well as Depression-hardened opponents. Say he was in Pico, California, fighting the aforementioned Rudy Ayon, and Rudy gets "cute" with him. Maybe sticks a thumb in his eye or hits him real low. The referee says he didn't see nothin'. The officials are yawning. The spectators are laughing and cheering. Well, Fritzie had better have a contingency plan or a pipe in his glove. Fritzie eschewed pipes—I think—but he was always ready to fight fire with fire. If an opponent wanted to modify the Marquis of Queensberry rules a touch, that was fine with Fritzie Zivic.

My dad insisted that Fritzie "almost never fought dirty first," but there was something in his blue eyes—and maybe a hint of a smile—

that made me doubt that assertion. Reading about Fritzie did nothing to ease my suspicions. And on the subject of boxing I was something of a savant—my family would say idiot savant. I subscribed to only two magazines, *Boxing Illustrated and Wrestling News* and *The Ring,* and read them more or less from cover to cover, including letters to the editor and the agate-type fight results, but seldom anything on wrestling. Occasionally the name Fritzie Zivic would appear in a story. In 1959, for instance, *Boxing Illustrated* ran a feature entitled, "The Fine Art of Dirty Fighting." It included an action photograph of Zivic as well as a drawing of him with glove-thumb horns sprouting from his head. "You *got* to fight dirty," noted Fritzie. "Look at the three best fighters—Jack Johnson, Jack Dempsey, and Harry Greb. All dirty fighters." Why? "Because fighting is a dirty business, both inside the ring and out."[5]

Every instinct I have, however, tells me that for Fritzie dirty fighting was more than a retaliatory response to overzealous opponents or a rough-and-tumble business. I suspect that, like other Pittsburgh fighters, he was not above a preemptive strike every now and again. That's exactly what my dad hinted had happened in 1936 when Fritzie met Billy Conn. "I didn't see the fight, but I heard that Zivic threw the first low blow" was the way he began the story. I can't remember all the details, but I do recall a rather anatomical discussion of thumbs, elbows, and groins, and of tactics that would have made Fritzie's Olympic brothers turn their heads in shame. Years later, when I decided to check on my dad's—or my—memory, I looked for an account of the fight in the *Pittsburgh Post-Gazette.* There boxing writer Harvey Boyle commented that the match "was to be a nice pleasant boxing bout between pals, but as it worked out, the boys used everything but knives, with the result that the town was treated to as swell a boxing feud as you would care to gaze at."[6]

Conn later remembered the fight as a learning experience. Zivic "was a great teacher," Conn recalled. It "was like going to college for five years, just boxing him 10 rounds. The minute you did something to him, he would holler and scream, you'd have to have the police to keep him quiet. He put an awful face on me, busted me all up with everything. He did everything but kick you."

Zivic recalled that Conn was a smart boxer but "couldn't knock your hat off," a point not lost on Joe Louis. "I thought I won the fight," Zivic insisted. "The referee gave it to me and the papers gave it to me but Conn got the decision of the two judges."[7]

That was the nature of Depression boxing. A fighter fought often, and if he was good he won most of them, but rare was the fighter who won them all. Today's champions are manufactured. On the way to the top they fight toothless once-weres and clawless never-will-bes. They pile victory atop victory like firewood in a shed. The idea is that at some point they will fight for the title with not a blemish on their record. Back then a loss here or there didn't make much of a difference. During the Depression everybody lost sometime, everybody could identify with a losing struggle. Even the great Joe Louis hit the deck before he won the title. And Fritzie Zivic was no Joe Louis. He was knocked out four times in his career, lost sixty-one decisions, and fought ten draws.

That didn't keep him from getting a title shot. On October 4, 1940, he battled Henry Armstrong, one of the finest fighters in the history of the sport, for the welterweight championship of the world. At the end of 1938 Armstrong had held three world's championships—the featherweight, lightweight, and welterweight. He was "Hurricane Hank" or "Homicide Hank," the windup fighter who started punching at the opening bell and just kept on going until the fight ended. He fought and beat the best at a time when the best were around to fight—Baby Arizmendi, Chalky Wright, Barney Ross, Lou Ambers, Ceferino Garcia—names mostly forgotten now but feared then. He even knocked out Fritzie's older brother, Eddie. "None of that bothered Fritzie much," my dad speculated.

Zivic prepared to fight a war in the shadow of a war. The major news of the day featured the German air blitz of England and the Brenner Pass meeting between Adolf Hitler and Benito Mussolini. The two Axis leaders met on the day Fritzie fought to discuss their winter military plans and how they would cope with an American intervention. Given Hitler's passion for boxing, I also like to think that they swapped opinions on the big fight. While foreign correspondents speculated about the outcome of the Brenner conference, New York sportswriters hinted that Fritzie needed a major ally if he hoped to defeat Armstrong. Henry knocked out seven opponents that year, and he was a 4 to 1 favorite to defeat Zivic. Even the *Pittsburgh Post-Gazette* reporters predicted that Zivic would not go the distance.[8]

But upsets did happen, and hope was alive in Pittsburgh—hope that Fritzie Zivic, like Frank Klaus, George Chip, Harry Greb, Teddy Yarosz, and Billy Conn before him, would bring a title home to the city on the three rivers. A large group of locals—including brothers Jack, Eddie, Joe, and Pete—followed Fritzie to Madison Square Garden to cheer him on, and many thousands of others tuned in their radios to the 10 o'clock broadcast of the fight. My dad's storytelling ability always led me to believe that he trained up to the city with "the little, great one," but I don't think he ever really said that. Perhaps he just had a good eye for the radio.

Over 12,000 fans watched Fritzie perform surgery on Henry Armstrong. Less than two weeks before he fought Zivic, Armstrong had defended his title against Phil Furn, winning with a knockout in the fourth round but suffering a cut. The cut was still red and tender when he began his fight with Zivic, but Armstrong's manager was brave and greedy and he wanted the payday. Fritzie went after the eyes, slashing Armstrong with uppercuts and quick, glancing punches designed to peel skin. Zivic later recalled he began the fight with every intention of fighting clean. It wasn't so much that he had had some sort of conversion epiphany on the road to New York, just that he knew Armstrong was a favorite at the Garden and he didn't want to be disqualified for dirty fighting. So he took the pledge: "Today, I will not foul." It was Armstrong that started the rough stuff—so said Fritzie, so said my dad. "He hit me low, choked me, give me the elbow, and everything," Fritzie recalled. Arthur Donovan, the referee, didn't say a thing. In the sixth, Fritzie fell off the wagon. He dug a hook into Armstrong's groin. "Pardon me," he said. He whacked him low again. "Pardon me," he apologized again.

Donovan saw what was happening. Separating the fighters, he said, "If you guys want to fight like this it's okay with me." Fritzie's heart soared. He hiked his trunks up to just below his nipples and went to work on Armstrong's eyes.

> I busted him up, cut him here and cut him there. I'd get him in the clinch. He'd have his head down trying to give you that head,

> I'd come up on the side. When the eye was cut, I'd rub it with the laces to open it up a little bit more. Then he's watching this cut and I'd cut this [other] eye. His mouth was cut real bad. He was too proud to spit the blood out. He swallowed it. Swallowing the blood made him sick.

Armstrong's face and chest were covered with his blood. Zivic's cheeks and shoulders were covered with Armstrong's blood. The upper lids of both of Armstrong's eyes were cut badly, and his eyes swelled so much that he had trouble seeing. He looked like he was fighting with two bruised plums in his eyesockets. But he kept fighting and bleeding. Moments before the final bell ended the contest and his reign as welterweight champion, Fritzie floored Henry. A Pittsburgh sportswriter said that at the end of the fight Armstrong's face "looked like dripping hamburger. . . . He must have been virtually blind from blood and the swelling of his eyes."[9]

Armstrong's memory of the title fight differed from Fritzie's only in culpability. Zivic "was just a nasty fighter, just a foul fighter," Henry recalled. "He did everything foul."[10]

Many of Fritzie's opponents felt the same way. But Zivic never lost a fight on a foul—came close, but never lost one. My dad seemed as proud of that accomplishment as Fritzie was, though the boxer wore the distinction like a badge of honor. "[The public] put a label on me as a dirty fighter, but I never lost a fight on a foul in my life. I'd give 'em the head, choke 'em, hit 'em in the balls, but never in my life used my thumb because I wanted no one to use it on me. But they accused me of that. I used to bang 'em pretty good. You're fighting, you're not playing piano, you know."[11]

But Fritzie did win one fight on a foul. It was his first match after winning the title from Armstrong. It was against Al "Bummy" Davis in the autumn of 1940. Fritzie's wife, Helen, told me that Bummy started the "dirty stuff." I don't know.

My dad never told me about that fight. He died before he got around to it.

2

RINKY DINKS AND THE SINGLE WING

RICHARD F. PETERSON

I DON'T REMEMBER how young I was at the time, but it's easy to see why my first memory of growing up on Pittsburgh's South Side is so vivid. I'm dressed in an Indian outfit, my mother's lipstick streaked on my face for war paint, my headband displaying one proud feather for bravery. As "Pop Goes the Weasel" plays somewhere in the background, I stalk around two diminishing rows of wooden chairs with other costumed children, anticipating the moment when the music stops. It's all great fun, diving into a chair, laughing as some disappointed cowboy or cowgirl, GI Joe or nurse, hobo or fairy princess walks off the floor. But then it happens, the first defining moment of my childhood. The music stops, I scramble for a chair, and one little Indian is eliminated from the game—or, as I clearly recall, one tantrum-throwing little Indian. My reaction to losing was to break out in a howling rage and fling myself to the floor.

As my embarrassed mother and aunt dragged me out of the bingo hall for being such a crybaby and poor sport, I was about to enter a working-class world of school and play where friendships and rivalries were established and defined by the way you competed in games. I was also on the way to becoming a bad-tempered loser just as Pittsburgh's post–World War II baseball and football teams were on the threshold of becoming the worst teams in professional sports. Losing at musical chairs was just the beginning of a boy's life in which playing at games, rather than being a diversion, would become the way of finding identity and pride in a world hostile to the spirit of youth. And as I played ball as if my life depended on it, rooting for Pittsburgh's sports teams became the way of sustaining some dream or hope of a life beyond steel mills and coal fields, even if the teams were as hopeless as the dream itself.

So many of my memories of Pittsburgh in the late 1940s and early 1950s are of playing ball on grassless city fields and poorly surfaced courts or hitchhiking out to Forbes Field, Pitt Stadium, and the Duquesne Gardens to watch the city's sports teams. The seasons of my youth on the South Side flowed by to the rhythm of games played with baseballs and bats held together with masking tape and nails, footballs made of newspapers folded and tied with twine, hockey sticks pieced back together after being shattered and abandoned at Hornet games, and slick-surfaced basketballs often lopsided and bubbled from too much wear. In the spring and summer I lived to play softball and baseball at Ormsby playground and Quarry Field and died watching the rinky-dink Pirates lose game after game. In the autumn I turned to schoolyard and alley football and followed the same old Steelers, at least until life and sports fell off into the dark winter days. Then I reluctantly followed minor-league hockey and college basketball, skated badly on abandoned tennis courts, dribbled away the hours at poorly heated church gyms, and waited for the spring.

Like the poet Donald Hall and countless other baseball Peter Pans, I also have strong memories of playing catch with my father, when we had time for each other, and going out to major league games together. But I can't recall some perfect Field of Dreams moment of playing catch to balance the Halloween nightmare of playing musical chairs or summon from my past some Forbes Field epiphany when I suddenly realized if I didn't become a Pirate some day I'd end up a wino roaming the back alleys and river banks of the South Side in search of my lost youth and bottles for deposit. Playing catch with my father or going out to Pirate games in the late 1940s gave me a chance to spend some time with a man who seldom had anything to say. Rather than cherished moments of magical exchanges and discoveries, my baseball memories of my father stand out because they were the times he was willing to talk about the few things that mattered to him in a life clouded by alcohol.

Gloomy and brooding, my father was an intelligent, unhappy man, a child of immigrant parents and an adolescent of the Great Depression who dropped out of school early, found work in gas stations on the South Side, and tried to drink away his troubles, only to become more miserable as he drank. After a day of fixing flats, greasing cars, and pumping gas, he'd walk around the corner after supper to Kalki's for a familiar barstool and evening drafts of beer, with an occasional boilermaker mixed in if he had the money or if the bartender was in a generous mood toward one of his regulars. By the time my mother was ready to leave for her graveyard shift as a waitress at Rodger's out on Centre Avenue, he'd be back home, seated at the kitchen table with his bottle of Iron City or Fort Pitt, ready to announce, as my mother walked out the door to catch the 77/54 out to Oakland, that going to sleep was the best part of the day.

On those few occasions when my father offered to play catch, he'd gradually open up about his own boy's life on the South Side. As we tossed the ball back and forth, he'd talk about his good old days when, as the Bluetail Kid, he pitched for a Lithuanian team that went up and down the South Side playing against rival Polacks, Hunkies, and Serbs. He told stories about his younger brother, Tony, who was called "Mustard Face" because he loved mustard sandwiches as much as he loved baseball, and his older brother, Joe, who was called "Joky" because he loved cards and dice more than playing ball. My father told me not to worry about being so damn short and skinny because he was puny-looking in his own day. If I took my mother's advice and stayed away from the booze when I grew up, I wouldn't end up with my old man's beer belly and high blood pressure, and if I paid attention I might learn a few things about throwing drops and in-shoots and maybe turn out some day to be a damn good pitcher like Rip Sewell or Murry Dickson or like Frank Petrauskas was a long time ago.

On the occasions when my father took me out to Forbes Field in the late 1940s, he enjoyed talking about the great Pirate teams of the past because there wasn't much to cheer about when watching the Pirates of the present, except for a brief early run at the pennant in

1948. Getting to Forbes Field was always an adventure, dotted with stops at Kalki's on Saturday or the Duquesne Social Club on Sunday. When we finally made it out to Oakland, we also had to stop at the Home Plate Café because they didn't sell beer inside the ballpark. But once inside Forbes Field, I'd watch the Pirates and listen to my father talk baseball at least until the seventh-inning stretch, which was usually my father's signal to head back to the Home Plate Café, where I was to join him after the game was over.

The Pirates were rapidly becoming my bumbling boys of summer, but at least for a while I had my father's stories of great Pittsburgh teams as proof that there was a time—maybe long ago, but a time—when ballplayers in a Pirate uniform could actually play baseball. There were stories about Fred Clarke's Pirates, who lost the first modern World Series in 1903 to Cy Young and the Boston Red Sox, though they were called the Pilgrims in those days; and even better stories about the 1909 Pirates, who beat out Frank Chance, Mordecai "Three Finger" Brown, and the great Chicago Cubs for the National League pennant and won the World Series against the Detroit Tigers. It was fun hearing my father talk about Honus Wagner, who ran circles around Ty Cobb, and about a rookie pitcher named Babe Adams, who won all three of his starts, including a shutout in the seventh game, to give Pittsburgh its first World Series championship in the very first year the Pirates played baseball at Forbes Field.

All that was before my father's time, but not the Pirates of 1925, of Pie Traynor, Max Carey, and Glenn Wright. This was my father's team, the team that played its way past John McGraw's New York Giants into the World Series against the defending champion Washington Senators. Branded cowards by fans and the press after losing three of the first four games, my father's Pirates made baseball history by coming back and beating the great Walter Johnson in the seventh and deciding game of the World Series on Kiki Cuyler's bases-loaded, ground-rule double in the cold, rain, and fog at Forbes Field. Two years later, even with Paul and Lloyd Waner in the outfield, the Pirates lost the World Series in four straight games, but that was against the New York Yankees and Murderers' Row.

Though Forbes Field went out by way of the wrecking ball after Bill Mazeroski recorded the last out of the last game on June 28, 1970,

I can still see the mammoth aging ballpark and still hear my father urging me to take it all in, as if it were the eighth wonder of the world. In his eyes it was still the biggest, best-damn-looking ballpark in baseball. To get a sense of its beauty, he'd tell me look out at the Pitt Cathedral looming majestically behind the left-field bleachers or at the trees in Schenley Park surrounding the red-bricked outfield wall. To get a feel for its size, he'd point at the towering scoreboard topped by the Gruen clock, at the deep recesses in center field, and at the iron gates in right-center field where fans could walk out of the ballpark at the end of the game. He'd tell me to look around at the massive steel and concrete grandstands, double-decked in right field and triple-decked behind home plate where the crow's nest still sat as a sad reminder of the year Gabby Harnett hit the home run that cost the Pirates the 1938 pennant and broke my father's heart.

Forbes Field wasn't some bandbox like Ebbets Field with cheap signs all over the place or the Polo Grounds with its ridiculous cigar shape and "Chinese" (easy) home runs down the lines. My father wasn't happy when they put in the Greenberg Gardens and shortened left field by thirty feet, but Forbes Field still had plenty of room for Rosey Rowswell's doozy marooneys, for doubles down the lines and triples in the alleys. Center field was still so deep that the ground crew rolled the batting cage out to the 457 mark and it rarely interfered with a game. And even when Barney Dreyfuss, the Pirate owner who built Forbes Field, had to shorten right field for a new grandstand, he put up a high screen down the right-field line to prevent cheap home runs. Forbes Field wasn't built for home-run hitters—that's why they had to put the Greenberg Gardens out there in 1947 for Hank Greenberg and Ralph Kiner—but the ballpark was a line-drive hitter's paradise with all its open space. No pitcher, not Babe Adams or Wilbur Cooper, not Dizzy Dean or Carl Hubbell, had ever pitched a no-hitter at Forbes Field and, so far as my father was concerned, no pitcher ever would.

I'm glad my father had his proud memories of Pirates past, because when I looked down with him from the bleachers or the grandstands at Forbes Field we saw a Pirate team on its way to becoming one of the worst franchises in baseball. It was a good thing that my father quit going to games with me after I was old enough to get out to Oakland by myself because the Pirates by the 1950s were the joke of the National League. After finishing last in 1950, the Pirates, like Stalin's Soviet Union, embarked on a five-year plan that doomed Pittsburgh fans to an emotional Siberia. With the fabled and controversial Branch Rickey as the baseball mastermind, the Pirates came in next to last in 1951, Rickey's first year in Pittsburgh, then finished dead last for the next four years. Desperate for success after being forced out of Brooklyn, Rickey was ready to trade anyone to any team willing to deal with him. He got rid of popular players like pitcher Cliff Chambers, infielder George Strickland, and outfielders Wally Westlake and Gus Bell for the likes of bespectacled Dick Cole, who should have worn his glove on his shin, prematurely bald Joe Garagiola, who discovered in last-place Pittsburgh that baseball is a funny game, and banjo-hitting Johnny Berardino, who parlayed a trip to the Pirates' minor-league Hollywood Stars into a successful acting career in television soap operas.

In 1952 I was a die-hard, thirteen-year-old, Knothole-gang witness to a Pirate team that was so awful it became the stuff of legend. One of baseball's all-time disasters, the 1952 Pirates, Rickey's infamous rinky-dinks, ended the season a whopping 22½ games out of seventh place with a record of 42-112. My poor idol Murry Dickson lost twenty-one games as the leader of a staff that used up twenty pitchers, fourteen of them, including minor-league strikeout phenom Ron Necciai, finishing a collective 5-38 for the year. The twenty-six position players included two nineteen-year-old rookies fresh out of Pittsburgh high schools. First baseman Tony Bartirome, destined to become a Pirate trainer after lasting one year in the major leagues, and centerfielder Bobby Del Greco, whom I played softball against in the Greater Pittsburgh League a decade later, combined for one home run and hit .217 and .200 respectively for a team so terrible Joe Garagiola described them as a ninth-place ballclub in an eight-team league.

The only bright spot for the Pirates in 1952 was a sore spot for Branch Rickey, who had a much-deserved reputation for being a tightwad when it came to paying veteran players. Ralph Kiner's home runs may have been the reason a handful of sorrowful Pirate fans still came out to Forbes Field, but Rickey didn't see it that way. The Pirates finished last in 1952 with Kiner and his $90,000 salary and they could damn well finish last in 1953 without him. Rickey's solution was to offer Kiner to Chicago in a ten-player deal that included Garagiola and two other Pirates for six Cubs—five were ex-Dodger farm hands—and $150,000.

On June 4, 1953, when Rosey Rowswell sent word of the Kiner trade out over the radio just before the Pirates and the Cubs were scheduled to play a Ladies' Day matinee, I was shocked by the news and felt betrayed by Rickey. Growing up in a working-class neighborhood, I saw Kiner as a baseball god. Short and skinny, I dreamed that someday I might become a Murry Dickson, but Ruthian Kiner was beyond my baseball fantasies. Like my baseball buddies, I cocked my right elbow at the plate and swung with an uppercut, but we knew that Kiner's towering home runs were the stuff of the Mighty Casey and Ozark Ike. Playing in a shot-and-a-beer, steel-mill town, Kiner was strictly Hollywood. Saying Fords were for singles hitters, he drove Cadillacs, dated starlets, including Elizabeth Taylor, and eventually married tennis professional Nancy Chaffee, who paraded around decaying Forbes Field with her leashed Afghan hounds.

If baseball in the 1950s had a Shakespeare looking to write about a star-crossed team, he could have turned to the Pirates and found plenty of material. Before and after the Kiner trade, the Pirates were the stuff of theater, though mostly low comedy. They even became the subject of a 1951 Hollywood movie called *Angels in the Outfield* in which a hapless Pirate team, led by a foul-mouthed, brawling manager, becomes a pennant winner when the angelic spirits of baseball greats descend upon Forbes Field to help win games as long as the manager keeps his temper.

With no angels in the outfield or anywhere else, my most vivid memories of Rickey's Pirates, as they finished last in 1953 without Kiner and last again in 1954 and 1955, are of inept players and ridiculous plays. There were all those bonus babies and rookie phenoms who should have been arrested for indecent exposure after putting on big-league uniforms. The Pirates signed the basketball All-American O'Brien twins, who flopped badly, and acquired the brothers Freese, who also failed to double the pleasure of Pirate fans. When not signing teenagers, Rickey picked up aging veterans better suited for an old-timers' game, like ex-Yankee slugger Johnny Lindell, who was trying to hang on, without much success, as a knuckleball pitcher, and ex-

Yankee World Series hero Joe Page, who had a 11.17 earned run average in his one hazy season with the Pirates. Even when the Pirates finally crossed baseball's color line and signed African Americans, the players turned out mediocre at best. While other teams had future Hall of Famers like Jackie Robinson, Larry Doby, and Willie Mays, we had Curt Roberts.

While my father grew up watching Hall of Famers Pie Traynor, Max Carey, and the Waner brothers, I'm stuck with vivid nightmares of Gene Freese doing his best impression of Fred Merkle by failing to run down and touch second base on what should have been a game-winning hit against the Phillies; of Tommy Saffell, in an opening-day game against the Dodgers, turning to play a ball off the outfield wall as the ball landed beside him; and of Danny Kravitz, who couldn't catch a foul pop-up behind home plate without a catcher's mitt glued to the top of his head. I listened to Rosey Rowswell re-create Pirate road losses from tickertape accounts of the games, and, on one unforgettable occasion, after high-school baseball practice, heard Bob Prince describe, in a voice of disbelief, the last inning of a game from Wrigley Field in which Sad Sam Jones completed a no-hitter against the Pirates by walking the first three batters, then striking out Dick Groat, Roberto Clemente, and Frank Thomas to end the game.

Although my father had stopped taking me to see the Pirates, he still listened to Rosey Rowswell and Bob Prince on the radio and watched televised games from his stool at Kalki's. Clinging to his own baseball memories, he could no more desert the Pirates than a devoted parent could give up on a child who keeps getting beat up by bullies and keeps bringing home bad grades from school. But the Pittsburgh Steelers were another matter. My father loved college football and talked with pride about poor Jock Sutherland's great Pitt Panther teams, and what a shame it was, Sutherland dying of a brain tumor in early 1948, just two years after taking over the Steelers for Art Rooney. But he refused to spend the money to take me out to Forbes Field for a Steeler game because he thought professional football wasn't always on the up and up. He'd let me go to Kalki's with him to watch the fights on the *Gillette Cavalcade of Sports* and the *Pabst Blue Ribbon Bouts,* and we even watched pro wrestling, which was as phony as Gorgeous

George. But he was not going to watch the Steelers because, as long as pro football used referees from the same region as the home team, the Steelers would get jobbed every time they played on the road.

Occasionally the Steelers justified my father's cynicism by losing a close road game on a questionable call—the National Football League actually changed its system of assigning referees after an unnecessary roughness penalty against the Steelers set up a last-second win for the Los Angeles Rams in 1955—but the Steelers of my youth usually didn't need much help from referees to lose football games. They weren't as awful as the Pirates, but they were consistent losers, the same old Steelers—a hard-luck team bought in 1933 for $2,500 out of Art Rooney's legendary racetrack winnings and plagued for decades by Rooney's cronyism. The Pirates may have bumbled their way through my South Side childhood, but the Steelers, even with some good players and a few great ones, managed to bungle every opportunity for a championship.

In 1941, after enduring eight straight losing seasons, Art Rooney, in response to a newspaper contest, changed his football team's name from the Pirates to the Steelers. When asked by a reporter what he thought of his newly christened Steelers, Rooney answered that they looked like the same team to him—they'd finished 1-9-1 for the year. That tag, "the same old Steelers," would hang around Rooney's neck like an deflated football for the next three decades—and for good reason. In the 1950s pro football entered the golden age of television with revolutionized T-formation offenses led by Sammy Baugh, Otto Graham, Bob Waterfield, and Bobby Layne, but the Steelers, stuck in the 1930s, still ran the obsolete single wing under Sutherland protégé Johnny Michelosen. They actually hold the historical distinction of being the last pro football team to use the single wing long after other teams abandoned it. When Rooney finally fired Michelosen after the 1951 season and hired one of his cronies, Joe Bach, to install the T-formation, they still seemed like the same old Steelers because under Bach and Walt Kiesling, another Rooney crony who took over in 1954, the Steelers developed the most predictable T-formation offense in football. They opened each game with the same play so often—a handoff to fullback Fran Rogel—that Pittsburgh fans, including one angry kid from the South Side, chanted, "Hi diddle diddle, Rogel up the middle" when the Steelers broke huddle and approached the line of scrimmage for their first offensive series.

Rooney's same old Steelers were the misfits of pro football in the 1950s, but they were the perfect misfits for a hard-fisted steel town. They actually were fun to watch at times, even when they were losing, because their defense, led by Ernie Stautner, Bill McPeak, Dale Dodrill, and Jack Butler, was mean and tough and routinely beat the hell out of other teams. Their games against Ed Sharkey, Bucko Kilroy, Norm "Wild Man" Wiley, and the Philadelphia Eagles were bloodbaths, where more players made it to the emergency room than into the end zone. On one memorable Saturday evening in 1955, after losing two weeks earlier to the Eagles in Philadelphia on a bad call (my father apparently was on to something), the Steelers—with quarterback Jim Finks wearing a catcher's mask on the front of his helmet to protect the broken jaw he suffered in the game in Philadelphia—put several Eagles in the hospital, won the game on two dramatic catches by Elbie Nickel, and took over first place in the NFL's Eastern Division. But the Steelers were so banged up after taking revenge on the Eagles that they lost six of their last seven games and ended up with another losing season.

The other intense Steeler rivalry, though it was usually one-sided on the scoreboard, was with the Cleveland Browns. Unlike the brawling Steelers, the Browns were all smugness and precision. While Stautner and McPeak managed to put a few dents in Otto Graham's pride, the Browns pretty much named the score against the Steelers. One of my best Forbes Field memories is looking down at Graham screaming at his offensive linemen, including Chuck Noll, because the Steelers were roughing him up on every pass play. But one of my worst Forbes Field memories is watching Marion Motley, after losing his helmet on a missed tackle, run through and bounce off the entire Steeler defensive team on his way to a touchdown. After the lopsided game, Motley boasted that running against the Steelers was like running downhill.

My boyhood Steelers were not content just to brawl their way out of contention each year. Their off-the-field bungling more than matched their on-the-field losses. This was a team that either drafted great college football players and cut them because they couldn't recognize their obvious talent, or passed over great players to make incredibly bad choices in the draft, or simply traded away high draft choices for another team's castoffs. During the Michelosen three-yards-and-a-cloud-of-dust years, after giving up the draft rights to Texas All-American Bobby Layne because he refused to play single-wing football, the Steelers selected highly touted quarterbacks like Notre Dame's Joe Gasparella and Tulsa's Jim Finks but used them as defensive backs. Under Joe Bach they selected future Hall of Fame running back John Henry Johnson, who became one of America's first football draft dodgers when he jumped to Canadian football rather than play in Pittsburgh. They also lost another future Hall of Famer, the great Pitt All-American linebacker Joe Schmidt, to the Detroit Lions simply because they waited too long in the draft.

Their biggest blunder, however, became the stuff of pro football legend. In 1955, the year of Clemente's rookie season with the Pirates, the Steelers drafted Louisville quarterback Johnny Unitas, a hometown boy who'd actually played high school football in Pittsburgh against one of Rooney's sons. But Rooney crony Walt Kiesling thought Unitas was too dumb to be a pro football quarterback and cut him a week before the season opener. Unitas ended up playing sandlot football for the Bloomfield Rams until he got a call from the Baltimore Colts, where he played the next seventeen years and was smart enough to win three world championship games, including the 1958 overtime thriller that, thanks to television, turned pro football into a rival to baseball as America's most popular sport.

Undaunted, the Steelers finally seemed to catch a break the next year when they hit pro football's jackpot and won the bonus draft pick for 1956. Year after year, I waited for the Steelers to win the bonus pick and with only two teams left in the lottery, the Steelers and the Lions, Rooney, who couldn't lose at the racetrack and couldn't win for the Steelers, finally pulled the right slip out of Commissioner Bert Bell's hat. At last my same old Steelers were poised to change their luck and their history. There were wonderful draft picks, great running backs waiting for the Steelers, like Ohio State Heisman trophy winner Howard "Hopalong" Cassady and Penn State All-American Lenny Moore. And when the announcement came, the Steelers drafted, to my disbelief and my father's I-told-you-so smirk, somebody named Gary Glick out of some place called Colorado A&M. Drafting Glick as a quarterback after the Unitas fiasco, the Steelers discovered that he may have been smart enough to play the position, but he couldn't pass worth a damn. He spent three mediocre years with Pittsburgh playing defensive back, while failing miserably as a placekicker.

The Steelers did, however, draft another future Hall of Fame quarterback in 1957 when they passed up Syracuse's sensational running back Jim Brown and selected Purdue All-American Lenny Dawson, but Dawson had no opportunity to play football in Pittsburgh. When ex-Detroit Lions coach Buddy Parker replaced Kiesling, Dawson was discarded and forgotten because Parker first traded for quarterback Earl Morrall, then, unhappy with Morrall, acquired Bobby Layne from the Detroit Lions the following year. With the brash, bloated Layne, who played without a face mask and threw touchdown passes that looked like wounded ducks, the Steelers did finally become more exciting on offense, especially when they convinced John Henry Johnson, also acquired from the Lions, that there were worst things than playing in a Steeler uniform. They even became more menacing on defense when they acquired Big Daddy Lipscomb, who would die a few years later of a drug overdose. Under Parker, the Steelers were no longer just the same old Steelers. With Layne leading the way, including the way to Pittsburgh nightclubs during the week, the Steelers ended the decade by changing their reputation from pro football's brawling losers to its brawling drunks.

My father may have been content to spend his Sundays in the fall drinking his beer and playing cards at the Duquesne Social Club while Joe Tucker's broadcast of the Steeler games droned on in the background, but I was determined to be at Forbes Field for Steeler home games. Win or lose, and mostly they lost, they were my same old Steelers. Getting money for Pirate games on Sunday was never a problem—I'd bum a dollar from my mother's tips, get her to pack a bag full of chipped ham sandwiches, throw in a large bottle of Tom Tucker pop, and I was all set to spend a long, sunburned afternoon in the left-field bleachers, watching the Pirates lose a doubleheader. I also had all those free Saturday Knothole games as thousands of us watched from the right-field stands and usually outnumbered the paying customers. But a Steeler ticket cost three times as much as a Pirate ticket and was too steep for my mother's Saturday night tips. So my football buddies and I had to come up with a plan to get into Forbes Field for nothing.

During the 1950s I saw almost every Steeler home game and didn't pay a dime. I'd get up Sunday morning and con my mother into believing I was going out to Forbes Field early to see if I could get into the game by peddling the Sunday *Press* or *Sun-Telegraph*. I'd plead with her to pack me a lunch just in case, smuggle some old newspapers under my coat, and head out to the ballpark. Once I met up with my football buddies, our ranks slightly depleted by the Catholics who couldn't talk their way out of Sunday mass, we made our way out to Oakland and headed into Schenley Park, where we walked around the outer wall of Forbes Field until we got to the iron gates. With the ballpark still unguarded, we found a Schenley Park bench and propped it upside down against the outfield wall so that the bench legs served as a ladder. We climbed up the bench, avoided the barbed wire fringing the top of the outfield wall, walked tight-roped along the ledge, and took a football leap of faith into the deserted right-field grandstands.

Once inside Forbes Field and with nearly two hours to kill before the ticket gates opened, we had to go somewhere to avoid the police and ushers who would soon be patrolling the ballpark. After exploring the rusted underground of Forbes Field, we eventually came across the perfect hideaway, perfect if you didn't mind utter darkness, absolute filth, and the sound of rats scurrying a few yards away from where you were hiding. Our black hole, where we disappeared until the gates opened at noon, existed beneath the right-field stands where the back wall of a storage shed for ballpark concessions intersected the slanted underbelly of the grandstand and left a small opening just big enough for a handful of South Side fugitives to crawl through and escape detection. Once through the hole, we spread out old newspapers to lie on, took a vow of silence so workers loading up supplies for the concession stands wouldn't hear us, threatened anyone with a reputation for chronic farting, and waited until the sounds of chains and rolling metal alerted us that law-abiding ticketholders were about to enter the ballpark.

Emerging from our tomb-like sanctuary, after praying for what seemed an eternity that the workers wouldn't hear us moving about to get comfortable and the rats wouldn't confuse our toes with the lunches they were no doubt smelling, we must have appeared an unholy sight to the paying Steeler fans dressed in their Sunday finest. With our clothes smudged with newspaper print, our hands and knees caked with filth, and our hair and caps coated with spider webs, we must have looked like escaped waifs from some western Pennsylvania coal mine or some displaced persons' camp. But appearances to the contrary, we were now a part of the Sunday crowd and, after our descent into the underworld, more than ready for another bruising Steeler loss.

The right-field grandstands at Forbes Field were long-distance viewing for baseball, but they offered the best seats in the house for football. Since we had no tickets and the stands were quickly filling up with paying fans, we improvised once again by climbing on top of a concession stand located near the fifty-yard line. From our little crow's nest, we looked down on the same old Steelers, ate our fingerprint-stained "sammiches," and yelled with all our working-class vehemence and teen-age vulgarity for the blood and broken bones of the Steeler opponents—for Jack Butler to undercut and maim Pete Pihos or Mac Speedie every time one of them leaped high for a pass, for George Tarasovic or John Reger to tear the limbs off that midget every time Eddie LaBaron scrambled out of the pocket, and for anyone, even Gary Glick, to break the legs of that goddam Ollie Matson every time he broke free on a kickoff return.

Forbes Field may have been the pleasure palace of my father's youth, but for me it was part amusement park, obstacle course, and torture chamber. It was also the towering centerpiece of an Oakland sports complex that included Pitt Stadium and the Duquesne Gardens. In Oakland, just a forty-minute walk from the South Side, I could escape from the boredom of public school and the unhappiness of family life, learn how to connive and hustle my way to the objects of my heart's desire, and gain early lessons about loyalty, toughness, and even pride in a hard-nosed city closely identified with smoke, soot, and losing professional sports teams. Forbes Field and major league sports dominated my boyhood adventures from April to December, but I also had the chance to go out to Oakland and watch games at Pitt Stadium in the fall and the Duquesne Gardens in the winter. It meant following college football and basketball and minor-league hockey, but, while the Pirates and the Steelers played like amateurs and bush leaguers, the Pitt Panthers, Duquesne Dukes, and the Pittsburgh Hornets actually had outstanding teams in the 1950s.

I never bothered trying to penetrate the concrete bowl of Pitt Stadium because I either got high school passes or could watch Pitt football for nothing if I didn't mind missing 30 percent of the game. By standing on a hill overlooking the north end zone, I could see the action at the far end zone, follow the game across midfield, to about the thirty-yard line where players and the game disappeared under the outer rim of the stadium. I saw Corny Salvaterra option Pitt into the Sugar Bowl and the Gator Bowl in 1955 and 1956, but half of his touchdown runs and passes at Pitt Stadium were invisible to my eyes, validated only by the roar of the crowd and somebody's portable radio. I groaned as Penn State's Lenny Moore and Syracuse's Jim Brown broke off dazzling open-field runs, only to watch them disappear once they crossed Pitt's thirty-yard line. And I looked down in disbelief as Freddie Wyant led West Virginia to a great 17-0 upset over Pitt in 1955, though in my mind's eye some of his passes are still waiting to be caught.

The West Virginia upset is still a vivid memory because of what happened when my college football buddies and I went into the stadium, as we usually did after a game, to play tackle football on the thick grass carpet—our high school field at South Stadium was all dirt and hard as concrete. As we were leaving the field, we stumbled across the discarded crossbar from the goalpost torn down by Mountaineer fans who'd come up from Morgantown for the Pitt game. Like bearers of forgotten treasure, we carried the crossbar down Cardiac Hill to Forbes Avenue, sneaked past the Juvenile Court building, and made the long hike high above the Monongahela River and the Jones & Laughlin mill to the Brady Street Bridge. Once we got to the middle of the bridge, we scratched our names, the date, and the score of the game into the crossbar and ceremoniously pitched it over the railing. We watched the crossbar plunge into the water, before floating downriver through industrial slime and human waste to its final resting place—not as a trophy on the campus of West Virginia, but as a piece of unrecognizable debris on the banks of the Monongahela or Ohio.

While Pitt Stadium may have seemed impenetrable or at least not worth the effort, the Duquesne Gardens, where I watched the Pittsburgh Hornets and occasionally the basketball Duquesne Dukes, was a freeloader's paradise. Getting into the rundown Gardens, located out past Forbes Field and Carnegie Tech on Craig Street, was as easy as rapping on a door. Originally built at the turn of the century as a streetcar barn, the Gardens had a series of side exits just waiting for the right moment. All my hockey buddies and I had to do was walk around to the side of the building, knock on one of the metal doors, and hope some paying Hornet fan, remembering his own panhandling youth, would push open the door and let us in for an evening of hockey.

If no one responded or, worse yet, an usher opened the door and told us to get the hell outta there before he called the cops, we went over to the building's fire escape and climbed up to the roof. On the top of the Gardens was a small structure resembling a doghouse. We'd swing open the door, lie down on our bellies, lean over, and look down on the hockey rink. There's no remembered sensation from my South Side youth stranger than looking straight down at the Hornets skating up and down the ice against the Cleveland Barons, Hershey Bears, or Providence Reds with the heat of the arena rising up to warm the upper torso of my body and the bitter cold of a Pittsburgh winter threatening my lower extremities with frostbite. I probably still have all my toes—we wore our battered "tennies" all year 'round—because some fan would inevitably look up and start pointing at the sight of hockey angels with dirty faces staring down at him. Knowing a cop was soon on the way, we'd bid farewell with our middle finger, beat it back down the fire escape, and start the ritual of rapping on the side doors all over again.

I had no serious interest in basketball because Pittsburgh hadn't owned a professional basketball team since the Ironmen back in the early 1940s. But if I got a student pass, I'd trek out to watch the Steel Bowl tournament at the Pitt Field House or take in the Duquesne Dukes at the old Gardens. Under Dudey Moore, the Dukes, who regularly played in the National Collegiate Athletic Association and the National Invitational tournaments (you could play in both until the 1952 season), were one of the best teams in college basketball. With All-Americans Dick Ricketts and Si Green doing most of the scoring, the Dukes won the NIT in 1955, the same year my South High Orioles won the city championship at the Pitt Field House and advanced to the western regional, only to lose to a powerful McKeesport team. In that game McKeesport players taunted Joe Muza as a "white nigger" because he was the only white player on the South High starting team. The irony of the taunt was that South High was mostly an all-white school in a city system segregated by neighborhood—and a lot of the black kids in Pittsburgh lived in the Hill District and Homewood and went to Fifth Avenue and Westinghouse.

Even the basketball Pitt Panthers, who rarely made it to a postseason tournament, generated some excitement by the late 1950s after undersized Don Hennon from Wampum, Pennsylvania, accepted a scholarship at Pitt. For decades, Pitt's only claim to basketball notoriety, as the football Panthers roared to national prominence, was the eccentric behavior of coach Red Carlson, who fed ice cream to his players at halftime and threw peanuts to Pitt students watching the game. But with Hennon and his soft running hook shot and his brilliant play-making, Pitt's basketball team made it to the NCAA tournament in 1957 and 1958. Hennon also brought his own notoriety to Pitt because his father, who was the basketball coach at Wampum, gained national media attention for his unorthodox training drills—his players dribbled blindfolded and ran up and down the court in galoshes. Without his blindfold and galoshes, Hennon was so quick and accurate that I once saw him throw a no-look pass to hatchet man Mike Ditka, who had better luck catching football passes. The ball hit Ditka in the back of the head, bounced on the fly back to Hennon, who promptly scored a basket on his running jump hook—with the assist going to Ditka.

When the Duquesne Gardens fell to the wrecking ball in 1956, the same year I graduated from South High, Pittsburgh's greatest sports loss was the Pittsburgh Hornets. The basketball games, the boxing and wrestling cards could find another building, but the Hornets, who came to Pittsburgh in the 1930s as an American Hockey League minor-league franchise, left town and didn't return until the Civic Arena opened in 1961. A farm club for the Toronto Maple Leafs, the Hornets weren't the first professional hockey team to play in Pittsburgh—the National Hockey League Pirates struggled for five years in the late 1920s and finally left after the 1929–30 season to become the Philadelphia Quakers. But the Hornets were popular in Pittsburgh. Hornet fans, including a half-frozen, top-of-the-world South Sider, were watching minor-league hockey, but it was winning hockey. With career minor-league all-stars like goalie Gil Mayer, wingers Andy Barbe and Bob Solinger, and defensemen Pete Backor and Frank Mathers leading the way, the Hornets won several division titles and in the 1951–52 season won the Calder Cup, symbol of minor-league hockey supremacy.

The Hornet players weren't big league, but they took on added importance for me because of my mother. My father may have brought the Pirates to life for me and the Steelers may have fit the hard-boiled character of my hometown, but the Hornets belonged to my mother. She didn't understand a thing about hockey, couldn't distinguish a red line from a blue line, but she knew her hockey players because they hung out at Rodger's after games at the Gardens. Throughout the early 1950s, my mother waited booths and flirted with future Hall of Famers like George Armstrong and Tim Horton, who were passing through Pittsburgh on their way to greatness in the National Hockey League, and like former Toronto Maple Leafs Wild Bill Ezinicki and Howie Meeker, who were on their last legs with the Hornets. With their toothless smiles and their stitched-up faces, they were her battered boys of winter. Her favorite Hornet, Pete Backor, even promised Lil Peterson's son a hockey stick. But poor Pete Backor, after one glorious season in 1944–45 with the Stanley Cup champion Maple Leafs, spent the better part of the next decade in Pittsburgh, waiting in vain for another chance to play in the National Hockey League, and poor Dick Peterson, almost fifty years later, is still waiting for his hockey stick.

After graduating from high school in 1956 and bumming my way through five years of temporary jobs and unemployment lines, I finally went to college at Edinboro State in 1961. As I spent most of my time in the late 1950s playing sandlot baseball and football and industrial-league basketball and trying to figure out what to do with my life, the Pirates, when I needed it the most, gave me something to cheer about. In the late 1950s, with Roberto Clemente, drafted by Rickey out of the Dodger farm system, and Dick Groat, another of Rickey's basketball All-Americans, emerging as stars, and young pitchers like Vernon Law, Bob Friend, and Roy Face surviving earlier beatings, the Pirates became a good team. When they added nineteen-year-old rookie Bill Mazeroski, traded Dick Littlefield and Bobby Del Greco for Rookie of the Year Bill Virdon, and gave up hometown hero Frank Thomas for Don Hoak, Harvey Haddix, and Smoky Burgess, they had the nucleus for a championship team.

With a residue of the few decent players to survive the Rickey years, supplemented by the good trades made by Rickey's successor, Joe L. Brown, appropriately enough for the Pirates, the son of the famous comedian Joe E. Brown, the Pirates, after nearly a decade of finishing last or next to last, made a run for the National League pennant in 1958 before finishing in second place. They fell back to fourth place in 1959, then won the pennant in 1960, their first in thirty-three years, and beat Casey Stengel's heavily favored Yankees on Mazeroski's dramatic home run after an improbable World Series of close Pirate wins and lopsided losses. In the fall of 1960, I snaked and danced my way through Pittsburgh's downtown streets in celebration of the Pirate victory, but by the next fall I was away at college and the Pirates were back in the doldrums.

The Steelers, with Buddy Parker giving away draft choices like they were green stamps, also made life interesting, but it wasn't until the early 1960s, when I was away at college, that they finally made their first run at a championship since they lost a conference playoff game in 1947 after finishing in a tie with Steve Van Buren and the Philadelphia Eagles. The Steelers finished second in the Eastern Conference in 1962 and lost to the Detroit Lions in the first Playoff Bowl—a ridiculously conceived idea, dubbed the Also-Ran Bowl by its critics, that matched the runners-up of the two conferences. But in 1963 the Steelers were in a position to win the first championship in the team's history if they beat the New York Giants in the last game of the season—they'd beaten the Giants, 31-0, in their first meeting in Pittsburgh. I remember sitting in a drafty lakeside cottage—there were no dorms at Edinboro for upper-class male students—and watching the Steeler game on a tiny black-and-white set, as the winter winds howled down from Lake Erie. My Steeler buddies and I looked on in dismay as the winds at Yankee Stadium blew Ed Brown's passes everywhere but into the arms of Steeler receivers Buddy Dial and Gary Ballman. The defense also played a terrible game and the Steelers lost, 33-17.

Though Bobby Layne had been forced into retirement by Parker at the end of the 1962 season, his reputation and influence still lingered on in Pittsburgh. After the Steeler loss, the story began to circulate that Brown and his teammates had decided to lay off the booze during the week before the Giants game. Pro football history may decree that Frank Gifford's miraculous one-handed catch was the turning point in the game, but some Steeler fans, including one very unhappy Edinboro college student, had a different view. We believe the turning point came before the game even started. All those Steeler fumbles and bad passes preceding Gifford's catch were the result of pregame jitters or, to put it more bluntly, the pregame shakes, and not the high winds and bitter cold at Yankee Stadium. After the game Buddy Parker lamented his decision a year earlier to retire Layne—and most Steeler fans were ready to drink to that.

By the time things finally turned completely around in Pittsburgh sports in the 1970s, I had finished my graduate degrees at Kent State and taken a teaching position at Southern Illinois University. Now a Pittsburgh sports fan in exile, I watched the Pirates on WGN out of Chicago, WTBS out of Atlanta, and KPLR out of St. Louis, or tried to listen to a fading and crackling KDKA at night as they won the World Series in 1971 and 1979. I was in Pittsburgh in 1972, visiting my mother, when Franco Harris made his immaculate reception, but I had to drive over 100 miles to Kent, Ohio, to see the game because Pittsburgh television was blacked out. I watched the Steelers win four Super Bowls and Pitt claim a college football championship after beating Georgia in the Sugar Bowl—all from my living room in Makanda, Illinois, population 400 and the home of Paul Simon, the former senator, not the singer.

Thanks to the National Hockey League expansion in 1967 I also had the chance to watch the misnamed Pittsburgh Penguins on television when they played the St. Louis Blues. Despite the tragic death of rookie sensation Michel Brière in a car crash and the threat of bankruptcy, the Penguins made the playoffs six times in the 1970s. Pittsburgh even had another shot at professional basketball, first in the early and late 1960s with the Rens of the ABL, then the Pipers, who lived up to their team name by leaving town after winning the ABA's first league championship. The Pipers, curiously renamed the Condors, returned, red-white-and-blue basketballs and all, in the early 1970s before folding for good after two years. As pro basketball faded out, Pittsburgh's college and even its junior college teams prospered with conference championships and tournament bids. In the 1973–74 season Pitt's basketball team went as far as the NCAA Final Four before losing to North Carolina State. Pittsburgh sport teams were so dominant in the 1970s, my first decade in complete exile from my hometown, that when the short-lived World Team Tennis came to town in 1974, the Pittsburgh Triangles won a league title in its second year—all these championships and I was spending my days in a emotional limbo surrounded by Chicago and St. Louis fans, the lovable losers and the spoiled brats of sports.

The irony of watching Pittsburgh sports on television is that the great Pirate and Steeler teams of the 1970s and their Hall of Fame performers loom small in my mind's eye, mere reflections of the television screen. But because I grew up with Pittsburgh sports in the 1950s, those Pirate rinky-dinks and the same old Steelers still seem as large as life, though the memories are often as painful. In a way, they even appear larger than life in my memories. They were the closest thing I had to heroes in an otherwise drab blue-collar world. They played out their follies at a magnificent ballpark, at one time a symbol of civic pride, but now just a Pittsburgh sports memory. They gave me pride and hope, no matter how foolish and misguided, because they were my Pirates and Steelers. No matter how often they disappointed and angered me, they still deserved my loyalty and love because they were all I had. I was thrilled with all the Super Bowl and World Series wins in the 1970s, but my strongest emotions and memories still belong to those bumbling Pirates and brawling Steelers of the 1950s.

I made the mistake once of asking my wife, who grew up just outside of Pittsburgh, why the Pirates and the Steelers had to wait until I left before they started winning all those championships. She thought my leaving was probably the best thing that ever happened to Pittsburgh sports. It was obvious to her that I was a jinx, and, once I got the proper jinx-removing distance from Pittsburgh, its sports teams went on a rampage out of relief and gratitude. She also believes that all the talk about the Pirates and the Steelers leaving town was just a warning in case I have some notion of returning to Pittsburgh after retirement.

Jinx or not, I'm glad I have my memories of Pirate rinky-dinks and the same old Steelers and wouldn't trade any of them away. Pittsburgh sport fans of later generations will have no trouble remembering championship plays because they're available on highlight reels and tapes, but only a die-hard Pittsburgh fan of the 1950s remembers the incredible sight of bonus baby Paul Martin throwing warm-up pitch after warm-up pitch into the screen behind home plate as Jackie Robinson quaked in his spikes in the on-deck circle. Pittsburgh sports fans will always be able to watch Roberto Clemente dazzle in the 1971 World Series and Lynn Swann make those incredible catches in Super Bowl X, but there's something oddly unique about remembering Steeler receiver Ray Mathews pointing to the lights of Forbes Field after a sure touchdown pass hit him in the helmet and fell to the same infield dirt Mazeroski would circle in the 1960 World Series.

After thirty years of exile, I'd like to come back to my hometown, but, because of my close identification with Pittsburgh sport teams, emotionally I never left. Thanks to those misfit teams of Branch Rickey and Art Rooney, I still feel a deep loyalty and pride in the city of my youth. I hate to lose but, win or lose, the Pirates and Steelers were the one certainty I had in a life of working-class uncertainties. No matter how unhappy or confused or inferior I felt, I could always go out to the ballpark. And no matter how many times I watched the Pirates and the Steelers lose, there was always that hope that this time they were going to win.

RICHARD F. PETERSON teaches at Southern Illinois University. He is the editor of *Crab Orchard Review* and the SIU Writing Baseball series. His current project is "Growing Up with Clemente," a memoir about Pittsburgh in the 1950s.

3

REFLECTIONS ON THE PRE-RENAISSANCE STEELERS

FRANK LAMBERT

THE PHRASE "Pittsburgh Steelers of the National Football League" conjures up images of the team's glory years in the 1970s, especially the four Super Bowl championships. As a favorite of Monday Night Football, the Steelers became the window through which millions viewed Pittsburgh, the Renaissance City, celebrated for its remarkable economic and environmental transformation in the 1960s and 1970s. Cameras captured the gleaming new skyscrapers of the Golden Triangle, the city's business district that boasted corporate headquarters of Westinghouse Electric, Alcoa Aluminum, Pittsburgh Plate Glass (PPG), Koppers, U.S. Steel, H. J. Heinz, and Gulf Oil, as well as the banking empire of the Mellon family. Once the site of scores of steel mills producing megatons of steel for international markets and belching clouds of hydrocarbons into the atmosphere, Pittsburgh had undergone a dramatic metamorphosis in how its citizens earned their daily bread and in the quality of the air they breathed. The popular press of 1965 toasted Pittsburgh's miracle. *Life* magazine referred to the transformation as a "Golden Clean-up." The *National Geographic* touted the city as a "Pattern for Progress." And the *Saturday Review* marveled at "How One City Did It."[1] Everywhere, it seems, the country took notice of the renaissance occurring at the confluence of the

Allegheny and the Monongahela. This impression was reinforced by the Steelers. When Americans tuned in on the Black and Gold games, they witnessed a team befitting a miracle city.

It had not always been that way. In the 1960s the Renaissance City had a decidedly pre-Renaissance football team. With the town's celebrated renascence well under way, the Steelers languished in the Dark Ages. When I arrived in Pittsburgh in September 1965 as a rookie punter traded from the New York Giants, I came to a very different team from those of the glorious 1970s. Put simply, we were not very good. Our preseason record of 0 and 5 suggested that we would struggle and lose; we would and we did. We ended the season with a 2 and 12 record. Not only did we fail, we did so on a heroic scale. Half of our losses, including each of our last five games, were by margins of three or more touchdowns. We committed two turnovers for every one we forced, throwing an incredible thirty-five interceptions in fourteen games—two and one-half per contest—and coughing up forty-two fumbles, an even three per game. When we did not give the ball away, we generally punted it away, certainly justifying my position on the team. Our league-leading seventy-eight punts, or five and one-half per game, eloquently bespoke a sputtering offense. We averaged about fourteen possessions each football game, and on more than ten of those possessions each Sunday we either turned the ball over or punted. That meant that I had the dubious distinction of putting the finishing touch on about 40 percent of our offensive efforts, a far greater role than that any offensive coordinator would plan for a punter.

Writing about those days from the distance of several decades and several careers presents a structural problem. As a former player, I could take an insider's view, recalling the personalities that gave the teams their color and appeal, the personal bonds that lent coherence, and the shared experiences that provided a common culture. As an American historian, I could study those teams from the outside in hopes that distance would contribute to a more objective, analytical account. At first glance, there seemed to be irreconcilable differences between the two viewpoints. After all, professional football players and historians live and work in different arenas and see the world through very different eyes. The former engage in contests that reward strength, agility, and speed, and they perform in stadiums before tens of thousands of partisan fans with millions more watching on television. The latter live in a world of ideas, producing and disseminating knowledge, spending most of their time working alone in libraries and archives and teaching relatively small groups of students in classrooms. Yet they have one thing in common: both are storytellers. Historians begin their stories by first exploring accounts left by the men and women who lived in the past, how they made sense out of their lives. Football players also tell stories about the past they helped create, albeit in a less self-conscious, but often far more colorful, way. They constantly reflect on past teams, games, or even plays, usually for the sheer pleasure of recounting moments of glory and agony, and often with great embellishment for added amusement or heightened drama.

Given the choice of perspective, I opted to look at the pre-Renaissance Steelers from the inside, as a former player. Others will analyze, and perhaps overanalyze, those years and their place in the larger history of professional football. I prefer to tell stories, tales of colorful characters, the men who played on the 1965 and 1966 teams. Guys like John Henry Johnson, John Baker, Ray Mansfield, Jim "Cannonball" Butler, and Buddy Parker. Those stories shed light on the character of the game, specifically changes in the team, the league, and the nation that have had profound influences on professional football and its place in American culture.

In 1984 I brought my two sons, then fourteen and seventeen, to the Alumni Day Game at Three Rivers Stadium, the first Steelers game I had attended since I left the team after the 1966 season. At a luncheon, several players from the 1960s reflected on the Steelers' miraculous change under Chuck Noll's leadership. Ray Mansfield, one of the few who played on our cellar-dwelling teams and the Super Bowl champions of the 1970s, identified the biggest change as one of culture. Chuck Noll, he said, taught them how to win. We wanted to win, but played not to lose, often finding ways to let tight games slip away.

The new Steelers always expected to win, played to win, and usually won. Mansfield made the important observation that professional football teams have cultures. That is, they have a set of underlying beliefs, values, and assumptions that define their characters. These cultures emerge from many shaping influences: the teams' traditions, their owners' personalities, their host cities' characters. Of course, individual coaches and players can have enormous impact on their team's culture and can contribute to important shifts. Chuck Noll changed the culture of the Pittsburgh Steelers. He reoriented the organization. Instead of relying heavily on trading for veteran players, he built a team through drafting young guys. And he instilled a winning attitude.

I was representative of the old Steelers in the way I came to Pittsburgh, through a trade. While Noll built his great teams through the draft, most of my teammates were veterans who arrived from other franchises. In 1964 I was elated when, following my senior year at the University of Mississippi, my favorite NFL team, the New York Giants, drafted me. The Giants were just that—giants, larger than life, legends, winners, Frank Gifford, Y. A. Tittle, Sam Huff. Men who had come from the beaches of Southern California, the plains of Texas, and the ravines of West Virginia—from everywhere—to play in the shadows of skyscrapers. But with only two weeks remaining in the preseason, I left the Big Apple.

When Coach Allie Sherman said he wanted to see me, I entered his office with only one question: Where? I was gone. I knew the New York Giants were going to trade me, but to what other franchise? The Giants had drafted me in the fifth round to replace their fine punter, Don Chandler, whom they had traded to the Green Bay Packers. Then in the tenth round of twenty, New York picked Ernie Koy, a powerful running back from the University of Texas who was also an excellent punter. His versatility made him much more valuable than a specialist, especially on a squad then limited by the National Football League to just forty players. I was expendable. And, as owners of virtually chattel property, the Giants could buy, sell, and trade players at will—their will. I could only hope to go to a winning franchise or at least to a premier city. Green Bay would be great, I thought. Vince Lombardi had turned that team around, and they were sure to be a contender in 1965. Some players made fun of the small town in Wisconsin, but for someone who grew up in Hattiesburg, Mississippi, its size was no problem. San Francisco would certainly be nice, a beautiful city in a gorgeous setting with a rich and cosmopolitan culture. Dallas, Washington, Chicago, Los Angeles—they all had unique attractions.

Pittsburgh had not been on my short list. Indeed, both the team and the city languished at the bottom of my choices, along with such other "rust belt" sites as Detroit and St. Louis. No one expected winning seasons from those franchises, forget about championships. And the cities, at least in my mind's eye, were gray, dirty industrial centers lacking excitement and culture. The fact was, I had never been to any of them. Indeed, prior to joining the Giants, I had been in exactly one of the fourteen NFL cities, Washington, D.C. But I did attend movies and from time to time saw on the Movietone newsreels Pittsburgh with its grim steel mills and belching smokestacks. Moreover, I knew that the franchise had enjoyed little success since Arthur Rooney established it in 1933 when the team was known as the Pittsburgh Pirates. Although the Pirates underwent a name change in 1939 and became the Steelers, their fortunes on the football field had not changed. They continued to lose. The fact was, I was joining an organization that had won no championships but recorded numerous losing seasons. Had I bothered checking the Giants' record books before departing for the Steelers' training camp at the University of Rhode Island, I would have learned that New York enjoyed a 36 to 23 won-loss advantage over Pittsburgh. Two weeks before I was traded, as a Giant I had contributed to yet another Steeler loss, a 16-7 defeat in an exhibition game in the Yale Bowl at New Haven. Now I was joining this outfit whose image fit the city it represented: hard-nosed, hard-working, dirty, unkempt, and tough.

An NFL trade in 1965, as I suspect it is any season, was a cold, impersonal transaction. It drove home the fact that professional football was a business and that players were assets that owners could buy or sell, keep or discard. With no free-agency protection, players performed when and where owners dictated with little recourse. When I joined the Giants at their training camp at Fairfield University, I soon realized that I was a commodity. In an article focusing on the college all-stars who were arriving in camp, a *New York Times* sportswriter suggested that "Lambert, the punter, will be an immediate *asset*" (my emphasis). A month later, another *Times* piece announced in language that could have been found in the business section that "Tom Lambert, who led the nation's collegiate kickers last year, *was obtained* by the Pittsburgh Steelers of the National Football League from the New York Giants today in *exchange* for a 1966 draft choice." There it was, in the impersonal passive voice: a transaction transferring an asset, not a person, from one corporation to another. And they didn't even get my damn name right.

In 1965 and 1966 the NFL Players' Association had not become the collective bargaining force that it would be in the 1980s and 1990s. In fact, I recall that we had just one meeting each year, the first of which occurred shortly after I arrived at the Steelers training camp at the University of Rhode Island. Our player representative, John Baker, presided. Now I'm not sure how Baker got that assignment; I don't ever remember voting for a player rep. Maybe it went to the person willing to take the responsibility. Maybe it went to the most paranoid player. I just don't know.

At any rate, the major grievance that John aired, apparently having received word from the national association, dealt with bubble-gum cards. He informed us that a percentage of the funds from the sale of those cards went into our pension fund, but between nods and suspicious glances he suggested that the owners were somehow interfering with the process. Blowing a conspiratorial bubble of his own, Baker claimed that this issue was part of a larger pattern of owners refusing to share the wealth with players. He pointed to the per diem funds we received during the preseason. As I listened, I had difficulty mustering a sense of outrage. Our pension plan was far superior to that of 99 percent of Americans. One was fully vested after playing five years, and to be credited for a year one had to appear in but three games. And I regarded the per diem as extra cash because we had no expenses during training camp. However, when Baker called on us to approve a list of demands to be submitted to the owners, all the veterans signified their approval with uplifted hands and several suggestions that management ought to go perform some pretty unthinkable—and perhaps even impossible—sexual acts. Though I failed to see injustice, I stretched my own hand upward as high as possible lest any behemoth in the room think this lonely kicker was opposed to his position. I knew that rookies should exercise free speech very judiciously—and kickers perhaps not at all—because on a professional football team the court of last appeal is a coliseum where the lions (*read:* veterans) far outnumber the Christians (*read:* rookies).

Though professional football was, and is, a business, it was also not as impersonal as transactions such as player trades suggested. It involved a personal dimension that sometimes included warm relations between owners and players. I had the great privilege of playing for two wonderful owners, Wellington Mara of the Giants and Art Rooney of the Steelers. Both were gentlemen who had benevolent, albeit paternalistic, attitudes toward players. At the time most NFL teams were owned by individuals, and at the time players had few rights outside those spelled out in their contracts. They were bound to play for the team that drafted them, and they had no say in whether or not they would be traded and to whom. In other words, players had no free agency, and owners had absolute sovereignty. That meant that owners were despots, maybe benevolent, but despots nonetheless. Some players likened them to masters of Old South plantations: what rights the field hands had were at the behest and whim of the masters. At least I had good masters. Like all figures of speech, the metaphor of slavery can lead to serious distortions. Professional football players, then and now, choose to play the game and are handsomely rewarded for the privilege.

The first conversation I ever had with an owner revealed the depths of my naivete in negotiating with successful businessmen. In 1965 college players were often drafted by two teams, one from the National Football League, the other from the American Football League. That was great for players because the interleague competition for talent drove up salaries. For example, All-Pro defensive lineman Big Daddy Lipscomb, who played for Baltimore and Pittsburgh in the late 1950s and early 1960s, made just $14,000 in his best year, and San Francisco star quarterback John Brodie made $35,000 in 1965. By contrast, that same year Joe Namath signed with the New York Jets for $400,000. Also in 1965 I was drafted by the New York Jets and the New York Giants and benefited from intercity as well as interleague rivalry. After drafting me, Sonny Werblin, the movie mogul who owned the Jets, called me in Houston, Texas, where Ole Miss was preparing for the Bluebonnet Bowl. He asked me about my contractual expectations. Hoping to cash in on having finished the season as the nation's leading collegiate punter, I boldly told him that I wanted a multiyear, no-cut contract with an income that matched that of the highest paid punter in professional football. His response caught me by surprise. "No," he replied in what I assumed was going to be a flat rejection, "you should not ask for parity, you should insist on being the *highest* paid professional punter." I politely thanked him for the lesson in contract negotiation and hung up. I eventually signed with the Giants for $55,000, an enormous sum at the time, especially for a kicking specialist.

When I was traded, Wellington Mara made the transition as easy as possible and went well beyond what my contract demanded of him. He said that he understood that I would incur all sorts of costs in moving from New York to Pittsburgh and pledged that he would reimburse me. Indeed, my wife and I had laid out considerable funds for education and housing, some of which were nonrefundable. We were both enrolled at Rutgers University and had paid tuition and fees and bought books for the fall semester. We had signed a two-year lease on an apartment in Nutley, New Jersey, and faced a loss of several thousand dollars in breaking it. We expected no mercy from the disappointed landlord who had salivated over the prospects of Giants tickets when I signed the lease. When I told Mara all this, he replied, "Look, you will incur costs you can't conceive of at the moment. Give yourself a few weeks to settle in, then send me a figure—you need not itemize the expenses—and I will reimburse you." It was that simple. A gentleman did not expect an itemized receipt from another gentleman. He followed through, and we made the move with no cost or loss to us.

Though Mara had made the financial transition as easy as possible, he did not emotionally prepare me for the Steelers. The physical appearance of the Steelers' facilities loomed in stark contrast to those of the Giants. The Giants played in storied Yankee Stadium while the Steelers performed in Pitt Stadium, as guests of the University of Pittsburgh. The Giants' locker room and practice arena was first-class. The Steelers trained at South Park, a public park in southern Allegheny County. I soon learned that pedestrian traffic was the least of our problems with the turf at South Park. The much more serious issue was the condition of the field—deep tracks left by horses as equestrians traversed the field when we were not practicing. In the winter, when the ground froze, those hoof divots scarred the surface with thousands of deep, sharp edges that snagged cleats and turned ankles. Ironically, practicing in such deplorable conditions actually prepared us well for home games at Pitt Stadium. By the time our Sunday afternoon games rolled around, the turf there had been churned up during the preceding week by a couple of high school games, a soccer match or two, and a Pitt Panthers game on Saturday afternoon. By November grass in Pitt Stadium was as rare as a tree in Brooklyn.

Training and playing facilities constitute one of the major differences between pre- and post-Renaissance Steelers. A stroll through old Pitt Stadium, before the artificial turf and before the new training center for the University of Pittsburgh, revealed a cramped, dingy dressing room that we used for home games. A tour of our old practice quarters out at South Park exposed another small dressing room, a couple of nondescript meeting rooms, and a training room equipped with tables for taping ankles, a few whirlpool baths, and little else. By contrast, the current Steelers enjoy state-of-the-art facilities and equipment at their Three Rivers headquarters. The conditioning room, filled with free weights and all sorts of exercise machines, is particularly impressive. There was no conditioning room in 1965. In fact, weightlifting was still foreign to the NFL, although it would soon become central to any team's conditioning regime. Most coaches and trainers in the mid-1960s feared that heavy lifting would build the wrong kind of muscle and would make players bulky and less flexible. In 1966 we took a small step toward rethinking conditioning by preceding each practice at training camp with isometric exercises. The thinking was that isometrics, which involves applying muscle pressure against either another muscle or an immovable object, could give the benefits of weightlifting without hazarding the risks associated with free weights. As I recall, players regarded the isometric routines more as a gimmick than as a means of making us a better football team. Perhaps we underestimated its power: we increased our wins from two to five.

The pre-Renaissance Steelers also preceded the high-tech culture of Silicon Valley. Now, with the assistance of computers, coaches analyze their own team's tendencies as well as those of opponents. They know what kind of plays the opposition prefers on every down and at every spot on the field. And coaches rely upon that information to prepare game plans and call plays during games. Quarterbacks have direct access to coaches sitting in booths high above the stadium, coolly analyzing play on the field against computer-generated profiles. It was a bit more primitive in 1966. Coach Bill Austin sent plays into quarterback Bill Nelson by shuttling running backs, a system that was far from foolproof. During a game against the Minnesota Vikings, Austin grew increasingly frustrated as Nelson repeatedly called plays other than the ones he sent in from the sidelines. Finally, after the Minnesota front four, the infamous "Purple People Eaters," stuffed one ill-conceived play, Austin snapped. As Nelson came off the field, Austin screamed, "Goddamn it, when I send in a play, run the fucking play." Nelson, equally frustrated, retorted, "What you're calling is no fucking good."

After that eloquent exchange, Austin called over Jim "Cannonball" Butler, one of the couriers. Upon inquiry, the coach discovered that Butler could not remember the plays while running onto the field and therefore, upon reaching the huddle, simply mumbled any play that came to mind. Though mystified at some of the calls Nelson dutifully followed through. As I recall, Austin found a new courier, but failed to increase our offensive productivity.

The closest I came to Three Rivers Stadium as a player occurred in 1966 before it was built. The city fathers had approved a plan to construct the new arena on the North Side and wanted the Pirates and the Steelers to participate in a grand groundbreaking ceremony. For their part, the Pirates, wearing their home uniforms, agreed to assemble at the work site. The players would "take the field" and assume their respective positions on the plot laid out for the new diamond. Fans could imagine their boys of summer in the glistening new ballpark, and sportswriters would have a great shot for the next day's paper. The Steelers' involvement in the publicity scheme fell in the lap of our director of public relations, Ed Keily. What Ed lacked in knowledge of the game, he made up with a fertile imagination and boundless enthusiasm. He envisioned various Steelers actually punting, passing, and kicking on the construction site, thinking perhaps that with footballs sailing around the place, faithful fans could see the dawn of a new age for their gridiron warriors. Toward that end, Ed called me during the off-season to enlist my services. He proposed that I stand, fully caparisoned in black and gold, on the Golden Triangle across the Allegheny River from the stadium site and punt a football across the river and into what would someday be the field of play. I had a better sense of my own abilities, however. Estimating the river's width to be about one quarter mile, I asked him if he had looked at the Allegheny recently. Further, I told him that if I could kick a ball that distance, the Steelers could not afford me. He said he would check out the river and get back to me. I never heard from him again on that subject. Years later, as a professor of colonial American history, I ran across George Washington's 1753 description of the "Alligany" at what would soon become the town of Pittsburgh. He estimated the width of the river to be "a Quarter of a Mile, or more," and noted that it was difficult to traverse because of "very rapid and swift running water." Indeed, it took him a full day to cross on a raft. Surely, kicking a football across such a body of water would have brought me immortality in the annals of professional sports, a feat at least equal to Washington's mythical toss of a silver dollar across the Rappahannock.

While physical facilities caught my eye upon first arriving in Pittsburgh, the team's culture, more subtle to fathom for a newcomer, marked another major difference between my old and new teams. The head coach of an NFL team sets the overall atmosphere, and the Steelers' Buddy Parker had a dark side that had cast a grim pall over the team. I saw it most clearly in the sharp contrast between the atmosphere he created for team meetings and the one that prevailed under Allie Sherman in New York. Though a serious coach who had the respect of his players, Allie recognized, especially during the drudgery of training camp, the need for lighthearted exchange between players and coaches, even sometimes at his own expense. One day he sat down at the projector to begin a film session. When he turned the machine on, the motor whirred but the light failed to come on. Thinking that the bulb had burned out, he ordered a new one. After installing it, again he turned the machine on, but, alas, the same results. Unbeknown to him, Rosey Brown, the Giants behemoth offensive tackle and practical jokester, had placed adhesive tape over the lens. Calling for a second bulb, this time uttered with some colorful oaths, Sherman was visibly frustrated at the delay. After installing the new bulb but again meeting with no light, he exploded. Rosey could take it no longer. One could hear from the back of the room a low, slow-building, guttural rumble that grew into a room-shaking laughter. Everyone, coaches and players alike, joined in the mirth, and we proceeded with the film session in a good mood. The practical joke was for all of us one of those shared moments that, insignificant in itself, contributed to team cohesion and camaraderie.

If I expected a similar kind of atmosphere when I joined the Steelers at their training camp, my first team meeting disabused me of that notion. When I arrived at the session, probably three-fourths of the players had already assembled. Parker was seated at the front of the room behind a desk, expressionless and silent. Sitting in folding chairs along one side of the room, his assistants were as silent as death. A few players talked in muted tones, but there was none of the horseplay and banter that had prevailed among the Giants. After I took my seat, we continued in virtual silence for about five minutes, awaiting the appointed hour for the meeting to begin. The arrival of John Henry Johnson just before Parker began the meeting broke the tension. He barreled in, talking a blue streak as was his wont. He was the kind of guy whose presence filled a room. One simply could not ignore John Henry. As he came in, he kept up one staccato burst after another with the featured word being his favorite: "mutter-fucker." He came as close as humanly possible to making it a one-syllable word and managed to work it into all its forms: noun, adjective, verb, and adverb. Indeed, John Henry said it so often that on one occasion a teammate suggested that we call his running plays, "mutter-fucker right and mutter-fucker left." A great football player on the field, John Henry was also a much needed breath of fresh air in an otherwise heavy, stale atmosphere.

Substandard facilities and heavy culture aside, in joining the Steelers I was most concerned about the team's prospects on the field. Whether pre- or post-Renaissance, football players want to win. I wondered what kind of talent we had, and how we would match up with the other teams. And, of course, at the personal level, like every other rookie, I worried about how I would perform. Could I compete professionally according to professional standards? By the time I joined the Steelers, I had already learned that the level of play in the National Football League was higher than I had imagined. First, only the best of the best were drafted, and then those selected few faced the harsh winnowing of training camps. Fighting for one more year in the league, veterans used all their wisdom and wiles to ward off rookie challenges much as an old buck defended his harem against young upstarts during the rut.

An experience at my first practice session with the Giants defined what "professional" meant in this league. As I prepared to punt, All-Pro center Greg Larson left his position over the ball, walked back to where I was standing, and began interrogating me: "How high off the turf do you want to receive the ball? Thigh high? Waist high? Chest high?"

Having been grateful in the past just to receive it at any level, I started to reply, "I have no strong preference," but sensing that this guy played the game according to a much more exacting yardstick, I mumbled, "Waist high."

Then, like a plastic surgeon asking a patient about desired outcomes of an impending tuck, he then asked, "Where do you want the laces when you catch the ball?"

Now suspicious that this line of questioning could very well be a trick the veteran played on naïve rookies, I, nevertheless, went along. "Up and slightly to the right," I answered.

"Fine," he said. "Now, how far do you stand behind the line of scrimmage?"

"Thirteen and a half yards," I replied promptly, hoping the half-yard added professional exactitude.

Armed with my answers, he returned to his position astride the ball and prepared for the long snap. He looked through his legs once, mentally setting his sights, looked ahead, took one more glance back at me, and then looked straight ahead as he passed the ball back in a tight spiral with as much velocity as I could generate from a standing position. That snap, and the ones that followed, reached my hands waist-high with the laces slightly to the right. I knew at that moment that this was a game qualitatively different from the one that I had previously played. And I realized that I must ratchet up my own performance.

What I knew about the Steelers as a team I had learned primarily from the press. In its inaugural season in the NFL, Pittsburgh had finished last in the Eastern Division with a 3-6-2 record, trailing teams that sounded like they belonged in major league baseball: the New York Giants, Brooklyn Dodgers, and Boston Braves. The Steelers fared little better in recent history, managing winning records in only four of the last fifteen seasons ending in 1964. Firmly established at or near the bottom of their division, the team had never won a division or league championship. In the season before I arrived, the Steelers finished sixth in the Eastern Division, above only the hapless Giants.

From all accounts the 1965 Steelers looked to a sure bet to continue their losing tradition. *Sports Illustrated* picked the team to finish last in the Eastern Division. Veteran NFL sportswriter Tex Maule offered a preseason analysis of winners and losers. Describing the Green Bay Packers, his choice to win the Western Division and Pittsburgh's opening day opponent, Maule emphasized coach Vince Lombardi's youth movement. Explaining why it had taken a couple of years to revitalize the Packers, Maule wrote, "Lombardi needed time to pump plasma into what was obviously a team operating on tired old blood." On the 1965 team "no less than half the 40-player squad will be men with less than four years' service in the NFL." By contrast, Buddy Parker, the Steelers' "ingenious coach, tries to fill his player needs with sleepers, discards, and trades." Maule observed that Pittsburgh, "often a contender but never a champion, puts no great store in high priced draft choices."

At no position was the point more obvious than at quarterback. The Steelers would open the season again with Ed Brown, the former Bear who in 1964 finished fourteenth among the NFL passers (there were fourteen teams) and had the highest percentage of interceptions. Parker's defense of his decision to start Brown served only to underscore additional weaknesses. The coach explained that "we didn't have the receivers," and Maule added that "rushers often poured through the middle of the Steeler line." Defense was the one bright spot. Perhaps remembering the cover of *Sports Illustrated* featuring a mud- and blood-splattered Y. A. Tittle on his knees after being sacked by Pittsburgh end John Baker, Maule noted that "the Steelers hit and hurt, even when they appear to be badly handicapped."[2]

Coach Parker's assessment was even harsher. Before quitting or being fired one week before the 1965 regular season opened, whichever the case may have been, the head coach walked away, declaring, "I can't win with this bunch of stiffs." As the season unfolded, Parker appeared to be an astute prognosticator, but as much because of injuries as lack of talent. When Bill Nelson, a gifted passer who would later lead the Browns to championships, took over for the aging Ed Brown, he played on battered knees that "made him a sitting duck for every pass-rusher." And our running attack was stymied by the loss of John Henry Johnson, who also suffered from a bad knee.[3]

While banged up and performing poorly, the Steelers were at least colorful. Like the city they represented, the 1965 squad was a diverse lot. We came from every region. The forty players on the roster came from thirty-two colleges in twenty-two states. About two-thirds attended colleges located east of the Mississippi River, and half from schools located on either side of the Mason-Dixon line, extended in the West by the Missouri Compromise line. Thirty-two guys were white and eight were black.

We were a melting pot of ethnic and religious backgrounds. Many of us were newcomers, either arriving to our first Steelers training camp as rookies or via a trade from another team. Altogether twenty-two of us had been in the league less than five years. Others were grizzled veterans like John Henry Johnson, John Baker, Ed Brown, Charlie Bradshaw, and Mike Sandusky.

Off the field, we came from many walks of life and few considered football much more than a brief stop before accepting a more traditional job. Bradshaw was a lawyer, the only attorney in the NFL at the time. Andy Russell held an MBA and looked forward to a successful business career. Ray Mansfield, an English major in college, talked about teaching. Ken Kortas determined to make his fortune while he played. Hailing from Chicago, home of the Commodities Exchange, Ken speculated in the futures markets. He regaled us with exotic tales of the risks and relative merits of corn and pork-belly futures. As the 1965 season came to an end, he informed us that he was seeking more direct profits in hogs. He planned to open a huge hog operation in Missouri, certain of quick, eye-popping profits from animals noted for their prolific breeding and large litters. He left for the off-season talking loud, walking tall, and brimming with optimism. A humbler Ken returned to training camp in 1966. I asked Ken about his porcine enterprise. With a snort resembling that of the animals he raised, he launched into a tirade against the beasts. "You cannot conceive of all the things that can go wrong with hogs," he replied. He then told us of diseases and deformities on the farm and rising costs and falling prices in the marketplace that personally conspired against *his* project. With the new season just weeks away, dejected ex-hog farmer Ken Kortas, wiser though poorer, once again prepared his own 300-pound hulk for rooting out quarterbacks.

The 1965 Steelers also were interested in a wide range of avocations. Many of the guys got caught up in a craze that year: racing little cars guided by remote control. It was quite a sight to see several enormous guys bent over, operating tiny cars flying around a miniature oval and cheering them on with an enthusiasm that increased in direct proportion to the consumption of beer. My own interests took another direction. I happened to enjoy reading, and throughout training camp read a great deal when not at practice or in meetings. At the time I was slowly working my way through the works of the nineteenth-century Russian novelist Fyodor Dostoevsky.

My pastime genuinely perplexed my roommate, a veteran linebacker. A great storyteller and beer drinker, he was frequently at the center of the many bull sessions that players engage in while away long hours during training camp. It mystified him that anyone would select a thick volume, a reference not to the book's content but to its physical measurements, and then devote hours reading it. "Why the hell do you read that stuff?" he queried one day, as if I were ingesting daily doses of arsenic.

I told him that I enjoyed Russian novels and liked to read in succession all the works of a single author, and right now, those were the works of Dostoevsky. But his interest piqued my own. "How about you?" I quizzed him. "What do you enjoy reading?"

Without hesitation, he said that he had read only two books from cover to cover in his entire life. Now that was food for thought. Two books in five years at the University of Minnesota said something of football in the Big Ten, but that seemed to me far less intriguing than the question of the two books themselves. Two books? Perhaps the Bible and a play by Shakespeare? Or *Huck Finn* and *The Hundred Greatest Athletes*? What pair of books found their way into my roomie's hands? I just had to ask.

"*The Old Man and the Sea,*" he replied proudly. "Twice." Though not a long list, I concluded that it had its merits.

Years after leaving the team, I had the good fortune of crossing paths with Byron "Whizzer" White, a former Steeler who also had a passion for reading and who, of all who once wore the Black and Gold, attained the greatest national distinction. The Steelers' first draft choice in 1938 from the University of Colorado, White was appointed Associate Justice of the United States Supreme Court by President John Kennedy. I met Justice White in the mid-1970s when I taught U.S. history at a prep school in Louisville, Kentucky. Each year we took high school seniors to Washington, D.C. Having led several of those trips, I had grown frustrated over the inaccessibility of members of the executive and judicial branches of government to high school students. Representatives and senators were most obliging; after all, kids' parents vote. But I wanted to open doors to the other two branches.

First, with the good offices of one of our parents, Attorney General William Saxbe agreed to spend a few moments with the students in his office. And, as it turned out, through a chance encounter, Secretary of State Henry Kissinger also met with us briefly. Second, I wrote Justice White. I informed him that he and I shared a common experience as former Steelers, and on that common, albeit flimsy tie I asked him if he would talk to the students about the Supreme Court. He promptly and graciously accepted. And then, in an auditorium in the Supreme Court Building, Justice White delivered a brilliant forty-five-minute lecture on judicial review, followed by about twenty minutes of questions and answers. Watching him in that hall that day, I could not suppress a swelling pride in having been with the Pittsburgh Steelers.

Not that all Steeler running backs were Supreme Court material. One of my teammates in particular comes to mind when I think of the sad fact that many players arrive in the NFL with little to show for their collegiate academic pursuits, if indeed knowledge was ever one of their quests. On one occasion, I had a first-hand glimpse at our team's literacy. As part of our intelligence-gathering efforts to learn more about our opponents, on Tuesdays each player would fill out a questionnaire describing the play of one person he had played against during the game on Sunday. For instance, an offensive guard would analyze the tendencies, strengths, and weaknesses of the defensive tackle he had confronted. These assessments would then go into a scouting file that would be available for us to review when we next played that team. At the request of an assistant coach on the day in question, I collated the completed questionnaires prepared after a game against the Dallas Cowboys. As I shuffled through them, one in particular caught my eye. It contained a series of phrases and clauses naked of all capitalization and punctuation. A couple of the statements I remember well. Writing about the Cowboys' tough linebacker, Chuck Howley, one of our running backs had wisely commented, "chuck howley he are hard to knock off he feet." His summary comment was, "chuck howley he are a good linebacker." While one can quibble about the grammar, the analysis was right on target. Indeed, as I recall, the author of those comments had not once knocked Howley off his feet.

In addition to high schools and colleges failing to make sure athletes were also scholars, America had done a lousy job of bringing the races together. Coming from segregated Ole Miss to the integrated NFL I was acutely aware of race. Courageous blacks confronted the country with its shameful record of unfilled promises and discrimination. Race became very personal for me as I joined the Steelers. As a white rookie coming from Mississippi, the state with arguably the most deplorable civil rights record, I wondered how black players would regard me. Specifically, I worried about encountering one particular person. Marv Woodson was a defensive back for Pittsburgh. He had been an All-America performer at Indiana University and then became the Baltimore Colts' first pick in the 1964 draft. I did not know Marv, but he and I knew about each other. We were both from Hattiesburg, Mississippi. A town of about 40,000 in south-central Mississippi, Hattiesburg's schools were rigidly segregated in 1965, more than a decade after *Brown v Board of Education*. I had attended the all-white Hattiesburg High School. Marvin, an African American, had gone to the all-black Royal Street High School. White politicians had made the patently absurd claim that the schools were "separate but equal," inviting skeptics to look at the two facilities' exteriors: Royal Street was a new brick structure and Hattiesburg High an old, multistory, dilapidated firetrap. The most cursory investigation revealed, however, that when the white school got new, late-edition textbooks, the black one received its discards, filled with torn pages and graffiti. And while I had the best football equipment that our liberal athletic budget permitted each year, Marvin wore what we rejected. Moreover, while Marvin was a far better athlete, I got more attention from local reporters, whose extensive coverage, action pictures, and feature stories of all-white Hattiesburg High dominated the sports pages. Apart from reporting game scores, the *Hattiesburg American* ignored Royal Street High and its players. Finally, Marvin did not have the opportunity to join me at the segregated University of Mississippi.

Perhaps projecting the anger and resentment I believe I would have had if our fates had been reversed, I dreaded our first encounter. As a veteran, he had the power to inflict pain and embarrassment on me, a lowly rookie. Instead, after I arrived, Marvin sought me out, extended his hand, and said, "Welcome to the Steelers. It's great to have a hometown guy on the team." Never before or since has a greeting meant as much to me nor revealed as much class.

In 1965 Americans were deeply divided over blacks' demands for civil rights. My home state of Mississippi had been the scene of some of the worst expression of racial hatred, particularly in the desegregation of my alma mater, the University of Mississippi. In 1962 James Meredith, an Air Force veteran from Jackson, applied for admission. When he was denied, he sued on the grounds of race discrimination and prevailed. But Governor Ross Barnett intervened, named himself acting registrar of the university, and personally turned down Meredith's application. President John Kennedy and Attorney General Robert Kennedy countered by sending 500 federal marshals and eventually more than 10,000 U.S. troops to the Oxford campus to guarantee Meredith's safe enrollment. I remember the martial atmosphere that prevailed throughout the state on the eve of Meredith's arrival, as Barnett, whose defiance was backed by pledges of militia support from thousands of arch-segregationists throughout the South, prepared Mississippians for the impending confrontation with the federal government. We were playing the University of Kentucky in Jackson on Saturday, the night before Meredith was to arrive on campus. Upon returning to the field after halftime, we heard 50,000 fans singing not the school's fight song or alma mater but a piece newly commissioned by Barnett, a state battle hymn. Before that night I had not associated football with political and social issues. But during the awful days that followed, when two people were killed on our campus, scores injured, and hundreds arrested, I came to realize that society's hopes and fears and politicians' power and authority were sometimes settled on fields of play.

Having grown up in Mississippi, where de jure segregation was securely in place despite *Brown v Board of Education,* I was unprepared for the de facto segregation we encountered in Pittsburgh. The city had a particularly tight housing market when my wife and I first arrived in 1965, in part because in a consolidation move U.S. Steel had brought many of their people back to the city. Quite by accident we found an apartment in the South Hills at a location convenient both to South Park and Pitt Stadium. Many less fortunate teammates holed up in motels and hotels hoping for apartments to come available. Shortly after we moved in, the superintendent stopped me one morning as I left for practice, proudly announcing that a unit was coming on the market and telling me to spread the word among the Steelers. I was delighted and immediately thought of Marv Woodson. Before I got out the door, however, the super called and said, "By the way, no colored are allowed here." Stunned, I replied in my naivete, "How can that be in Pittsburgh? In Mississippi, of course, but here? How can you do that?" As if sensing that I might defy him by bringing a black teammate to look at the unit, he took me to the vacant apartment and pointed to a stack of paint cans in the corner. "If anyone we do not want here comes around to look at the vacancy," he explained, "I just point to the paint cans and tell them the place is still being repainted and is not available." That, I realized, was how the color line was painted north of the Mason-Dixon line.

I soon discovered that professional football softened the hard edges of racism. There is a degree of equality on a football team not seen in the rest of society. Players, black and white, have similar educational backgrounds, earn money based primarily on performance, and perform as equals in a game that demands teamwork and cooperation. To be sure, the National Football League had been slow to recruit black players and coaches, reflecting a similar lag in college football. Before the 1960s, although many outstanding African Americans played in universities across the country, none had been selected as a Heisman Trophy winner. Then, in 1961, Ernie Davis of Syracuse won that cherished award. More important, in the 1960s the NFL drafted the nation's best football players regardless of race, and black athletes immediately demonstrated their talents, dedication, and hard work.

Regardless of race, professional football players engage in a brutal sport, and the 1960s Steelers were past masters of violence. From reading popular sports magazines, I knew something of the Steelers' reputation as tough guys, on and off the field. The issue of *Sport* on the newsstands when I was traded carried a feature story on "Those Hell-Raising Steelers." I soon learned that "hell-raising" was a long and revered part of the team's culture. The pre-Renaissance Steelers were a hard-living, hard-hitting lot whose antics off the field often reflected their ferocity on the gridiron. When Big Daddy Lipscomb arrived in Pittsburgh in the early 1960s, the 300-pound giant found a home where he could sate his enormous "appetites with unbridled zeal." As one sportswriter put it, "In quarterback Bobby Layne and other Steelers roughnecks, Lipscomb had new drinking pals. After practices they would repair to the South Park Inn, where Layne would buy everyone except Lipscomb a drink." He bought Lipscomb a whole bottle of V.O.[4]

One of my teammates, Brady Keys, remembered Big Daddy's Pittsburgh adventures. He said that when he arrived at the giant lineman's place each morning to pick him up for practice, "an orgy was often in progress." Keys recalled that "there would be three or four women, and they would be half naked." He continued, "Big Daddy had enough energy for them all. He was always drunk. And he always had cash lying all over the place. Big Daddy did three things: he drank, he screwed, and he dominated football games."[5] The first two of those activities fit many of my teammates. Regrettably, the latter applied to only one or two.

Steeler lore reinforced the team's image. An important part of a team's culture are the stories that players and coaches circulate about the past. Players select and repeat those stories that current team members find amusing, entertaining, and relevant. The stories amuse and instruct, teaching new players what it takes to be a man in the NFL. At the core of the 1965 Steelers' culture was hard-hitting, hard-drinking, blue-collar masculinity. Not only was that a self-image, it was a widely held perception among those who followed professional football. In fact, a year before I joined the Steelers in 1965, a *Sports Illus-*

trated cover made graphic the team's hard-nosed style of play with its famous photograph of Y. A. Tittle. Many viewed Pittsburgh as a team that played "dirty" football. My guess is that if one considered the matter with some degree of objectivity, rarely possible when discussing sports or politics, the facts would reveal that the Steelers had no more personal fouls or player ejections or fights or brawls than other NFL teams. That said, sometimes because of insufficient talent to make plays, our players committed infractions. Defensive back Brady Keys had a reputation around the league for holding pass receivers that he tried to cover. I rather thought that he simply knew his own limitations, and when he could not cover a young, fast receiver he grabbed the guy's jersey to prevent a sure touchdown. True, some of his offenses were so blatant as to bring a chorus of boos from fans, but teammates saw those as prudent choices by a wily old veteran. On such matters perspective was everything.

In 1965 the two figures who loomed largest in Steeler lore were ghosts of the past—former quarterback Bobby Layne and recently fired coach Buddy Parker. Both had had long, colorful, and successful careers in the NFL. And both were known for their off-field antics as much as their performances on Sunday afternoons. Veterans trafficked freely in Layne lore. He was a Steeler's Steeler—tough, talented, and competitive, with a decided emphasis on tough. His teammates said that while his passes were "ugly," meaning that they rarely had the classic tight spiral, they were accurate. He played the game hard and expected everybody else on the team to do the same, never shrinking from publicly berating those who missed assignments. Lacking the physical size and power to lead by intimidation, he relied upon his good friend and offensive tackle Ernie Stautner as an enforcer. On more than one occasion Layne ordered offensive linemen who failed to provide adequate pass protection to leave the field, knowing that the miscreant would obey because Ernie would enforce the edict. Perhaps the 1965 Steelers loved to repeat Bobby Layne stories because we desperately wanted players with his passion for excellence and winning.

The most oft-repeated story about Layne said as much about the Steelers as it did about the celebrated quarterback. It seems that Layne and his sidekick, running back Tom "the Bomb" Tracy, were out on the town "unwinding" late one Saturday night before a home game the next afternoon. By the wee hours of Sunday morning, the pair was thoroughly relaxed as they sped through the streets of Pittsburgh, a city that still had streetcars in operation. Unfortunately, Tracy, the inebriated driver, plowed into the side of a parked trolley car. It was at this point that the person relating the story always warmed to the telling, enacting how Layne with his inimitable cockiness left the car unscathed, staggered over to the streetcar, and shouted at the operator for not watching where *he* was going. Then, after a pregnant pause, the storyteller would inform his listeners that Layne went out that afternoon and "played a helluva game." It's difficult to say what about the story resonated with players. Perhaps it was triumph despite one's own self-destructive behavior, or the ability "to soar with the eagles after hooting with the owls." I do not recall much analysis after those stories, but it was hard not to share an imaginary swagger with old Bobby.

Buddy Parker tales dribbled toward the dark side, kind of football horror stories. He had made his bones as a top NFL head coach during the 1950s as coach of the Detroit Lions, who regularly challenged Paul Brown's Cleveland Browns for the league championship. When he came to the Steelers in the late 1950s, he brought with him such top players as Bobby Layne and John Henry Johnson.

He reduced the game to bare essentials. The team that made the fewest mistakes (measured by penalties, fumbles, interceptions) and who maintained the best field position (determined in large part by the kicking game) usually won in the NFL. He had little toleration for mistakes. According to one story veterans repeated often, Parker once fired half a dozen players at halftime. It seems that the Steelers' play that Sunday had been particularly hapless. In the locker room, the livid coach paced in front of the players, pausing from time to time to point to an individual and shout, "You!" When he had so identified five or six guys, he said, "Don't bother coming out for the second half, you're cut."

Before I first heard that story and knew better, I managed unwittingly to cross Parker. I had joined the Steelers at training camp at the University of Rhode Island on the Wednesday before a Saturday preseason game against the San Francisco 49ers. Parker devoted much of Friday's meetings to the kicking game, going over blocking assignments and return schemes. Then during practice we went over each aspect carefully. When it came time for the punting team to go through its drills, I assumed my place. Parker again talked about assignments, walked us through what we could expect from the 49ers' punt blocking and return tactics. Finally, he glanced in my direction, said, "Okay, punt a couple," and turned his back on me to watch the proceedings unfold. Speaking to his back, I said, "I do not punt on the day before a game." Far from being insubordinate, I was merely informing him of a longstanding preference, maybe part superstition, for abstaining on the day before combat. Parker spun around and glared at me in disbelief and, I thought, contempt. For what seemed like minutes but actually only a few seconds, he fixed me with a stare that penetrated my soul. Finally, probably sensing that athletes were a superstitious lot, he shook his head and shouted, "Well, throw the goddam thing!"

Our team added its own propensity for outrageous behavior to the folklore. The most memorable incident requiring a cover-up involved a bit of after-hours fisticuffs between two of our players. It occurred, ironically, after we had attended a dinner promoting Catholic Charities in Pittsburgh. The Steelers had very close ties to that wonderful organization that did much good in the community, especially in working with youth. First, Art Rooney's brother was a priest and head of Catholic Charities. Second, we players contributed our fine money to that particular charity. I do not recall if that designation resulted from a vote or from executive fiat, but we all considered it a sage strategy. Throughout the season, coaches fined various players for a variety of infractions, such as practicing or playing without having one's ankles taped ($50), losing one's playbook ($500), or failing to reach a target playing weight ($50 per pound). Poor play or faulty judgment during a game could also cost a player money. Coach Mike Nixon threatened to fine me after one game when we were penalized five yards for having too many men on the field. As punter I was responsible for counting our players to make sure we had eleven. Fortunately, the kick after the penalty was assessed resulted in our having decent field position, and I escaped without financial damage. At the Catholic Charities dinner in question, we dutifully attended and basked in the warm glow that our indiscretions on and off the field would help fund worthwhile initiatives for others. The idea that our failing and our penance would benefit mankind—or childkind—struck me as properly Catholic. Afterwards, we went spiritually our separate ways.

It is safe to say, however, that two destinations attracted most guys. A significant number returned to their apartments and homes to be with their wives or girlfriends. A larger group repaired to the team's favorite watering hole: Dante's Bar. A blue-collar bar on the south side of Pittsburgh, Dante's was the sort of bar where guys went without their spouses. It attracted groupies who wished to make it with football players, and we had plenty of accommodating guys. I went home.

The next morning Coach Nixon convened a special meeting before our regularly scheduled prepractice film session. From his somber demeanor it was apparent to all that something was amiss. Some players shot questioning glances at one another. Others avoided all eye contact as they stared at their hands. After a long pause, Nixon finally spoke, informing us that after the charity dinner two of our teammates had an altercation that rendered one incapacitated for the upcoming game because of a, well . . . crushed cheekbone from the fist of the other. It seems that the two, fullback Mike Lind and guard Ray Lemek, had shared a ride to the previous evening's event. Afterwards, the former looked for the latter for a ride to a bar. Apparently, however, Lemek left without Lind, understanding that his rider had made other arrangements. Highly offended and sorely angered, the aggrieved Lind went in pursuit of Lemek, bent on redress for the slight. Professional football players, like other males of the species throughout history, live by a code of honor. Any word or deed, no matter what the intent behind it, can trigger an immediate demand for satisfaction by the offended party. Unlike eighteenth-century gentlemen, however, twentieth-century NFLers choose to settle things with fists, elbows, knees, feet, and other manly anatomical weapons as opposed to sabers, pistols, or swords. Upon finding Lemek at the aforesaid watering hole, Lind demanded immediate satisfaction, and upon receiving something less than what he deemed acceptable to assuage his fevered spirit, he proceeded to pummel Lemek's face with a savagery characteristic of people who make their livings from such bellicosity, albeit governed by rules intended to make the violence just. Nixon, a former Pennsylvania state representative, assured us that he had contacted local officials and sympathetic members of the press to keep the affair from public attention. Most of us gave the incident little thought. Having been in the sport at some level for decades, I knew this sort of behavior was not unusual. When I was playing at the University of Mississippi, a similar incident occurred on the practice field. The second-team center landed a brutal blow between the interstices of the face mask of the first-team center who was playing middle linebacker at the time. After the injured party left for the hospital—also with a caved-in cheekbone—the head coach said simply, "Gentlemen, let's keep our hands to ourselves." He then told the survivor to put on a first-team jersey, and we resumed practice as if nothing had happened.

Unfortunately our ferocity was matched by our fecklessness on the field. We approached each Sunday with optimism and believed that we had a solid game plan that could produce a victory. But we managed, through penalties, fumbles, and interceptions, to beat ourselves. One game in particular stands out in my mind as representative of how we self-destructed. In preparing for a home game against a hapless Philadelphia squad, our coaching staff noticed that the Eagles' punt-return team left itself vulnerable to a pass because the players moved quickly to set up a running lane for their returner. Therefore, we installed a fake punt and worked on it all week. With Roy Jefferson playing end on our punt-coverage team, we had our best receiver in position to pop open over the middle for a pass that I would toss after beginning the motions for a punt. After executing the play successfully all week long, we were confident it would work and were eager to try it in the game. Our game plan called for us to use the play the first time we had to punt. But, on that cold December Sunday afternoon, we reached new levels of ineptitude. In the first quarter the Eagles intercepted three passes and returned them for touchdowns, a new NFL record. By the time we faced our first punting situation, we were down 35-0. As I left the sidelines, I asked Coach Nixon if he wanted to go with the fake punt. "Hell, no!" he replied, "Punt the goddamned thing." So many of our balls had been intercepted I feel he suffered from shell shock.

Frustrated by our ineptitude, Art Rooney replaced Nixon after the 1965 season. In 1966 the Steelers started the season with high hopes fueled by a new head coach, Bill Austin, one of Vince Lombardi's assistants at Green Bay. He brought to the task a great deal of energy and a determination to transform us into a more disciplined football team. Toward that end, he imposed a grading system for position coaches to evaluate the performance of each player under his tutelage. To illustrate, consider the play of a defensive back. If that player did his job on a given play, say prevented a completion, he received a zero (0). If he did something exceptional, say made an interception, he got a plus one (+1). And if he really excelled, say, ran an interception back for a touchdown, he was awarded with a plus two (+2). Conversely, if the back got beaten for a completion, he received a minus one (–1), and if he got beaten for a touchdown, he got a minus two (–2). An overall grade of 0 meant that the player did his job consistently. Cumulative scores above or below 0 reflected exceptional play either positively or negatively. On Tuesdays after reviewing films of the previous game, the ratings were posted for all to see. Players congregated at the bulletin board to see how they and their teammates performed. Usually, however, mistakes had been highlighted twice previously: once during the game itself and again during the film session. The posted ratings served as a visual, permanent record of one's performance.

Illustrative of the gap between Austin's expectations and our performance was the occasion when one of our guys received a –2 for the game without leaving the sidelines. One of our captains, defensive end John Baker, had missed several games because of an injury. As we prepared for a home game against the Cowboys, however, Baker worked out and was deemed ready for limited action. Defensive coach Lavern "Torgy" Torgeson decided to use John only on the goal-line defense, that is, when the opposing team had the ball inside our five-yard line. Throughout the week, sportswriters and sportscasters had trumpeted John's return, unaware that he would see only limited duty. They conveyed the notion that his service would no doubt end our losing ways. I remember the day well, a cold, wet Sunday in late November. When not playing, parka-clad players milled about perpetually searching for a measure of warm, dry comfort. The Cowboys got their offense going, and quarterback Don Meredith drove them down the field. A pass resulted in first and goal at our two-yard line. Clearly a situation calling for our goal-line defense, our big guys lumbered onto the field all, that is, except John Baker. Meredith came to the line of scrimmage, noticed that we had no defensive end on one side, called an audible, and walked the ball into the end zone. Austin was livid. His anger turned to head-shaking bewilderment, however, when Baker explained his failure to enter the game because he was unsure if first and goal from the two-yard line constituted a goal-line situation. The "Jesus Christ!" that Austin roared transformed Pitt Stadium into an evangelistic crusade for a brief moment. On the following Tuesday, we all saw Baker's score posted by his name: –2. And he never removed his parka.

The following year, after I had left the team, Austin again sought to transform the Steelers into a finely tuned, winning machine. This time he brought to training camp a team of psychologists to administer a battery of tests. It was a scientific experiment. The idea was to see if there were any personality quirks that threatened team solidarity and, if so, to deal with them in a way that promoted cohesion. In a team meeting introducing the testing, Austin expressed his belief that the Steelers could go all the way this year and that he wanted to take every measure to ensure success. Hence, the psychological testing. My old roommate was still on the team, and he is my primary source for what happened during the testing. He said that the exams consisted of such questions as "When did you stop wetting the bed?" and "Do you love your mother?" Because the instruments were designed to be taken at the examinee's own pace, players finished at different times and left the room. My ex-roomie said he finished in fifteen minutes, and that virtually everyone else had completed the task shortly thereafter. After turning in his paper, he remained in the room and conversed for thirty minutes or so with a couple of the assistant coaches. As he started to leave, he noticed that three teammates, hulking defensive linemen, with pencils dwarfed in their outsized mitts, were still taking the test. Curious as to what could possibly be taking so long, my buddy walked undetected behind the trio and peered over their shoulders. To his surprise, they were all on question number 9 of the 100 or so total. He watched silently as the three sat motionless, hovered over their papers. Finally, one said to another, "Hey," calling one of his pals by name, "what do you think the answer is?" My narrator thought in disbelief, "My God, we are in deep trouble. These guys are cheating on personality tests!" Unfortunately, the screening program failed to improve performance on the field: the Steelers' record fell to 4-9-1, one less win than that of 1966.

At the end of the 1966 season, I decided to leave professional football to pursue other interests. While the won-loss results of the pre-Renaissance Steelers were frustrating, the challenges, competition, and camaraderie of those Steeler teams are memorable. We simply lacked the talent and leadership to bring a championship to Pittsburgh. It would take a new coach and new players, perhaps best exemplified by another player named Lambert, for the Steelers to enjoy the kind of renaissance befitting the city they represented.

FRANK LAMBERT is professor of history at Purdue University and the author, most recently, of *Inventing the Great Awakening*. He was a college All-American at the University of Mississippi and a punter for the Pittsburgh Steelers (1965-66).

4

PITTSBURGH POISON

THE WANER BOYS

THOMAS E. SCHOTT

PAUL WANER AND his younger brother Lloyd were just little kids in 1909 when Forbes Field, a ballpark for the new century, opened in the Oakland–Schenley Park section of Pittsburgh, about three miles east of downtown, in farm fields split by a ravine and populated partially by cows and partially by people pushing out the boundaries of the growing city. The modern concrete and steel showcase cost $2 million and seated 25,000 fans. In the simpler time of this field's birth, ballpark names connected with their place or team. This new field commemorated Gen. John Forbes, a British general in the French and Indian War, who in 1758 captured Fort Duquesne on the site where stood Fort Pitt. By the 1920s, when the Waners began to grace its outfield, beautiful Forbes Field, with its elevator-served three-tiered grandstand, had been dubbed the "Hialeah of ball parks."[1]

Forbes Field, like the Waners themselves, is now but a memory. All that remains are traces: parts of the brick outfield wall, the base of the flagpole, and, in almost its exact location, home plate, encased in glass on the first-floor walkway of the University of Pittsburgh's Forbes Quadrangle. Mervis Hall stands in right field. Roberto Clemente Drive runs about ten feet under what used to be the infield. A plaque in a cement walkway marks the spot where one of the most famous home runs in baseball history, Bill Mazeroski's World Series–winning shot of 1960, sailed over Yogi Berra's head and into the trees behind the left-field fence.[2]

Paul and Lloyd Waner's plaques are in the Baseball Hall of Fame in Cooperstown, New York.

Why anyone should have ever called Paul Waner "Big Poison" as a physical description of the guy is a mystery. The story goes that the Pittsburgh Pirates' rightfielder got tagged with the nickname by a loud-mouthed fan at the Polo Grounds who put the Brooklyn spin on the pronunciation of the word "person." But a big person Paul Waner was not. The elder of this most famous of baseball brother acts stood only five feet, eight-and-a-half inches tall and weighed 153 pounds dripping wet. "Little Poison," the moniker applied to his brother Lloyd by the same fan at the same time, was just as unlikely. Just about the same size, five-foot-nine and 150 pounds, Lloyd Waner had arrived at the Pirates in 1927 even smaller: 132 pounds. Pie Traynor, Pittsburgh's Hall of Fame third baseman, took one look at the rookie at spring training and pronounced him "too small, too thin, and too scrawny." Both were shrimps by today's standards, and even by the standards of the 1920s when they broke into the big leagues.[3]

Shrimps or not, few opposing pitchers found the antidote to the kind of poison the Waners dished out from the batter's box. For thirteen years together on the club, the Waner boys terrorized them. Line-drive hitters with superb bat control, they hit to all fields. "Paul had the best bat control of any hitter I ever faced," said Hall of Fame left-hander Carl Hubbell. "He could foul off your best pitch, your 'out' pitch. Then he had you." And they both ran like the jackrabbits of the plains of Oklahoma where they had been born and raised. Either was as likely to beat out a high infield chopper for a hit as to rattle a shot off the outfield boards in the gaps. One of them, or so it seemed, was always on base. By all accounts, both had extraordinary eyesight, "Cats eyes," groused an opposing manager. "Probably can see in the dark."[4]

In fact, at least one didn't see all that well. Paul had an astigmatism, but he didn't like wearing glasses on the field, he once explained to an astonished Casey Stengel. He admitted they brought the ball into sharper focus, made the ball seem just about the right size. But without glasses, he said, the ball appeared "about as big as a grapefruit. . . . I liked the big blur because I just aimed for the middle of it." Lloyd's eyes were just fine. The brothers consistently made contact with the ball. Over the course of their careers—eighteen seasons for Lloyd and twenty for Paul—they struck out (another way of saying failed to put the ball in play) a total of only 449 times between them, an average of about twelve times each per season.[5]

During their careers the Waner boys amassed a total of 5,611 hits, far more than any other long-standing brother combo in the big leagues—517 more than the three DiMaggio brothers, 753 more than the three Alou brothers, and 1,394 more than the five Delahantys who played around the turn of the century. (Also 1,624 more than Hank and Tommie Aaron, if anyone's counting.) No other pair of brothers ever got over 200 hits each in a season. The Waners did it three times. Only the DiMaggio boys surpassed them in career doubles, and they join the Aarons in surpassing their career totals of runs scored and runs batted in. Otherwise, the Waners are tops in all these departments, plus far ahead in triples over all. "They just killed you with zillions of doubles and triples," Hubbell said.[6]

Paul hit with more power, and although he wasn't a home-run slugger, opponents dreaded him. Billy Herman, a Hall of Fame infielder with the Cubs and Dodgers, echoed Hubbell. "Pound for pound Paul Waner was the best hitter I ever saw. Nothing worked on him—we never found a way to get him out."[7] In an age of prodigious batsmen such as Joe Medwick, Mel Ott, Johnny Mize, Chuck Klein, and Bill Terry, he led the National League in doubles twice, triples twice, in total base hits twice, in runs scored twice, and RBIs once—this in addition to his three batting crowns. (It would have been four batting titles if today's rules governed in 1926, his rookie year, when he played in 144 games and had well over 500 at-bats. Instead, fans witnessed the incredible spectacle of a catcher, Cincinnati's Eugene "Bubbles" Hargrave, walk off with the honor with only 326 at-bats.) From 1926 through 1934, and then again in 1936, 1937, and 1939, Paul Waner's name appeared among the top five in some major offensive category. Lloyd, who carried a less potent stick—he was more of a spray singles hitter—also occasionally turned up on the same lists.[8]

There is hardly a single list of lifetime offensive achievements for the Pirates that one Waner, but usually both, doesn't appear on. For example, both are in at least the top eight for runs, hits, singles, and triples, not to mention games and at-bats. Paul has the highest lifetime average as a Pirate, .340. He shares the all-time Pirate lead in doubles (556) with the legendary Honus Wagner; he is second in base on balls (909), third in extra base hits (850), and fourth in total bases (4,120). Paul Waner also holds the single-season Pirate record for hits (237 in 1927), doubles (62 in 1932), and RBIs (131 in 1927). Lloyd holds it for singles (198 in 1927). With only slight exaggeration, it's safe to say these guys were superstars and franchise players before anyone ever invented the descriptions.[9]

It's almost impossible to talk about baseball players without talking about numbers. If the stories and memories are the soul of baseball, numbers and statistics are its heart and lifeblood. The game lives on them, devours them, worships them. More than any other sport, baseball statistics have a way of enshrining the game's heroes and forever tarnishing the game's incompetents, of putting flesh on memories. They embody the history of seasons, of teams, of series, of single ball games. They whisper the heartbreaks and shout the triumphs that linger in the minds of fans for decades. They encapsulate the careers of every player, magnificent or insignificant, every manager, every team. And now, with the advent of the computer and a level of sophistication and precision never before possible, baseball statistics for the first time allow statistically valid comparisons of players from different eras.[10]

And of course they enable more finely honed comparisons of players in the same era. The subjective appraisals of players, dear to the hearts of all baseball fans—who was or is the best clutch hitter, the best base runner, the better fielder, and so forth—the source of countless arguments and heated partisanship, can now be verified with a much higher degree of confidence.

On the basis of modern statistical research—or by traditional measures, for that matter—the Waners were as poisonous on defense as at the plate. Few realize just how good they were. During the years 1926–40, they dominated other National League outfielders. No other centerfielder of the period had fewer errors in as many games than Lloyd Waner. He led the league four times in putouts; Paul led once in assists. Together they stand number one and two in total putouts during that time—no other pair of outfielders is even close—number one and five in the number of assists, one and five in highest fielding average, two and five in number of double plays. And in total chances and successful chances, the two brothers are in a class by themselves.[11]

"No better center fielder ever lived and that includes Tris Speaker," said Pie Traynor about Lloyd Waner in 1951, and referring to the American League centerfielder universally regarded then as the best ever. Traynor was right, though. Speaker was flashier, but Waner was steadier, made fewer errors, and, most important, covered more ground. He got more hitters out—about 6 percent more per season. And that's all that counts in the field.[12]

In the forty-eight years that have passed since Traynor made his observation, little has happened that would cause him to change his mind. Indeed, only one centerfielder who played for ten seasons or more since Lloyd has surpassed him in terms of successful chances per game, Hall of Famer Richie Ashburn of the Philadelphia Phillies. When it came to patrolling center field by this measure of excellence, Little Lloyd Waner did it better than all the rest of the flamboyant speedsters since: Kirby Puckett, Lance Johnson, Devon White, Willie Mays, even the immortal Joe DiMaggio.[13]

Like most ballplayers of the early part of the century, Lloyd and big brother Paul learned how to play the game in rural America. The boys spent their boyhood years in Harrah, Oklahoma, a little town a few miles northeast of Oklahoma City. Oddly, the town is named after a man who made both of the land runs in Indian territory in 1889 and 1891 and failed to stake a claim either time. The town's favorite sons had been playing ball in Pittsburgh for a couple of years when Harrah became one of the first small towns in Oklahoma to get electricity.[14]

Both Paul and Lloyd were born before Oklahoma became a state, Paul on April 16, 1903, the third of five children in the family, and Lloyd exactly thirty-five months later to the day. Their upbringing for that part of the country was atypical. The Waner family had money. Their father, Ora Lee Waner, owned a profitable 400-acre wheat and alfalfa farm. (All his life, the boys, Paul especially, resented any implication that they sprang from Okie stock of the Tom Joad variety. Why, Paul pointed out, they both had gone to college, and growing up each had his own horse and gun.) The brothers came by their baseball abilities honestly: their father had played professional baseball with the Oklahoma City team in the Western League in 1898. As a kid back in Illinois, Papa Waner had apparently played well enough to receive a job offer from the Chicago White Sox, but he turned it down. His destiny lay in Harrah, Oklahoma, encouraging and teaching his sons how to play.[15]

The boys learned how to catch with an old catcher's mitt and their father's wicked curve balls; they learned how to hit with hoe handles and wet corncobs. According to Paul, no curve ball thrown by any pitcher in the major leagues was as hard to hit as corncobs. "A cob, thrown hard enough, just naturally takes all kinds of unnatural shoots and jumps." Hours of this every day of the week, "that was where I learned to follow the ball."[16] Every month or so their father would have them compete in a hundred-yard dash, showing them how to run on their toes for greater speed. "So you had that combination of things," Lloyd later remembered. "The constant playing, the desire, the love for the game, the encouragement and good coaching from our Dad; it all helped us to develop what God-given abilities we had."[17]

Both brothers developed an almost identical hitting style, and neither thought it anything special. No young player today, though, would be allowed to adopt the Waner way. Not only would it look strange, but it would also violate several supposedly inviolable tenets drilled into players from the first days of Little League. The Waners were not interested in swinging for the fences, neither had ever heard of bat speed. Their approach to hitting a baseball was as natural as corncobs and ax handles. They choked up several inches on the handle and awaited the pitch with the bat resting on their shoulders. The pitcher "can't throw until he pulls his arm back," Paul explained. "And until he gets the ball to the plate, you can't hit it." All you had to do was wait until then.[18]

"Paul used to lay the bat right on his shoulder and keep it there until the last second, and then with those strong wrists he'd whip it around and make that ball zing. I did it the same way," said Lloyd. Naturally, some of the managers around the league decreed inside pitches to the Waners on the theory that they "wouldn't be able to get the bat around on it. But the inside pitch never bothered us; in fact we hit it better."[19] Indeed. Burleigh Grimes, shaking his head over Paul Waner's uncanny talent with the bat, confessed, "I once threw a side arm spitter right into his belly and he hit it into the upper deck."[20]

Paul preached incessantly on the importance of hitting down on the ball, not up. This would produce a level stroke, he said, and line drives. "Be relaxed and don't wave the bat, don't clench it," he would advise young hitters. "Be ready to hit down with the barrel of the bat. Just swing it and let the weight drive the ball."[21]

Like all great hitters, the boys shared a certain disdain for the pitching profession. Paul didn't think many pitchers were strong enough to overpower hitters. The design of the game, sixty feet between pitcher and hitter, made sure of it. "I used to pay no attention to the pitcher while he did all that winding up and messing around. I acted just like he wasn't there." He refused to waste his time giving pitchers the death glare.[22]

Other subjects given major attention today Paul Waner dismissed. Batting stance? It had "very little to do with it. I never paid attention to it. Just walk up there and hit the ball."[23] Carefully selected bats for better bat speed? Bat didn't matter at all, said Waner. Elbie Fletcher, a teammate in the late 1930s, says, "One day, just to prove his point, he told us to pick out any bat we wanted and he'd use it in the game. Each time he went up to the plate we'd toss him a different bat. Well, he went four for five."[24] Paul tells the story of how he got six hits in a game (a feat that has happened only about forty times in each league this century). Having a smoke in the corner of the dugout interrupted, "I hustled out to the plate and just grabbed a bat on the way, any bat, I didn't even look. And I got a hit. So I thought, well, maybe that's not a bad way to do. The next time up I did the same thing, just grabbed a bat blind, not looking, and off came another hit. So I did that all day. Six bats and six hits." He doesn't mention that two were doubles, one a triple. Nor did he know that he is only one of five Pirates to have done this in a nine-inning game ever.[25]

What it came down to was bat control: the Waners could put the ball where they wanted it go. Paul preached hitting down both foul lines, and then for the holes in the outfield if they tried to cover the lines. "It took a lot of practice to hit where we wanted to," Lloyd said.

"Paul could. I could hit the baseball where I wanted to—but I had to wait for my pitch, or go with the ball where it was pitched." The story is told that Paul once asked a rival catcher where he wanted the ball to go. Going along with the gag, the catcher told him and then called for the exact opposite pitches. Paul hit four doubles in that game exactly where he said he would.[26]

One thing is certain: when Big Poison stroked those doubles, he was either under the influence of alcohol or hung over. It's anyone's guess what the ultimate effect John Barleycorn had on Paul Waner's career numbers, not to mention his health, because there is abundant evidence that he was a full-blown alcoholic throughout his time with the Pirates and beyond. He kept a flask sewn in his uniform, which he would nip on while in the outfield. He had become a daily drinker during his three years in the minor leagues; he didn't stop drinking until four years before his death in 1965, although according to John Hernon, a grizzled Pittsburgh sportswriter, he "was in and out of AA" during his playing time. His AA time could never have been for long. Somebody calculated that Waner was free of whiskey for only seven weeks during his twenty-one years in the majors.[27]

But Waner had a Hall of Fame career regardless. The stories of Paul and booze are legion. Bill Veeck, then working for the Cubs front office, swore he once saw Paul playing inebriated. And not because of the double and game-winning home run Waner hit in the game but because of what he did after he hit the two-bagger. Veeck saw him "take a wide turn at second base and go sliding into the bullpen mound in the left-field foul ground" better than 60 feet from his destination at third base. On the other hand, Casey Stengel maintained Waner had to be a graceful player "because he could slide without breaking the bottle on his hip."[28]

Ray Parmalee, a pitcher for the Giants, claimed the best way to pitch to Waner was talk to him before a game to see if he'd been drinking. If he had, he would pull the ball to right; if not, he'd go to left. "So we'd pitch him just the opposite," Parmalee said. "Not that it made a great deal of difference."[29] Howie Grossklos, a teammate in the 1930s, said he never saw Paul intoxicated, but imbibing seemed to improve his visual acumen. So hungover one day that he couldn't see the scoreboard, Waner still went four for four.[30]

Paul's dexterity with a baseball bat while incapacitated beyond the ability of ordinary mortals to do much of anything is a common theme. The story goes that once before a game with the Cubs, "Paul arrived, lubricated to the ear-drums, and, calling Gabby [Hartnett, the Cubs' catcher] aside, said, 'Gabby, the old boy is a little bleary today so as a special favor, I'm going to ask you to tell the pitchers to keep 'em away from my head.' 'Our pitchers don't throw them at your head,' said Gabby, 'but I'll tell them to be extra careful today anyway.'" They were, and Waner stroked four doubles to beat them.[31]

Paul Waner received his first offer to play baseball professionally from the Oklahoma City team in the Class A Western League. He was a sixteen-year-old pitching for his high school team. But Papa Waner insisted that his boys finish school first. It wasn't until a few years later, in 1921, that Paul actually signed his first contract to play professional baseball, with Joplin of the Western League. But he didn't report. Still in school at East Central State Teachers College in Ada, Oklahoma, Paul stayed put. But for his father Paul might have been tempted. He really didn't want to be a teacher, though. "What I wanted to be was a lawyer," he said, "and I figured sooner or later I'd go to law school. Eventually I was going to go to Harvard Law School. . . . That was my ambition, anyway."[32]

He wasn't kidding. Despite his later well-earned reputation as a habitual late-night, sometimes all-night denizen of watering holes in every National League city, Paul Waner had a serious, reflective side. As a kid he had entertained the idea of becoming a poet, even made a few sales to magazines. He read the Greek and Roman philosophers, developing a particular fondness for Seneca. But baseball got to him first.[33]

Waner's local reputation as a spectacular first baseman, outfielder, and pitcher for independent and college teams inevitably attracted the attention of Dick Williams, a professional scout from the San Francisco Seals, a Triple-A franchise in the Pacific Coast League. According to Paul, it happened only indirectly, by pure luck. Dick Williams had never even seen him play. He had been over in Muskogee checking out another prospect before launching himself onto a ten-day bender. On the train back to San Francisco, the local train conductor appraised the bleary scout about a phenomenal local player named Paul Waner. Williams grasped this straw to concoct a story to cover his ten-day silence: he had been in Ada looking Waner over, he told the Seals . . . and he didn't see how the kid could miss.[34]

Then he wrote to Paul, instructing him, "Tell me all about yourself: your height, your weight, whether you're left-handed or right-handed, how fast you can run the hundred and all that. So I'll know." Paul did, carefully following directions not to send the letter to the ball club, but to Williams's home.[35]

The following spring, to Waner's surprise, a contract and a train ticket to the Coast arrived in the mail. Within days, after solemnly promising his father to return to school if he failed, Paul made his way to San Francisco. The Seals had intended to try him out as a pitcher but speedily changed their minds once they saw him hit. Paul was nineteen years old, and somebody was willing to pay him $400 a month to play baseball. He never went back to college.[36]

Three years later, in 1926, the Pittsburgh Pirates paid the then-astronomical sum of $100,000 to purchase Paul Waner's contract from San Francisco. The pint-sized outfielder had torn up the Coast League three years running, never hitting below .356. His record for 1925 with the Seals, his last in the minors, reads like a string of misprints. In the 174-game season he hit .401, with 167 runs, 280 hits, 75 doubles, and 130 RBIs, and 36 assists in the outfield. He would have been a magnificent bargain all by himself, but as it turned out, the Pirates got Lloyd along with Paul, a steal. Big Poison beat Little Poison to Pittsburgh by one year.[37]

Neither of these brothers had anyone dearer to them than the other. Any number of commentators mentions it. Ray Berres, a former teammate, remarked on the "fondness or love they had for one another and how often they referred to each other as 'Little Brother' and 'Big Brother.'" Paul wasted no time talking up his kid brother's baseball prowess as soon as he got out to San Francisco. The Seals signed Lloyd to a contract in 1925 and "Little Brother" watched from the bench while "Big Brother" hit .401. Upset that the Seals had welshed on their verbal commitment to him for a $1,500 signing bonus, Lloyd asked for his release early in 1926, Paul's rookie year with Pittsburgh.[38]

By this time Paul had convinced Barney Dreyfuss, the Pirates' owner, that his younger brother played better than he did. Dreyfuss didn't need any convincing. He immediately signed Lloyd to a contract with the club and farmed him out to Columbia, South Carolina, in the South Atlantic League. Lloyd's one year there amply proved to the Pirates that the nineteen-year-old was ready to play ball with the big boys. In a shortened season he hit .345 with twenty-eight doubles and fourteen triples, and he patrolled the outfield with uncanny grace and speed.[39]

Lloyd reported to the Pirates spring training camp in Pasa Robles, California, the following year—all 132 pounds of him. His brother says the club really just wanted to have a look at him. No one had any thought of his actually making the team. Not only did he make the team, he made the starting lineup, too. As fate would have it, the regular leftfielder, a seven-year veteran by the name of Clyde "Pooch" Barnhart, reported to camp about 110 pounds overweight. Although management managed to sweat and run the weight off him, it left him "so weak he could hardly lift a bat." So Lloyd Waner started the season in left field. He wouldn't leave the starting lineup for the next thirteen years.[40]

The 1927 Pittsburgh Pirate team stood at the tail end of a long and honorable tradition of baseball in the City of Steel. Major league baseball had been there continuously since 1882, when the Pittsburgh Alleghenys had been accepted into the American Association, a rival of the National League. Actually an earlier edition of the Alleghenys first brought professional baseball to the city in April 1876, playing their first game in Union Park. This team had disbanded after only a couple of years. In 1887 Pittsburgh became the first American Association club to defect to the older and more prestigious National League.

The Allegheny Mountains certainly stood a lot higher than their namesakes on the diamond for the rest of the nineteenth century. It would not be stretching the truth to describe those teams as almost uniformly miserable. Only once in the thirteen years from 1887 to 1899 did a Pittsburgh team finish higher than fifth. And in 1890, when most of the team had jumped ship to the rival Pittsburgh Players' League club, they sank to the lowest point in franchise history. That team lost 113 games while winning only 23; it finished 66½ games out of first (and 23 behind the next-to-last club). The next year, having nabbed a valuable player through an administrative oversight that failed to reserve him to his proper team, the Pittsburghers got accused of being "piratical" by their frustrated rival. The nickname stuck, and it's been the Pittsburgh Pirates ever since.[41]

The team entered into its most glorious decade as the twentieth century began. Having benefited by the player fallout from the dissolution of the Louisville Colonels, the Pirates stayed in the chase until the waning days of the season in 1900. They finished second to Brooklyn, only 4½ games off the pace. This fine season was but a prelude to three straight pennants, from 1901 to 1903. Several former Louisville players formed the backbone of these teams, especially shortstop Honus Wagner, outfielder/manager Fred Clarke, and pitcher Rube Waddell.[42] In addition to the players, Pittsburgh benefited in another way from the breakup of the Colonels. It "acquired" Barney Dreyfuss as owner, as well as the fourteen Louisville players who came over with him. As owner of the Louisville club, Dreyfuss obtained half ownership of the Pirates at the merger; a year later he bought the other half. Shrewd, knowledgeable, and far-sighted, he became the power behind the Pirates. During his thirty-two years as owner, his team would finish out of the first division only six times.[43]

The 1902 Pittsburgh team ranks among the greatest in baseball history. It finished an astonishing 27½ games ahead of second-place Brooklyn, still a major league record for a full season almost a hundred years later.[44] The team led the league in all of the major offensive categories, while Wagner and others garnered most of the individual honors. The ace of the pitching staff, Jack Chesbro, who would soon jump ship to pitch in the rival American League then in its infancy, won twenty-eight games. Other desertions to the new league diluted the Pirates the following year, but the team still waltzed to the pennant by 6½ games. And then it had the distinction of being the first National League to play in, and lose, a World Series to a team in the new American League—the Boston Pilgrims, five games to three in a best-of-nine series.[45]

The Pirates didn't have a real contender for the pennant again until 1908, when the team finished tied with the New York Giants, both a single game out of first behind the Chicago Cubs. Many knowledgeable fans regard the pennant race that year as the most exciting ever.

The flag was still in the Bucs' grasp on the last day of the season, and had they beaten the Cubs that day the pennant would have been theirs. But they lost. The season finally came down to a single game replay between New York and Chicago, which the Cubs won, 4-2. Chicago's winning percentage of .643 stood .007 points higher than the .636 of both Pittsburgh and New York. It could hardly get any closer.[46]

The following year Pittsburgh celebrated its brand-new ballpark in Oakland and Schenley Park by bringing home its fourth league title of the decade in magnificent style, winning a club-record 110 games. Only one other team in National League history won more during a season, and that just three years before when the Chicago Cubs won 116 games. Although the hitting on this Pirate club was adequate—Wagner won another batting title and drove in a hundred runs—pitching made the difference. Two pitchers, Howie Camnitz and Vic Willis, produced forty-seven wins between them; a third, Lefty Leifeld, won nineteen games. Rookie right-hander Babe Adams won twelve games and lost three, and then went on to win three games in the World Series. The pitching staff had an earned run average of 2.07 overall. Most teams today would be delighted with an ERA twice that. The Bucs went on to defeat the Detroit Tigers in the World Series, four games to three. But an era had ended. The Pittsburgh Pirates haven't come close to duplicating the feat of four flags in any nine years since.[47]

Of the 1909 champions, only Adams, then forty-three years old, remained on the team sixteen years later in 1925 when Pittsburgh again won the National League flag. This magnificent team hit .307 and scored 912 runs, leaving the rest of the league in the dust—the second-place Giants finished 8½ back. The World Series against the Washington Senators went a full seven games, with the Pirates becoming the first team to come back from a 3-1 deficit to win the Series. Kiki Cuyler's winning hit in the rain-drenched final game, a ground-rule double drilled down the line in right in the bottom of the eighth, capped a three-run rally. Washington went quietly in the ninth; Steel City went bonkers. Little did the delirious fans realize that it would be thirty-five years, many of them lean indeed, before they again tasted wine so sweet.[48]

It is one of the ironies of baseball in Pittsburgh that during the period 1926–35, when as many as four or five future Hall of Famers adorned the lineup daily, the team could bring home the flag only once.[49] Pittsburgh's rabid fans naturally expected another winner in 1926. And Paul Waner's extraordinary rookie season that year couldn't blunt the disappointment of the World Champion team's third-place finish in the race behind St. Louis, a dark-horse pennant winner, and the Cincinnati Reds.

Baseball fans usually have long memories. But the arrival of the Waner Brothers, Act II, the following year immediately blotted out what from the perspective of a Pirate supporter must have seemed an aberrational season. No commentator on National League baseball for that year fails to mark it. Paul and Lloyd had help, of course: Traynor hit .342 with 106 RBIs and played brilliant third base, shortstop Glenn Wright drove in 105, pitcher Carmen Hill won twenty-two games, Ray Kremer won nineteen with a league-leading 2.47 ERA. And the staff workhorse Lee Meadows also won nineteen, with 299 innings pitched and twenty-five complete games. But the Oklahoma brothers' combined numbers are staggering. Their 460 hits were 28 percent of the team's total; they scored 30 percent of the runs and got 25 percent of the extra base hits that year. Lloyd hit .355, second on the team's to Paul's league-leading .380, and third in the league. Big Brother Paul also led the league in hits, triples, and RBIs. Understandably, the National League elected him Most Valuable Player at the end of the season. The Rookie of the Year Award had not yet come into being. No question that Lloyd would have won it hands down.[50]

But (as some might say) cruel Fate decreed, the Pirates had to tangle with the New York Yankees in the World Series. The Yankee team was greater than the sum of its parts, but what parts they were! In this year of Charles Lindbergh and the *Spirit of St. Louis,* the New York Yankees showcased an arguably more renowned and adored hero: Babe Ruth. Not that George Herman Ruth was not a colossus before 1927, but this season he hit sixty home runs: the benchmark for power hitters for a generation, a number that just by itself conjures up mental pictures of monumental blasts into the upper decks and sometimes clear out of ballparks. And images of a barrel-chested hell-raiser with those short, spindly legs and choppy stride slowly circling the bases: a legend.

But the team itself became a legend, still regarded by many as the best of all time. The Yankees won 110 games and led the league in every offensive category but doubles and stolen bases. "Those fellows not only beat you, but they tear your heart out," moaned Washington first baseman Joe Judge after a pair of drubbings by the Yanks (12-1 and 21-1) on July 4. "I wish the season was over." Ruth all by himself hit more home runs than thirteen of the fifteen other major league *teams* in 1927, and his twenty-four-year-old teammate Lou Gehrig hit forty-seven, more than anybody else but the Babe had ever hit before. By the by, Ruth hit .356 and Gehrig .373. Gehrig drove in 175 runs and Ruth 164. At season's end, the duo topped the American League in home runs, slugging percentage, runs, bases on balls, RBI, and total bases.[51]

And Ruth and Gehrig were but half of a "Murderers' Row" that also dished up leftfielder Bob Meusel (.337 and 103 RBI) and second baseman Tony Lazzeri (.309, 18 HRs—third in the league—and 102 RBI). And then there was Earle Combs, the centerfielder and best lead-off hitter in the game. He hit .356 and finished third in total bases (331) and in runs scored (137). "He and Gehrig finished 1-2 in the American League, respectively, in hits (231, 218) and triples (23, 18). Combs led the league in singles (166); Gehrig led in doubles (52). . . . Meusel ranked number two in stolen bases (with 24); Lazzeri tied for number three (with 22). And so on."[52]

And all this before you even talk about the pitching, which was what really made this team indomitable. Yankee hurlers had the league's best ERA, 3.20, a spectacular achievement at a time of livelier baseballs and pulled-in fences. Fifteen years would pass before another pitching staff in either league did as well. The Yankees also claimed four of the seven best pitchers with ERAs under 3.00. The staff ace, Waite Hoyt, went 22-7, just one of five Yankee pitchers with winning percentages over .700. Thirty-year-old rookie Wilcy Moore, a relief specialist who started only a dozen games, compiled a 19-7 won-lost record and a 2.28 ERA, lowest in the league.[53]

Reportedly Babe Ruth commented when he first saw the Waners in Pittsburgh, "Why they're just kids. If I was that little, I'd be afraid of getting hurt." His was a common reaction. "Hey," yelled a fan from the stands before the first game of the World Series. "Are them little

Fritzie Zivic lands a solid right to the head of Henry Armstrong during their title bout in 1940. Zivic went on to win the fight and the welterweight championship. (*Courtesy of Helen Zivic.*)

In the age of Jack Dempsey, no fighter was more feared and respected than Harry Greb. Gene Tunney remembered his first of five fights with Greb as "terrifying." Here, Greb glowers into the camera in 1922 (*Carnegie Library, Pittsburgh.*)

(Opposite, top) From the hill overlooking the north end zone, Pittsburghers could watch the games in Pitt Stadium free of charge, though they could not see a third of the field. This shot was taken from the roof of the Veteran's Hospital during a Pitt-Notre Dame game in the 1950s. (*Copyright, Robin Rombach,* Pittsburgh Post-Gazette, *2000, all rights reserved. Reprinted with permission.*)

(Opposite, bottom) The view from the seats along the first-base line of Forbes Field. Pitt's Cathedral of Learning looms over the left-field wall. (*Pittsburgh Pirates.*)

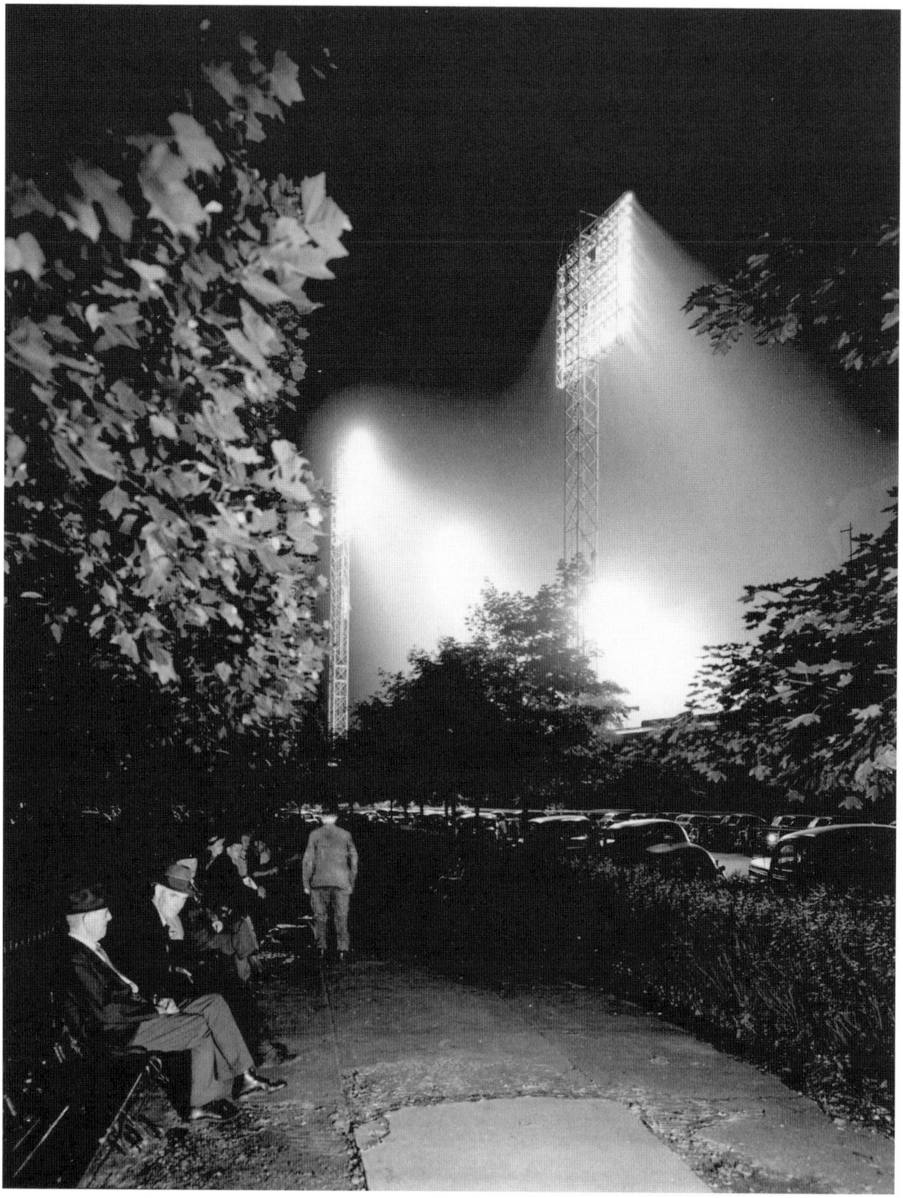

Night game at Forbes field, a chill in the air, and the Bucs inside. Richard Peterson spent much of his youth trying to figure out a way to get inside for free. (*Pittsburgh Pirates.*)

Ralph Kiner was a perfect Pittsburgh Pirate—tough, competitive, and hard-hitting. For seven consecutive years he led the National League in home runs. He also played day in and day out, through pain, illness, and hot summer days. (*Pittsburgh Pirates.*)

Harold Tinker chased baseballs throughout the Negro Leagues and played against and with some of the game's greatest African-American players. His Pittsburgh Crawford team included Hall of Famer Josh Gibson, fifth from left. *(Courtesy of Harold Tinker and Lou Swartz.)*

Paul and Lloyd Waner, Big Poison and Little Poison, brothers from Oklahoma whose bats made Pittsburgh feared throughout the National League. Together they accumulated 5,611 hits, more than the five Delahanty brothers or the three DiMaggio brothers.

(*Charles M. Conlon, Copyright* The Sporting News.)

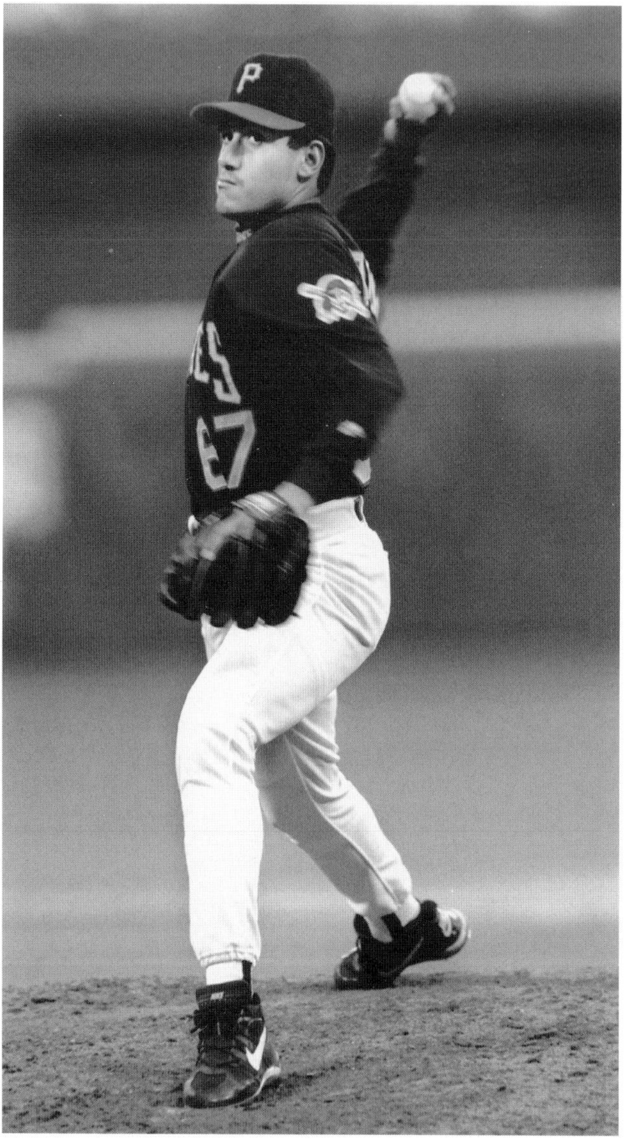

July 12, 1997. A night to remember. Francisco Cordova (above) and Ricardo Rincon pitch 10 hitless innings against the Houston Astros. Mark Smith's pinch-hit home run in the bottom of the 10th capped the first combined, extra-inning no-hitter in major-league history.

fellers going to have to play against them great big guys?" Yes, they did, and if the final tabulation had considered just the Waner brothers' contribution to the effort, the Pirates might have fared far better. The Yankee juggernaut made swift work of the Bucs, sweeping the series in four games. Pirate partisans try to put a better face on it, but it's not easy. Only two of the four games were close, the first and the last, both one-run victories. The Bucs lost the second game by a score of 6-2, with Lloyd scoring the first of the runs and Paul driving in the second in the bottom of the eighth. Game 3 featured a three-run homer by Ruth and a sterling pitching performance by Yankee left-hander Herb Pennock, who retired the first twenty-two batters he faced before giving up a pair of hits and a run. The Yanks coasted, 8-1. The Pirates struggled gamely in the fourth game, only to lose in the bottom of the ninth on a wild pitch, 4-3. It was over. The Yankees had won on steadiness: good hitting, good defense, and great pitching. The Pirates couldn't claim any of these.[54]

The Waner boys, however, had done their part. Lloyd went six for fifteen with a double and a triple, and he scored five runs, half of the team's total for the Series. Brother Paul got five hits in fifteen at-bats and drove in three runs. They didn't realize until their return to Ada, Oklahoma, how successful they had actually been. "Darned if they didn't have a parade and all for us in our home town," Paul related. "Everybody was so happy that I was hard put to figure it out. . . . It turned out that there had been a lot of money bet there . . . on the Waner brothers against Ruth and Gehrig. And our combined batting average for the Series had been .367 against .357 for Ruth and Gehrig."[55]

The Waners never played in another World Series. During the rest of the time the boys were on the team, Pittsburgh finished in second place four times. "That was tough to take," said Paul. "It'd just tear you apart. We'd make a good start, but before the season was over they'd always catch up with us. And when you're not in the race anymore, it gets to be a long season, really long." The closest the team came to winning again was in 1938. "God, that was awful! That's the year Gabby Hartnett hit that home run," Paul remembered. "That home run" put the Cubs in first with four games to play. It all but broke the Pirates' backs. With all the fight taken out of them, they lost to the Cubs again the next day and finished two games off the pace.[56]

And after a couple more years, it was over for the Waners in Pittsburgh, too. The Pirates cut Paul loose after the 1940 season and traded brother Lloyd soon after the 1941 season started. They both hung on for a few more years with various teams during the war before calling it quits. ("Hey, Paul!" yelled a fan from the bleachers during the 1944 season. "How come you're in the outfield for the Yankees?" "Because Joe DiMaggio's in the Army," came the instant reply.) Subsequently Lloyd worked as a scout for the Pirates and the Baltimore Orioles; his brother managed one year in the minors and spent several more years as batting coach for the Milwaukee Braves, St. Louis Cardinals, and Philadelphia Phillies. Big Poison was elected to the Hall of Fame in 1952, Little Poison in 1967.[57]

Both had gotten out of baseball before the institution of the pension plan. The most Lloyd Waner ever made from baseball was $13,500 a year. The best salary Paul ever drew was $19,000. For ten weeks in the winter after the 1927 World Series, the Waner boys traveled as a novelty act on the Loew's Orpheum vaudeville circuit. For that they received $2,100 a week.[58] You're almost tempted to say the boys missed their calling.

THOMAS E. SCHOTT, a lifelong baseball fan, is a historian and writer living in Brandon, Florida.

5

"I LIVED BASEBALL"

HAROLD TINKER AND THE PITTSBURGH CRAWFORDS

ROB RUCK

WITH COOL PAPA BELL flying around the base paths, Josh Gibson drawing accolades as the black Babe Ruth, and Satchel Paige walking the bases loaded, telling his fielders to sit down, and striking out the side, Pittsburgh became the crossroads of black baseball during the 1930s. Two teams emerged from the sandlots to carry the city's sporting banners across the country and into the Caribbean basin—the Homestead Grays and the Pittsburgh Crawfords. Between them, the two teams won over a dozen Negro National League championships and accounted for over two-thirds of the Negro Leaguers belatedly selected for the Hall of Fame. A group of black men in Homestead, mostly steelworkers, formed a team called the Blue Ribbons in 1900. In 1910 they became the Homestead Grays, and by 1930 Cumberland Posey Jr. had transformed them into black baseball's champions. The Grays played at West Field in Homestead, Forbes Field in Oakland, Greenlee Field on the Hill, and on sandlots throughout the region. Whether playing independent ball or as a member of the Negro National League, the Grays were the club that every other black team measured themselves against. In 1925 a challenger to the Grays emerged atop the city's Hill. By 1930 these Pittsburgh Crawfords were ready to take on the Grays. Harold Tinker played center field and captained the squad.

These recollections are from conversations that began in 1979 when I met Harold Tinker while working on my dissertation. They all took place at his home, with the exception of an interview he taped for *Kings on the Hill: Baseball's Forgotten Men,* a documentary about the Negro Leagues, which was done at the Central Baptist Church.

My dad, William Edlow Tinker, lived to be 102. Mother, if she had lived two more weeks, would also have been 102. They were remarkable people. The thing I remember about them is that they were not just church folks. They were Christians. They lived holy, and though we lived in the South, we were never taught hate for anybody, white, colored, anybody. They loved my mother and father in Birmingham. It was Mr. and Mrs. Tinker in all the big stores.

My mother's name was Mamie Willhite Tinker. She graduated high school. All of my mother's family was like that; her father was a preacher. Dad didn't go to high school. I believe that they were slaves on my father's side, on Tinker's plantation in Newburn, Alabama. But he left the countryside for Birmingham. That's where I was born, on March 23, 1905. Dad was a barber, and a real estate man, and an undertaker. My dad had one of the finest houses among colored people in Birmingham. It was a beautiful bungalow with hardwood floors and indoor plumbing. We even had a horse and buggy, and when you rode around in a horse and buggy in those days you were a well-to-do man. He was a fine horse, a chestnut with a white star on his forehead. Dan was his name.

I had all the fun—played baseball in the street in front of my house. That was our diamond right there. We had nickel rockets, canvas-covered balls that held up pretty well. You could buy a baseball for a nickel. I'll never forget it. The last beating my dad gave me was over a baseball—crying for a baseball at the wrong time. He had a deacon from the church come home with him on a Sunday and of all the times, I went in there and asked him for a nickel to get a baseball. And you know you don't play baseball on a Sunday. We never did, and then to show off when he told me go back in the kitchen, I laid down on the floor and started carrying on. He said Brother so and so, would you excuse me, and he reached down and took me out the back door. I knew something was about to happen. He took me to the stable and reached up and got that little whip you use for riding horseback and he laid stripes on my backside. I was bouncing for an hour. I had welts on my back and my legs. I never got another after that. I must have been about seven.

It was all black in our neighborhood. Most people worked in the mills and coal mines. It was just like Pittsburgh. The baseball field where the Birmingham Barons played, Rickwood Field, was about three-quarters of an hour ride from us. My sister's boyfriend took me to my first professional game. Buster Caton was playing shortstop for the Birmingham Barons. It's funny I can't remember who was playing center field. I think it only cost a quarter. We sat in the bleachers, colored bleachers. They had good colored attendance. There wasn't no Black Barons then, I remember that.

Everything was segregated, but my mother and dad didn't dwell on that stuff. As a matter of fact, I didn't know all those things that was happening in the South until I got up here and they told me about what was happening down there from where I came up. We would stay mostly in a black neighborhood. Most of the time when you would go through a white neighborhood, you'd know you was going to have some trouble. They'd throw rocks at you, and if they came in our neighborhood we'd throw rocks at them.

I think my dad overtaxed himself because he didn't give enough time to the things that he should have. He was taken advantage of. He lost out in his undertaking establishment and we ran into hard times. I'll tell you what, we lost our home. That was a tragedy. As a child, I wouldn't know too much about it. We had to move out, but we didn't move until Dad came and made a place for us in Pittsburgh.

Dad came up here for about a year, brought my oldest brother, Leon, with him. It was 1916. Leon had a job at Hornes Department Store as a shoeshine boy. He made a lot of money from tips. Dad got a job there as a porter. He cleaned furniture, dusted, swept up. Then he got in with another man, a church member at Central Baptist, and worked at Mason's Barbershop, right up on Wylie Avenue. He kept both jobs, went from one to the other.

We lived on Sweetbriar Street down there in the valley in Duquesne Heights. I was a kid. I was so busy flitting and flying and racing, it didn't seem too difficult to me. Of course, I didn't have no kids to play baseball with. We lived down in the hillside at the bottom of Sweetbriar Street, down by the woods. We didn't have no neighbors and that was kind of rough on me. But I found out that I could go up on the top of the hill and look over, and you could see that North Side diamond [Exposition Park]. I don't know what team was playing there then but I stood up there and watched them from across the river. That's how crazy I was about baseball.

We had to get acclimated here. We went to school with mixed kids and that was something new to me. I had to get used to going to school with white kids. It was strange for awhile, but we didn't have no trouble. I didn't encounter anything until I went to Miller Street School on the Hill. One of the Jewish boys called me something and I tried to fight him and he knocked me down. I had never fought anybody. I never did fight, even in sports.

Only one time and you know who that was? Pappy Williams, the magistrate. The Bailey Hotel started a basketball team, the Bailey Big Five. They were kids and wanted me to join them. I quit the Courier Big Five and went to practice with them at the Columbus Temple down there on the Hill where that Italian team played. We had a practice on Sunday and, you know, Pappy kept taking advantage of me, slapping me, giving me his elbow every time, and I said no, I don't have to take this, and said to myself the next time he gets near the ball, I'm not going to think about the ball. I drew back and hit him with my open hand and he was knocked down. He was a bigger man than I was. He was so startled that he didn't retaliate. He laid there rubbing his eyes for a few minutes. I went and put on my clothes and went home. That's the only time I ever retaliated in a game.

I never did believe in retaliation. I did hurt a couple of guys. I hurt a third baseman from Mount Washington. I was going for a triple and he was standing point blank in front of the base with both of his feet. I went into that bag and his feet went up and he landed on his head and I never will forget that. But I didn't mean to hurt him. That bag belonged to me.

The worst thing I ran into was in Ingomar. That was the day the Grays took Josh. [During the summer of 1930, the Grays recruited Josh Gibson away from the Crawfords.] I never will forget this. I was late 'cause I had to work late at RKO, and they had a car stay for me and bring me to the game. It was 10-0 in the third inning and Josh had already hit a couple of triples and that inning I got there they scored five more runs. This redhead was playing third base for Ingomar and you know what he did? He came over to our bucket, our water bucket that you drink out of, reached down and washed his hands. He could have caused a riot right there. I was glad that I got there 'cause some of those guys, that boy Neal Harris, would have probably bopped him. We beat 'em, 25-2.

We moved to Mahorn Street on the Hill and lived there for at least six years. I learned how to play the outfield at a field at the foot of Mahorn Street. That's the first Negro-built park in Pittsburgh. There was two brothers who built it and Sellers Hall [Hall played for, managed, and promoted black teams in Pittsburgh] had his Stars play there. That's the first place I saw Oscar Charleston [one of the first Negro Leaguers selected to the Hall of Fame, Charleston played for and managed the Pittsburgh Crawfords during their heyday]. When I first moved on Mahorn Street it was an open field and that's where all the kids and everybody played. That's where they had carnivals when they came to Pittsburgh.

I didn't play baseball because it was a pastime. I played it because I loved it. I played it with what they call reckless abandon. I ran over hills, I ran into fences, I dove into pigpens. I'll never forget that. Oh, I can smell it now! Mother always knew where her baby boy was—all during the day, even in the morning—I was down at the field because I was baseball nuts.

My first game at Forbes Field was when Honus Wagner was still playing. That was his last season. I can see him with those bowlegs. You think I'm bowlegged, you should have seen him. I remember Babe Adams, Carson Bigbee, and, later on, Billy Southworth. I sat in the bleachers if I got in. I never sat in no reserve or anything. No segregated seating. There were quite a few black fans in the bleachers. Seventy-five cents in left field; it was a little closer to the game. It was fifty cents in right field. That's where I first saw Casey Stengel, playing right field for the Pirates. He had a glove just like mine. It was raggedy. He held it up to us in right field and said, "Barney Dreyfuss don't even pay me enough to buy a good glove." He was a clown then.

I don't remember now how I had gotten in that day. I don't know if I got in through a hole in the fence or might of had fifty cents. Snuck in a couple of times. Those big cops almost got us, but we all ran separate ways so they couldn't get all of us. All they did was scare you. I saw them catch kids and let them sit down. We were the knothole gang, pretty near every day. Momma knew where I was. I'd walk down from the Hill. I could walk five miles and not think anything of it. You would get there and get your hole and if you didn't have a knife you were in bad shape. You had better have a knife because if most of the kids got there ahead of you, you wouldn't have no hole. It was like a reserved seat for a kid. I remember seeing Max Carey. He was the first outfielder that I admired. Saw more games through knotholes than any other way.

Harold Tinker played basketball and competed in track and field, too. Though black Pittsburgh was not as well known for basketball as baseball, the Hill was home to the Monticellos and then the Loendis, squads that gained informal recognition as the nation's top black team. Cum Posey was involved with both of them as a player and promoter.

I competed for the Saratoga Club. Bet you never heard of it. We were just a little bunch of boys from around here that got ourselves together to play basketball. We played the preliminary games to Cum Posey's Loendi Club down on Washington Street. We had about eight members, lasted for about four years. We paid dues, held meetings at the Centre Avenue YMCA, and played ball. We were taught to be industrious, to be independent to an extent. If you wanted to do something, you had to contribute to it. We didn't have TV. That made a whole lot of difference in this world.

Cum Posey needed somebody to practice against and he asked Earl Johnson if he got a kid team. It was on a Sunday and we [the Saratoga Club] were practicing at the Morgan Community Center where Earl was the athletic director. He told us he was going to let us practice against the Loendi and we grabbed our coats and ran down that hill half-dressed. I'll never forget that experience!

After a while, I was playing with the best colored teams in the area, the Ritz Club, the Saratoga Club, Courier Big Five, Bailey Big Five. Bill Nunn was running the Courier Big Five. I played ball with them for about three years. We were beating all the best teams in the area with the Courier Big Five when we got besides ourselves and booked the New York Renaissance [in New York City]. They annihilated us, 72-24. I'll never forget it. That was the worst night of my basketball career.

I lived baseball. I managed to get a ticket to the seventh game of the 1925 series, when the Pirates rallied in the rain during the eighth inning of the seventh game. They were the first team to win the championship after trailing three games to one.

I studied the centerfielder's every move and I listened to Pirate games on KDKA on a radio I made out of a cigarbox, some wire, and a magnet. I was fourteen years old, maybe fifteen, when I saw the Grays play. I sat down there in Forbes Field as a kid and I watched them play. They had the reputation of being the greatest Negro team in the country. Now, we didn't have no future in baseball. If you played for the Grays then, you had reached the heights. And I didn't see nothing to be gained by playing with them. I had an ambition. I wanted to put together a team that would defeat them. To be in the spot that they were in. And I worked toward that end. That was my life's desire. And every team that I became a part of, I took that nucleus of players that I knew in my heart would be coming toward that aim.

King Staples, an outfielder who had been playing sandlot ball for several years, saw me chasing balls down at the field near our home and he said to Momma, "Harold's a real ballplayer and I want to give him a chance to play, take him out to Westinghouse." Momma said, "I can't let him go, that's too far away. Down there, I know where to get ahold of him." He said, "Mrs. Tinker, I'll look out for him." I'll never forget that day he took me. She said, "King, don't let anything happen to my boy."

I went to play for WEMCO [Westinghouse Manufacturing Company]. I was the youngest player. I was fifteen, they were all eighteen, nineteen, twenty-five, and like that. Some were older than that. It was more or less a company team. That's what it was. Westinghouse was the sponsor. Something to get their employees interested in recreation. I imagine that's why they did it.

I played first base and I didn't know anything about first base. But I'll never forget the first game I played. I made a couple of sensational catches. They were sensational partly because of my inexperience. I was playing baseball in track shoes and I came in for a line drive, first line drive I ever fielded in a sandlot game, and the ball was over my head after I started in. I had misjudged it. I tried to put on the brakes, you know, with my heels, and you know how track shoes are. I stood on my heels and my feet went up and my hand flew up and I caught that ball. They thought I was a sensation. I chased one of the balls that day very much off the playing field and rounded it up. And they wouldn't let me go. They said, "Play!"

I played with WEMCO for two seasons, then there was the Pittsburgh Monarchs. As a matter of fact, the first time I ever remember getting paid for playing was with the Pittsburgh Monarchs. A couple of my friends were playing with the Monarchs and they told 'em about me and I wound up playing with them. Then I played for ET, the Edgar Thomson team in Braddock. Earl Johnson was the manager. Now he was a great track star. [Johnson was a welfare worker for the Edgar Thomson Steel Works, a U.S. Steel plant in Braddock, which ran extensive sporting programs to win the hearts and minds of their employees and the surrounding community. Johnson, who won a bronze medal in the 10,000 meters at the 1924 Paris Olympics, also ran for ET's track and field team and wrote a column for the Pittsburgh Courier.*]*

We got remuneration there, just a couple of bucks. We were in a league and played almost every day. When I played for Edgar Thomson, I couldn't come home. I left work and caught a streetcar and went directly to Rankin every night. Earl was a very progressive fellow and he took the nucleus of the Monarchs, who had disbanded. There was Charlie Hughes, Ormsby Roy, Neal Harris, Claude Johnson, William Kimbro, and myself. We were all from right there on the Hill, except for Charlie Hughes, who lived in Lawrenceville.

Well, we played a team, the Crawford A. C.—Athletic Club. They got their name from a bathhouse on Crawford Street. Jim Dorsey, who was the caretaker at Washington Park, was connected with this bathhouse and he told them to name their team the Crawfords. The Crawfords, that's all it was. Not Pittsburgh anything.

And those kids came to play Edgar Thomson. And we were so amazed at them that we could only beat them 2-1 or something like that. And these kids were really hustlers. Now Neal Harris's brother, Bill, one of them Harrises, he played third base for the kids, and that had something to do with us coming from Edgar Thomson, because he insisted to his brother Neal, "Why don't you come down, and we'll make this a real ballteam?" So we brought those boys from Edgar Thomson and went down to play with those kids at Washington Park.

The first time we played with them as the Crawfords, there was a mob of people there. They were all along those walls on Webster Avenue and Bedford Avenue. We took up about eight or ten dollars passing the hat. And we didn't have no idea about making any money, but we had a boy named Harry Beale who was very alive and he suggested getting a permit to play at a new field up on Bedford Avenue, Ammon Field. And I think the first time we played there, we took in something like twenty dollars. Boy, we went crazy! Harry got permits so we could play there two and three times a week, and we carried the crowds. That's how we began to really grow. We played some of the best teams in Pittsburgh. That's how good we had gotten right away. Teams like Book Shoe, and J. L. Thomas in Bloomfield, Dormont after a few years. Now, the Grays didn't beat Dormont regular, but we never lost to Dormont.

If they knew we were playing, they were there. People followed us around to games. Not just black people. We had fans coming from down in Lawrenceville, because we had a very heated rivalry between Immaculate Heart and the Crawfords. And a lot of those white fans, when they knew we were playing, they came up to see us.

You know sandlot baseball at that time was a great thing. It had to be great for a team like the Grays to pay salaries. And the Grays were so popular that everybody wanted to see the Grays. And that was the kind of stuff that we wanted.

We were in our rising days, and then we got Josh. In my spare time I was playing for a team on the North Side. And I went over there to play with them one day, and this boy was playing with another team, Josh Gibson. That day I saw him over there, he was playing on a very rough ballfield, just rocks and stones. He was playing third base and they were hitting shots down there and he was coming up with them like he was playing on Forbes Field. He'd let them run a little and—phiffft!—he'd throw. And I was amazed at his agility. That and the way he was built. I remember thinking to myself, this boy is a marvel. Where did he come from? This boy was digging ground balls out and he amazed me by the way he played, not by his hitting. And then near the end of the game, he hit a home run. He hit that ball out of existence. They didn't even go after it. It went over a mountain. And I said to myself, This is a part of my plan. He needs to be with us. After the game, I said, "Josh how would you like to play for a real team?" And he gave me that little childish grin of his and said, "Yes, sir, I guess so." And I said, "Well, you come up to Ammon Field next Tuesday and you'll have a job with the Pittsburgh Crawfords." Those people up there went wild over him and so did we, from the very first day.

We had a boy named Wyatt Turner. He was a smart catcher, but he couldn't hit. He wasn't an excellent hitter, not then he wasn't. So, right away, seeing Josh throw, we let him [Josh] catch. He had caught before. So we placed him behind the plate and from the very first day he played, he became a tremendous success. He hit balls out on Bedford Avenue, and up in that hospital. He was the most tremendous hitter I've ever come across in baseball—I'm barring none.

We were playing a team from Port Vue, up the river from McKeesport. That team got ahead of us some kind of way and they stayed there until about the sixth inning. They were two runs ahead; I was the first man up and I got on base. The next man up hit an infield single and moved me over to second. Josh was due up. He was the cleanup batter. Quite naturally, you know, you walk a man when you got an open base. They didn't have an open base, but they knew Josh. So the man threw two pitch-outs. Josh called time and he called over to me.

I met him on the infield grass and he said, "Can I hit the ball?"

I said, "What do you mean, Josh? The man is giving you the intentional walk and we need two runs to tie."

"I don't know. The man is pitching out too close to the plate."

"Josh, you mean to tell me you could reach out and hit the ball where he's throwing it?"

Josh smiled and said, "I can hit it."

I told him, "Well, Josh, if you feel you can hit it, you go ahead and hit it." I walked back to second base, and the next pitch that boy threw him was a pitch-out on the outside, way out, and Josh didn't hit that ball over the right-field fence—he hit that ball over the center-field fence. The people went crazy. I couldn't believe it . . . the ball was really out there.

Josh was built like metal. There was no fat on him. If you ran into him, it was just like you run into a wall. Yes, sir, that's the way he was built. His muscles were hard. He was a sinewy type. He wasn't big. He was big, muscular, but there wasn't no fat on him. He was a powerful boy.

Cum Posey took Josh away from us. That game in Ingomar where we beat 'em, 25-2, Josh left before it was over. Cum Posey's brother See showed up at the game and came over when he was sitting on the bench between innings. He talked with him, and then Josh came over to me and said, "Hooks, they want me to play at Forbes Field tonight."

I said, "They do?"

He said, "That's what he was talking to me about. Should I go?"

I didn't want to let him go. I looked at him and said, "Josh, I don't want to let you go, but you go, 'cause this is a break. Here's your opportunity."

I think Cum thought that after he took Josh he could take a chance on playing us because before that summer was over, that's when he gave us our first chance to play him. We almost interrupted his winning streak. They had 43 straight games, no, 42, that was the 43rd. We had been trying to get a game with the Grays for over a year. We had been beating the same teams that they did.

Now I'm not saying it because I was managing, or because I was a member of it, but they were really one of the greatest—I'm talking about local sandlot teams. Now the Grays had imports. They brought guys from New York and down South, but we were all from Pittsburgh, mostly right there on the Hill. We were more or less coaching ourselves. I was the captain and played center field.

Harry Beale [one of the original Crawfords] was a level-headed guy and he realized he didn't have the ability for the kind of ball we were playing. He knew where his ability would help us best and that's what he did. He was sort of like the business manager. If Harry said it, we did it. Then another man came into the picture. His name was J. W. King. He was an ice man, a coal man in the Hill District. He took care of all our expenses. That's how much he thought of us. He would give us what we wanted. He furnished the transportation in his ice truck. He was always there. Mr. King was a grand old man.

Now the sad part of it is that Gus Greenlee saw the potential of that team and he stole us off of that old man. That's just what happened. He talked us into leaving this man flat and he took the team over. He had a lot of bait to dangle in our eyes. We were all young men and he told us we would get paid. We would travel in limousines, which we did. And we wouldn't have to worry about expenses, or what it cost to run the team. So two or three fellas on the team listened to him. I didn't want to go because of what was going to happen to Mr. King.

We had some stormy meetings. We voted and it didn't go anyplace. But after a few meetings, most of them decided, "Let's go."

Everyone on the Hill knew that Gus Greenlee was heading the numbers, but I didn't have any idea what the numbers were. I had no concept of what it was until the day I went to get my first paycheck for the Crawfords and somebody told me to go upstairs over the Crawford Grill. I went upstairs and walked in that room and all I could see was, well, from here to the back of this church, were tables with adding machines and those people were sitting there counting up their money in the numbers and I stood there and was amazed. I had no concept that the numbers were such a big business.

When Gus took the ballteam, he let us know that it was his intention not to leave it as a sandlot, a semi-pro team. He was going to the top. He told us, "Now, you have to do one of two things. You have to quit your job and play ball, or quit the team and go to your job."

I had five children. I wasn't making a whole lot of money, but I was making more money than Gus Greenlee wanted to pay me. He gave me a contract for eighty dollars a month. Well, that was a long time ago, when eighty dollars was eighty dollars. I was making twenty-five dollars a week year-round. I couldn't take the chance. What was I supposed to do in the wintertime? The only thing that Gus could give was to let me write numbers, and I wasn't going to get involved in that.

Now I had an ambition and I said, "When I fulfill that ambition, I'll be ready to quit." And that was to beat the Homestead Grays. I didn't say I was going to quit and I didn't say I wasn't going to quit my job. He gave us a couple of weeks to think it over.

So we played the Grays in McKeesport. And that's the first game that they saw Satchel Paige. Harry Tincannon—his name was Kincannon but we called him "Tincannon"—started that game against the Grays. Harry was a good pitcher. Matter of fact, we had played the Grays down in Forbes Field the first time and Harry lost that game, 3-2. We should have won that game but Bill's brother, Vic Harris, made a running catch of a drive off of Charlie Hughes.

Harry started and they got three runs off of him and they warmed this Satchel boy up and we didn't know nothing. I knew Bobby [Williams, the Crawfords' manager] knew him and he brought Satchel in, and I'll tell you he was throwing nothing but fastballs. He didn't need no windup. He didn't use no windup. He could flail that ball. And the Grays hardly hit a hard foul for the rest of the ball game. We scored five runs and beat 'em, 5-3. By the grace of God, that's when we beat the Grays.

Satchel was really something. I can see him with those big feet. He had about a size sixteen. And he'd plant that big foot out there and he'd kick and the dust would fly and the ball would hit the catcher's mitt. I think he distracted the hitters and threw them off balance with the move that he had.

We played the Grays in McKeesport and had another game afterwards.

We played two games a day sometimes. We went from McKeesport to this field for a twilight game. And Gus was sitting on the bench. And that night, I'll never forget that night. I came in between innings and went over and sat down beside Gus. I said, "I got something to tell you."

He said, "What is it, Red?" They called me Red.

I said, "This is my last ball game."

He said, "What do you mean, this is your last ball game?"

I said, "I had an ambition and I realized that ambition today."

And he said, "What are you talking about?"

And I said, "I had an ambition to beat the Grays with a ball team that was developed by me and we did it today. You've given us an ultimatum to either quit our jobs or quit baseball. And I have to quit baseball because you don't pay me enough to support my family."

He said, "Kid, you think it over. You don't want to do that."

And I said, "Yes, I do."

He said, "I'll tell you what I'm gonna do. As long as you feel like playing, you come up and dress every Sunday that we play and I'll pay you."

Just for dressing and sitting. I appreciated that. I think perhaps that Gus didn't want me to go, really, because he knew that I was popular with the fans in this neighborhood. Maybe he just didn't want me to leave like that. So I did. Through the rest of that year I came up with them on Sunday. But that was my last game with the Crawfords. That was one of the toughest things I ever did. If I hadn't reached my life's ambition that day to defeat the Grays, I don't think I would have been able to do it.

Gus was a worldly man and he was a kind-hearted guy. I'll give him that. If you got in trouble, he'd be the first one to go to. He'd help. He did that for a lot of people. And he was straightforward. If he told you something, that's what he meant. I don't think he ever went back on anything he promised anyone.

The first job I ever had was going over to J&L [steel mill] and you know how long I worked? From nine until twelve. Come lunchtime, I went home and I knew I wasn't going back. I didn't have any business over there. I was too young for steel.

My next job was working as a porter for fifteen dollars a week one summer at the Hershey's candy factory on Centre Avenue in East Liberty. Somebody must have told me that they needed a young boy to work as a porter. All the porters were black. Long hours. There was no such thing as a union among the porters.

I was seventeen years old when I moved out. I got married. I was an idiot. That's when I dropped out of [Schenley High] school. We were both seventeen. I left school in the last semester of my junior year. I had already been at Pathé [Film Company], might have been there a year. We had three children but we separated. I had my daughters for a while, but she won custody of them and moved to Cleveland.

My dad took me to the Urban League office and the Urban League found me that job [at Pathé]. That was the one agency that was finding jobs for Negro people that needed jobs. I know that it was a popular place. I used to hear Dad talk about it. They gave me a letter introducing me. I took the letter and the recommendation and went into the Pathé Film office. They questioned me and said you can go to work. I started that day. They needed a porter, cleaning up the offices. I did that for about a year and a half. There was only one other colored porter that worked on Film Row. That's where all the movie companies had their distribution centers down on the Boulevard of the Allies in Soho. The films were flown in from California. We inspected them and sent them to the movie houses.

After a year and a half, I was promoted to assistant shipper, putting the film in a container. Oh, they were heavy. Ten reels of film in a steel box. I had the best attendance record at Pathé. I worked when I was sick, hurting, when there was snow and ice. I walked down over that hill when we had that 29 degrees below zero, got frostbitten this side of my face. I was the only one at work that day.

As a porter I made sixteen dollars a week; assistant shipper meant a five-dollar raise. Later on I became a head shipper. That was unusual. It was common knowledge where colored were acceptable. . . . Jobs like clerks and things, they wasn't available, even if you were well trained. When I was a head shipper, I made less than the other shippers, who were white. I knew I was underpaid and I told my boss that I wasn't making enough money to support my family. You know what he said? He said, "Harold, you'll have to learn to live within your means." He said that. But my coworkers treated me like they treated each other. There was one boy, name was Marino, who lived over on the South Side. He came and picked me up and drove me to work and wouldn't even take gas money!

I remarried in 1929, to Pearl Houston. She brought two children to the marriage and we had four girls and two boys of our own. We were living kind of poor. But I was never without a job during those critical times. I was never without a job. Most of those boys I played with on the Monarchs, and the Crawfords, too, were on welfare. What did they call it? They didn't give you the money, you had to do some kind of work—the WPA, the CCC. But I never had that experience of not having an income.

I made a few dollars playing baseball and basketball, but I never did have money as the basis of my interest in basketball and baseball. We played for the reputation and the desire to go to the top.

I was on my break at a lunch counter room near work one day in, I think it was 1936, when a union organizer came in and said that he was trying to organize the back-room employees on Film Row. All he needed was someone to sign the first union card. I stopped eating and said, "You mean a union for all the employees?"

He said, "Yes," and I said, "Give me that card!" Later on, I was elected to the executive board. Went to New York City for union business, the only time I went there except to play basketball. I had a lot of courage because I knew I was right. I faced those big guns and I talked to those guys like I talk to you.

I was making seventeen dollars a week less than the other head shippers. They were white, but we were all doing the same work. That was the first thing they straightened out after the union came in. I stayed with the union for all my working career. That was a blessing, too. I got a pension from the union and they've doubled that pension since.

In 1941 the family rented a small, run-down house on a street a few blocks from the Terrace Village housing project. President Franklin Delano Roosevelt attended the October 11, 1940, ceremonies dedicating the 1,800-unit housing project, which was an integrated community of working-class families in its early years. So was the street on which the Tinkers lived, but white families soon began to leave the area and the projects became heavily black.

They were exodusing shortly after we came in. As soon as we moved in, I went right to work improving it because I was young and industrious. About a year and a half later the landlord came by, and he was astounded by what I had done with it. The man said, "You've done so well with this house, how would you like to buy it?"

I said, "I'd like to buy it, but I don't have a nickel."

He said, "Don't worry about it. I'm going to sell it to you and all you have to do is just pay it as rent till you've paid it off." Been here ever since.

Harold Tinker played for several sandlot clubs and returned to baseball in 1949 when several black men living in or near the Terrace Village housing project organized the Terrace Village Baseball Club. By then, he had become more active in the church and was ordained as a minister at Central Baptist.

I was putting in my time for the Lord instead of on the ball field. When I saw in the paper that they were organizing, I told my wife, "I'm just going over there to see what they're doing." I knew what I was going over for, but I didn't want her to think that I was gonna go back. All I did was sit there and Bill Berry, I'll never forget it, said, "I see we have one of our popular ballplayers and managers in our meeting tonight. I'd like to suggest to our committee that we try to get him to accept the job of managing the Terrace Village team." I was astonished because I didn't ask anybody or say anything, but it was really what I wanted. I told them, "Well, you probably know that I have retired. I'll think it over and I'll let you know."

The great thing about this Terrace Village ball team was that we had an idea to progress. We had an aim in the beginning that we were going to the top of the heap. We weren't gonna be satisfied with just being a sandlot team. The next year we had a book program just like the Pirates have.

It was a good healthy community thing. We decided that it was going to be for all of the boys in the community, regardless of race, creed, or color. We didn't know anything about any particular white boys in the community who wanted to play sandlot ball, but they came. Lou DiPerna, Doc Shanafelt, Bill Barry, Billy Caye, Joe Studnicki. Our slogan was to "Beat yesterday."

Most of those boys with the original Crawfords would have played in the high minors. None of them—wasn't none of them couldn't have made the minor leagues. And of course, quite naturally, three of four of them would have been stars in the majors, including Josh, and Josh never made it. He never got that opportunity. And Campanella couldn't have held Josh's glove, and we went crazy over Campanella. Campanella used to sit on his haunches and throw 'em out, but he couldn't throw 'em out like Josh could. And I know Campanella hit home runs, but he never hit home runs like Josh. And all he needed was the chance to do it in the majors. He would have been something. I believe that. And I'm sitting on holy ground right now and I sure wouldn't say it if I didn't believe it.

I knew the time when the Crawfords were coming along—that was a sad time for this country. Not only for blacks but for the majority of poor people—it was sad. And they could come to a ball game and forget about all their woes. That's what satisfied me. I made a lot of people happy. Every time I made a great catch, they'd say, "Look at him." Man, they'd be turning somersaults, and those folks were worried to death. And I was just as proud of making them happy and when I'd come in, you'd think I had a million dollars because I had seen something happen to people who were down. That's how much baseball meant to them.

We really were the Kings on the Hill—no one like them. God bless them. God rest them. But you know, it brings back a lot of glorious memories, to think the way we came up from nothing, to be somebody.

ROB RUCK is the author of *Sandlot Seasons: Sport in Black Pittsburgh* and *The Tropic of Baseball: Baseball in the Dominican Republic*. The project director for the documentary *Kings on the Hill: Baseball's Forgotten Men*, Ruck teaches history at the University of Pittsburgh and Carnegie Mellon University.

6

LET'S GO BUCS!

HOME, FAMILY, AND THE PITTSBURGH PIRATES

LAURIE GRAHAM

> But what is the nature of the tale oft-told that recommences with every pitch, with every game, with every season? . . . It is the story we have hinted at already, the story of going home after having left home, the story of how difficult it is to find the origins one so deeply needs to find.
>
> —A. Bartlett Giamatti, *Take Time for Paradise*

THREE RIVERS STADIUM, Pittsburgh. Top of the ninth. One out. The Bucs lead, 3-2. But the Reds have the bases loaded. It is the fifth game of the 1990 National League playoffs, and the Pirates are down three games to one. If they lose tonight, they're out of it. Reds catcher Jeff Reed comes to the plate. Pirate reliever Bob Patterson takes his measure. The Reds are 90 feet from tying the game, 180 from taking the lead. The crowd tenses. Reed slaps a hard bouncer toward the hole between third and short. Bobby Bonilla, playing third for Jeff King, lunges to his left, cuts it off, and fires to Jose Lind at second. Lind takes the throw and, holding his ground against the hard-sliding Chris Sabo, relays it to first. Sid Bream gloves it inches above the dirt. The crowd roars! Double play! Game over! The Pirates win!

Ebullient, in no hurry to leave, the fans file down the ramps to the stadium exits. Horns honk, cheers erupt in the streets. The television monitors, the scoreboard screen project the frozen image of one fan's hand-held sign: "WE BELIEVE." I make my way with the crowd out of the stadium and along the river to the Sixth Street Bridge, which links the north Allegheny shore to downtown. In the last century my great-great-grandfather, a bridge contractor, helped to erect an earlier bridge on the site. The present bridge, one of three nearly identical eyebar chain suspension bridges known as the "Three Sisters," dates to 1928. Stepping onto the bridge I lean against the railing and look back at the lighted stadium. Teenaged voices cry, "Go Bucs!" from the cars behind me. I think back to the 1979 World Series. Then, too, the Pirates had been down three games to one. And they had come back. They could do it again. And yet, I realize, even if this game is the end, if this is the game I must pin my memories on, it is enough. The Pirates have brought me home and I am as happy as I have ever been.

To be a Pirate fan, for me, has been to hold the faith through sometimes extended periods of drought and, even with the intermittent triumphs, to have been the underdog. There has been in my lifetime no real Pirate equivalent to the term "Bronx Bombers" or "Big Red Machine" (though the "Lumber Company" of the 1970s came close). It was during one of those periods of drought that I first came to the Pirates. I was seven or eight at the time. My family was living near Chicago, in Evanston, in a big white stucco house on Lincoln Street. My father was a salesman for a bolt and nut manufacturer, not a surprising choice of occupation. His grandfather had founded a bolt and nut company in Pittsburgh, which had remained in the family until 1929. The company's brick-fronted plant building still stands on Neville Island, just down the Ohio from downtown. I remember my father in a brown gabardine suit and white shirt, a patterned tie, lowering himself onto one knee as I stood near the table in our dining room. He put his hands on my shoulders and looked into my eyes. "Are you going to root for the Pirates with me?" he asked. He was about to take me to my first ball game—the Cubs versus the Pirates at Wrigley Field. I knew and cared little about baseball at the time. But even at that age I knew not to betray the kind of eagerness I saw in his face. And besides, even then I could feel the exhilaration of the contrarian. It would be me and my father against the crowd.

In my memory the scene is bathed in green—grass, ivy, scoreboard. I remember how grown-up I felt, how worldly, in the seat beside my father, pulling for the visiting team. The Pirates scored repeatedly in the top of the first. As the inning came to a close, the scoreboard operator tipped the huge panel into place. Pirates 9 (an extraordinary figure, but the one that is lodged in my memory). At the end of the first he tipped a large zero into place beneath the 9. I remember turning to my father and saying, "I guess we're going to win, aren't we, Daddy?"

"Don't be too sure," my father replied.

I don't remember now who won. I just remember that it was close.

Family lore tells another story, this time of my mother at Wrigley Field. She and a friend had been given seats in Mr. Wrigley's box and were rooting lustily for the Pirates. It was more than Mrs. Wrigley, seated in her own box, could tolerate. She sent an usher to remove them. My mother stood her ground. I can just see her in her dark glasses, her sundress and flats, standing by her seat, feet planted, her hands on her hips. I can imagine her reply to the usher, her emphatic "I will not!" For years afterward I felt proud of my mother for bucking an unjustified authority, for her willingness to make a spectacle of herself, in the other team's ballpark, in support of her team. (Now, of course, when someone cheers for the visiting team at Three Rivers Stadium, I find the behavior totally irritating.)

Pirate fans had little to cheer about in those days, though they had had their heroes. Honus Wagner, the "Flying Dutchman," born in 1874 in the industrial Pittsburgh suburb of Chartiers (now Carnegie), was the greatest shortstop of all time, and an original member of the Hall of Fame. Other pre-1950s Hall of Famers included Fred Clarke, Pie Traynor, the Waner brothers, Max Carey, Kiki Cuyler, and Arky Vaughan. Barney Dreyfuss, visionary owner of the Pirates for over thirty years, had initiated the first World Series in 1903, against the American League Boston Pilgrims. (They lost to Boston and the legendary Cy Young five games to three.) The Pirates won the National League pennant in 1927 and were World Series Champions in 1909 and 1925. They beat the fabled Walter Johnson in game seven to take the Series in 1925. In August 1921 Pittsburgh's KDKA radio, the country's first commercial station, broadcast the first baseball game to be heard on radio, between the Pirates and the Phillies. The Pirates won, 8-5.

But from 1950 to 1957 the Pirates finished no higher than seventh. They won no more than 66 games in a season, and bottomed out in 1952 when they won only 42. They finished 54½ games out of first that year, and 22½ games behind the Boston Braves, who finished seventh. Joe Garagiola's well-known comment is used often to characterize that hapless '52 team. "According to our statistics," he said, "we should have finished ninth [in an eight-team league]. That's how bad we were. We found a different way to lose every night. It was exciting. A fly ball would go up, and we didn't know who was going to catch it or if somebody was going to catch it."[1]

I remember those spring mornings in Evanston, before I would leave with my mother and brother to spend the summer with my grandparents in Pittsburgh. I would run down the back stairs into the kitchen to learn from my father, who was eating breakfast, how the Pirates had done the day before. The news, more often than not, was bad. We would pore over the paper together, though for me the most telling stat was how many games the team was out of first. It was on those mornings, too, that I absorbed some of my father's resentment of the Chicago sportswriters, whose woeful Cubs, as often as not, left them no one to dump on but the Pirates. Even into my thirties, a teasing Cubs fan could tap a deep-seated fund of defensiveness and frustration inside of me. I remember a boyfriend, actually a White Sox fan, who would needle me occasionally about the Cubs. I knew he just wanted to get my goat, but I couldn't suppress my fury. I would bark frantically at him to be quiet. I knew I had outgrown my resentment only when, on a trip to Jackson, Wyoming, in the early 1990s, I met a friend of a friend—a lifelong Cubs fan who had started to follow the Pirates on ESPN during their early '90s playoff years. She gave me a Cubs pencil as a joking gesture of conciliation and, instead of throwing it out, I kept it and even rather cherished it.

Clearly though, as I was growing up, I loved my team not because they were a winner—a far easier thing to do—but because they were mine and they linked me to my family and to a place. I was not brought up to think of Chicago as my home. Aunts, uncles, cousins, grandparents on both sides of the family were Pirate fans. My favorite grandfather, a lawyer, had four particular passions: horseback riding, Shakespeare, the Bible, and the Pirates. I see him now in the living room of the house near Pittsburgh, in the dark, upholstered velvet rocker with the wide wooden arms, listening to the game on the big console radio at the other end of the room. He was my image of permanence and probity. He used to gather my brother and me onto his lap in that big velvet chair and read to us from the Bible. On the occasions when he asked us what we wanted to hear, we chose almost invariably the first chapter of the Book of Ruth. I remember the sound of Ruth's words as he read them: "Whither thou goest, I will go; and where thou lodgest, I will lodge." We were drawn to that articulation of the kind of commitment we felt in the safe haven of our grandfather's arms.

But I was governed, too, by a less lofty passion. Until 1953 I had my eye on Ralph Kiner, who was (unless it was Kirk Douglas) my first love. I remember watching him at Forbes Field, out of the corner of my eye, doing my best to be sure that my mother would not guess at my crush. Kiner had, after Babe Ruth, more home runs per at-bat than any other player. During that period of pitiful Pirate teams, fans came to Forbes Field just to see him hit. After his last at-bat, they went home. I think of him playing first base in 1951 (he was customarily an outfielder, but played first base for a third of that season). I remember those young, clean-cut all-American good looks, the big number 4 emblazoned on his back. I would lean forward on one of the folding chairs in my grandfather's front-row box and rest my arms on the rail. I could almost touch him. I lost Kiner forever when he was traded to the hated Cubs in June of 1953—of all places! What I didn't know was that the ultimate baseball reward was to come.

If the Pirates played in New York instead of Pittsburgh, Bill Mazeroski's home run, not Bobby Thomson's, would be the real "shot heard 'round the world." In 1960, after all those abysmal years, the Pirates had won the National League pennant and faced the Yankees in the Series. It was their first pennant in thirty-three years. I was a sophomore at Mount Holyoke at the time. I knew that the Pirates were the underdog. Every team was an underdog against the Yankees, who had played in twenty-four World Series in the past thirty-nine years. Their 1960 lineup included Mickey Mantle, Roger Maris, Whitey Ford, Yogi Berra, Tony Kubek, Bobby Richardson, Moose Skowron, and Elston Howard.

Pirate fans don't need to be reminded of the disparity during that Series in total runs scored. The Pirates took the first game, 6-4, and then were crushed in the following two: 16-3 and 10-0. After two more Pirate wins, 3-2 and 5-2, the Yankees struck again, winning the sixth game in a romp: 12-0. On October 13, 1960, I asked permission to watch the seventh game on the television in the living room of my college dorm. (In those days of "gracious living" one night a week in the dormitory dining room, at a time when colleges still acted *in loco parentis,* you didn't go around watching television in the middle of the afternoon—at least at Mount Holyoke you didn't.) Another girl with connections to Pittsburgh was in the living room when I arrived. I don't remember her name.

It was a rollercoaster ride: the Pirates up early, 4-0, then falling behind, 5-4, by the sixth. After the top of the eighth, they were down 7-4. We sat cross-legged on the Oriental rug in front of the television in a sea of growing despair. Only two more Pirate innings to pull it out. In the bottom of the eighth the Pirates came to life, scoring five runs after a bad-hop single that should have been an easy double play. We screamed and cheered in disbelief. Then our hearts sank as the Yankees came back to tie it in the top of the ninth. 9-9. We sat, eyes glued to the screen, tense with hope and apprehension. Could anyone really beat the Yankees? Pirate second baseman Bill Mazeroski led off the bottom of the ninth. Ralph Terry's first pitch was a ball. The next pitch was a high fastball. Mazeroski pulled it over the left-field fence. We leaped and screamed, incredulous, danced giddily around the room. It was the closest I had ever come to an experience of pure joy. For the rest of the day I repeated the words aloud, to myself or to anyone within earshot, "The Pirates won the World Series, the Pirates won the World Series" (no doubt driving a few people crazy in the process). Even hearing the words I couldn't entirely absorb the fact that it was true.

I have never been in Pittsburgh for a World Series. During the 1971 and 1979 Series against the Orioles, I was living in New York and working as an editor at Scribners. I followed the '71 Series in my studio apartment by radio and newspaper (I didn't yet have a television), and watched the '79 Series on my nine-inch black-and-white portable. I remember sitting at my butcher-block table for the seventh game, huddled over the television, alone. I knew no Pirate fans in New York, apart from the guys in Scribners' mailroom, who liked the Pirates "because they had so many black and Hispanic players." I still have copies of the New York papers, now somewhat brittle and yellowed, from the day after the '79 Series win. The huge *Daily News* headline:

STARGELL, BUCS WORLD CHAMPS. A photo of Willie Stargell scoring the home run that won game 7 on the front page of the *New York Times.* "Pops . . . hit one for 'The Family,'" columnist Dave Anderson wrote, referring to the theme of that Pirate year, inspired by the song "We Are Family" by Sister Sledge. The leader of the Pirate "family," Stargell had twelve hits in the Series. Four of those were doubles, three were home runs. Again the Series underdog, the Pirates had been down three games to one. The Orioles' front office was answering the telephone: "World Champion Baltimore Orioles." Even now I feel gratified thinking of the air going out of that balloon.

Though of lesser proportions, the 1971 Series had been a comeback too, thanks in part to Steve Blass (who, as a member of the Pirates' broadcast team, is still a highly visible member of the Pirate family). Pirate pitching had given up twenty-four hits and sixteen runs in the first two games against the highly favored Orioles, losing the first game, in Baltimore, 5-3, and the second by an ignominious 11-3. Blass, who would pitch the third game in Pittsburgh, had kept the pitching charts for both games but, confronted by that grim tangible record, decided simply to lose them. "I never brought them back to Pittsburgh," he said.[2] Instead, he answered with a three-hit complete game, and eight strikeouts, in front of a record 50,403 cheering Pirate fans. In game 4 Bruce Kison pitched 6⅓ innings of relief, allowing only one hit, as the Pirates came back to win the first night game in World Series history. After Nellie Briles pitched a nine-inning, two-hit shutout to win game 5, Baltimore took the sixth game in the tenth by a score of 3-2. With the Series tied at three games apiece, it was Blass's turn again. He rose to the occasion and then some, turning in another stellar performance, a four-hit complete game, as the Pirates took the Series with a 2-1 win. After a nineteen-win season the following year, Blass would, unaccountably, lose the strike zone, and by 1974 his career was essentially over. I am often struck by the graciousness with which he replies even today to frequent requests to explain an unexplainable and crushing disappointment. Why not ask him about those World Series wins?

Overriding all other '71 Series memories is, of course, Roberto Clemente, "The Great One." His "discovery" by the national media is a familiar story now. "After 17 major-league seasons," Jerry Izenberg wrote in the *Newark Star-Ledger,* "Roberto Clemente is an overnight sensation."[3] The '71 Series had highlighted for a national audience what Pirate fans already knew. Roger Angell wrote in *The Summer Game* of "the shared experience, already permanently fixed in memory, of Roberto Clemente playing a kind of baseball that none of us had ever seen before—throwing and running and hitting at something close to the level of absolute perfection." He batted .414 in the Series, with two home runs and hits in all seven games. "I want everybody in the world to know," he said, "that this is the way I play all the time. All season, every season. I gave everything I had to this game."[4]

Clemente believed he had never received the respect he deserved for the quality of his play, and he attributed his being underrated largely to the fact that he was Latino. We tend to forget nowadays the racial and ethnic stereotyping Clemente was subjected to by some sportswriters and fans, and even players, especially during his early years with the Pirates. At the time Clemente was drafted by the Pirates, in 1954, some clubs still had not integrated their major league rosters; others set informal quotas on minority players. Baseball has been not only a reflection of America's virtues, but also an embodiment of some of its deepest flaws.[5]

On New Year's Eve, 1972, only months after getting his 3,000th and final hit, Roberto Clemente died in a plane crash on his way to deliver relief supplies to earthquake victims in Nicaragua. I remember the shock on hearing the news, how impossible it was to take in. The sense of loss, the mental image of the terrible dark sea that took him. I think of him now, standing on second base after his 3,000th hit, lifting his cap to the cheering crowd. His stance is solemn, proud. I think of Bart Giamatti's words about baseball from the epilogue of *Take Time for Paradise*. "It sends its players out," he wrote, "in order to return again, allowing all the freedom to accomplish great things in a dangerous world."[6] In the case of Roberto Clemente, life and metaphor are one.

The year 1990 marks a dividing line in my life as a fan. Until then I had lived in other cities. But shortly after that playoff game against the Reds, I found an apartment in Pittsburgh, on a bluff overlooking the confluence of the rivers, Three Rivers Stadium, the skyscrapers of downtown. It was a difficult time for me. My husband had died several years before, and I knew I didn't want to start again in New York without him. The playoff games against the Reds had brought me home. For the first time in my life the Pirates would be literally my home team.

I couldn't have articulated it when I was a child, what it was that made Pittsburgh home. I'm not even sure I was conscious of it at the time. Pittsburgh then meant simply family. But when I came back to the city in 1990 I realized that it was something more. Looking out over the city one afternoon shortly after my return, I felt what I am convinced is a genetic link to the place where generations of my family had lived and worked before me. I felt at one with the hills, the converging rivers, their towboats and their bridges, the freight trains passing below me along the Monongahela, even the new glittering skyscrapers that had not existed in my youth. I remember feeling the city almost literally inside of me. The Pirates, too, were part of the city's identity. Not only did they link me to my family and to a place. They were, in the deepest sense, a part of me.

The Pirates would win no more games in 1990. They lost the final playoff game, in Cincinnati, by a score of 2-1, giving the championship series to the Reds, four games to two. For three years running, the Pirates would reach the playoffs only to fall short: to the Reds in 1990 and to the Braves in '91 and '92. Andy Van Slyke. Bobby Bonilla. Barry Bonds. Were they simply not good enough? I don't know. But certainly, in 1990 and 1991, the bats died. I remember the chill, dark night of game 7 in 1991, as Pirate pitcher John Smiley gave up three runs in the top of the first. I think we knew even then that the game was lost. In 1992, well, the reader might expect me to say something about Francisco Cabrera's game-winning hit for Atlanta in game 7. But in this respect I resemble the renowned evolutionary biologist and Yankee fan Stephen Jay Gould, who refuses even now to discuss Mazeroski's 1960 Series-winning home run. If you want to hear about Francisco Cabrera, you'll have to ask somebody else.

For me, the playoffs of '90, '91, and '92 underscored the city's consciousness of loss. During the 1970s and 1980s much of Pittsburgh's industrial base was shattered. In the 1980s alone 130,000 jobs were lost; 176,000 people left. In the steel industry, an entire multigenerational way of life—and the sense of identity that went with it—largely disappeared. I remember reading the paper after the final playoff game of 1991. Some Pirate fans sitting in the upper deck had offered congratulations to a clutch of Braves fans before the game was even over. I didn't like that graciousness in losing, the anticipation and acceptance of loss. The acceptance of that creeping suspicion that, as a city, we might not be good enough to win. I didn't want to see that Pittsburgh inferiority complex, born of years of being identified as a smoky city. I wanted us to be proud. Much of the work of Pittsburgh has been hard. Much of it has taken courage. But Pittsburghers have gotten it done. We are part of the nation's bedrock.

For much of the 1990s Pirate fans have had another possible loss to contemplate, a loss more devastating than that of any single game. For much of the 1990s we have faced the possible loss of the franchise itself. It wasn't the first time we had had to face such a possibility. We had pulled back from the brink less than a decade before. In the mid-1980s, drug scandals and what were perceived as overpaid, lackadaisical players had soured the team's image. In 1985 the Pirates finished last in the National League East, 43½ games behind the division-winning Cardinals. Attendance for the season was 735,900. The team was bleeding red ink. Eager to sell, Dan Galbreath, whose family had owned the pirates for nearly forty years, was ready to put the team into bankruptcy if a buyer could not be found. He could no longer promise to sell only to a group dedicated to keeping the team in Pittsburgh. It was only in the nick of time that a consortium of private individuals and local corporations, with an additional loan from the city's Urban Redevelopment Authority, saved the franchise for Pittsburgh.

The tenuousness of the franchise remained a subtext, though muted, even during the playoff years of the 1990s. National sportscasters cackled if a playoff game did not completely sell out, refusing to acknowledge the economic hit the city had suffered in the 1980s. Many fans were saving discretionary income for the Series—though of course we never got that far. I found myself monitoring attendance, and as the stars of the early 1990s—Bonilla, Bonds, Drabek, Smiley—left for other teams, somehow trying to save the team on my own, seldom missing a game, feeling that somehow my presence at the stadium was connected with the team's survival here. I was seldom seen without a Pirates T-shirt—I had them in every design, and some brought better results on the field than others. Finding a way to win games—even by wearing the right T-shirt—was crucial to a franchise at risk. A loss could mean lower attendance at subsequent games; lower attendance could mean the loss of the franchise itself. But they also served two related purposes. In my T-shirt I was a walking advertisement in support of the team, and part of the T-shirt's purchase price would be a small contribution to the team's coffers. It was a heavy responsibility, that superstitious self-identification with the team's destiny (and I write about it in the full knowledge that the reader may think I've gone over the edge). It took several years for my subconscious to realize that I was not a talisman, that I couldn't do it on my own. Still, even today, an unease lingers, tells me that I must not let up, that I must earn the privilege of keeping the Pirates here.

In 1994, saddled with some $60 million in debt, the consortium of Pirate owners that had saved the team in 1985 triggered their option to sell. The city had 180 days to find a buyer who would keep the team in Pittsburgh. The sharks started to circle, super-rich men from other cities determined to snag a franchise for their own hometowns. I remember after the final home game of the '95 season, as 11,000 fans stood silent in the rain, not wanting to leave, sensing that they had just seen the last game ever to be played in Pittsburgh. The scoreboard screen read something like "Opening Day. Pirates vs. Phillies. April 8, 1996. See you next year!" But few thought that promise could be kept.

On April 8, 1996, the Pirates played that home opener at Three Rivers against the Phillies. The team had been bought less than two months before, on Valentine's Day. The group of investors was headed by a 33-year-old member of a California newspaper family named Kevin McClatchy, who had vowed to keep the team in Pittsburgh on the condition that a new stadium be built to give the team the revenue streams it needed to survive. Some fans, and many in the local media, distrusted him, fearing that he had bought the team only to move it to Sacramento. But he has kept his promises to Pittsburgh, winning a number of hearts in the process. He lives in Pittsburgh now and seldom misses a game, sitting in the front row of the stands behind home plate.

I have never expressed my own gratitude to Kevin McClatchy. I've had ample opportunity, as he is very accessible to Pirate fans. But each time I've been around him, I've been seized by an attack of shyness and backed away. So perhaps this is my opportunity to say what I had in mind to say to him on the night of the groundbreaking for PNC Park: "Thank you, Kevin, for sticking it out."

As Kevin McClatchy became the Pirates' future, Jim Leyland, the team's manager for eleven seasons, became the Pirates' past. Leyland hadn't the stomach for the further dismantling and slow rebuilding that McClatchy saw as essential to creating a winning team in Pittsburgh. The team couldn't afford to buy a passel of high-priced free agents. Leyland had come to the Pirates in November 1985, a virtual unknown, after eighteen years of "scuffling" in the minors and four years of coaching with the White Sox under Tony LaRussa. The Pirates lost 98 games in his first season as manager. (At least that was better than the 104 games they lost the year before.) By 1990, he had led them to the first of three consecutive Eastern Division championships. In 1991, season attendance reached an all-time high: 2,065,302. Regarded as one of the best managers in baseball, he wanted a World Series ring before he retired. He no longer had the time or the patience to do it with a young team.

For a moment it seemed the ultimate betrayal. With the loss of many of its stars, Leyland had become the face of the team, the one constant holding things together. As a person he was the embodiment of how we, as a city, envisioned ourselves: unpretentious, straightforward, self-deprecating, tough when he needed to be, a family man, a believer in work. He was proud of his players, proud of their effort. I think back in particular to a rainy, cold afternoon in April 1991. It was the last game of a four-game series against the Cubs. After the top of the eighth, the Cubs had a 7-2 lead. Only a smattering of fans remained in the stands, in ponchos, or huddled under umbrellas. Then in the bottom of the eighth the Pirates scored four runs to make the score 7-6. In the bottom of the ninth, they scored again to tie the game. The fans were jubilant. But in the top of the eleventh Doug Dascenzo's RBI single and right fielder Andre Dawson's second grand slam of the series put the Cubs up 12-7. The crowd fell silent. Surely the game was over. I remember the crush of disappointment. But in the bottom of the eleventh the Pirates chipped away at the lead, two runs and then another and another, until, with the score 12-11 and the bases loaded, catcher Don Slaught sent a drive over the centerfielder's head. They had come back twice from five-run deficits to win the game. "They showed why they're professionals," Leyland said through tears in the interview after the game. He could hardly look at the camera. "Nobody gave up. . . . They always give their best. I'm proud of that."[7]

He wore his heart on his sleeve. "Do you think I'm proud that the whole country sees me with tears rolling down my face?" he asked in his goodbye to the fans of Pittsburgh. "Let me try to explain something to you. My dad was one of 16 children. He was raised in a family that got very emotional when one of its members accomplished something. That's the same way he raised us. He always preached family to us. And he always challenged us to make something of ourselves. I think that's why I'm like I am. It's like I worked hard all my life to make my dad proud. That's all I ever wanted to do."[8] When Leyland was introduced at the All-Star game at Three Rivers Stadium in 1994, Pirate fans gave him a thunderous standing ovation. I remember the sweet look of congratulation on Giants' manager Dusty Baker's face. Leyland got his World Series ring in 1997, with a Florida team that had far deeper pockets than the Pirates. But I'm not sure that by then it was all that much fun anymore.

For the Pirates 1997 was a year of joyful overachievement. The team had a cumulative payroll of $9,100,000, less than the White Sox were paying their surly slugger Albert Belle. Predicted to finish last, they were the kind of scrambling, hustling team that Pirate fans love. And they were in contention for a division title (in an admittedly weak National League Central Division) the entire year. On July 12, in perhaps the season's greatest moment, a sellout crowd of 44,119 saw two Mexican pitchers, Francisco Cordova and Ricardo Rincon, pitch the first combined extra-inning no-hitter in major league history.

Watching a no-hitter may be baseball's most exquisite tension. Each batter, each pitch, inning after inning bears such a burden, the possibility of that slight mistake that will mean the end. Cordova pitched nine hitless innings that night. The Pirates were playing the first-place Houston Astros. In second place, only one game out, they would be tied for first with a win. By the fifth, the stands buzzed with the awareness of a possible no-hitter. I can still see the image of a disgusted Jeff Bagwell, slamming down his bat after popping to right for the final out of Houston's ninth. But the Pirates had yet to score, and didn't score in the bottom of the ninth. Cordova's night was over. Manager Gene Lamont sent in Rincon to pitch the top of the tenth. He gave up a walk, but no hits. In the bottom of the tenth, with two on and two outs, journeyman outfielder Mark Smith came off the bench and sent an 0-1 fastball from John Hudek high into the left-field stands. Forty-four thousand voices roared their delight. "The best baseball game I ever saw," said owner Kevin McClatchy. "It was like something out of a movie."[9] There was a sense that these young, overachieving, low-salaried (in major league baseball terms) players were playing for the pure love of the game. Just before the All-Star break, Pirate right-hander Jon Lieber had struck out the mighty Albert Belle in all four at-bats in the first game of a three-game sweep of the White Sox. (It was the first year of interleague play.) They were, in the words of left-fielder Al Martin, "a blue-collar team in a blue-collar city."[10] The '97 Pirates were Pittsburgh's and baseball's darlings.

After nearly two years of rancorous debate, public and private funding is in place to build a new ballpark for the Pirates, as well as a new stadium for the Steelers, and the structures are now going up on their respective sites. The odds of keeping the Pirates in Pittsburgh long-term look better than they have for some time. I understand the arguments against using public funds to build professional sports stadiums. Too many people struggle here to hold life together on minimum wage. Why should their tax money be used to support a sport whose economics are barely under control? In an era when a pitcher can command a seven-year contract at $15,000,000 a year, when too many teams are owned by fabulously wealthy media conglomerates, how can a small-market team like the Pirates survive? I understand all this. But there is a realistic hope of increased revenue-sharing to narrow the gap between the "haves" and the "have-nots." Pittsburgh is building for a new high-tech future now. We can't afford to lose any more of our assets. The Pirates have been Pittsburgh's team for 113 years. I have to wonder how we could ever let them go.

I think back on the 1998 season. On the whole, it was disappointing. They had lost the magic of 1997. But still there was much to remember. Catcher Jason Kendall's aerial corkscrew slide to avoid the tag at home. Jose Guillen's strike from right field to nail the runner at third. The elegant line of first baseman Kevin Young's torso as he completed a home-run swing. Backup outfielder Turner Ward crashing though the wall to catch a fly ball, disappearing completely as the wall panel closed behind him like a door. And then, there was nineteen-year-old rookie Aramis Ramirez and his first major-league hit. Ramirez was 0 for 24 in major-league at-bats. The Pirates were holding on in the seventh to a 1-0 lead against the Mets. With two outs and the bases loaded, Ramirez headed toward the plate. The crowd rose in a standing ovation. A vote of confidence and encouragement. But also a lot of pressure to put on a rookie. The first pitch was a called strike one. Still the crowd cheered and applauded. On the next pitch Ramirez lined a double into left field. The crowd roared. "The people were real happy," Ramirez said after the game, "like me. I wanted to smile, but this is the big leagues. I acted real serious, but I was real happy."[11]

"A great baseball moment," said former pitcher and Pirate color commentator Bob Walk.[12]

"I don't think I've ever seen that," said manager Gene Lamont. "It gave you chills. I think the fans wanted to show him they like young, hungry players, which he is. The kid surely had to like it. I know I did."[13]

It was a moment that confirmed all that is right and beautiful in baseball, the gift of hope and possibility, the sense, even if just for a moment, that the world is good. Baseball is a game of new beginnings. Each game, each inning, each at-bat brings new opportunity, a clean slate, another chance. You begin again.

The 1999 season was a season of promise unfulfilled. What could have been closer to a contending team was decimated by injuries, including the horrific season-ending ankle injury to All-Star catcher Jason Kendall. "It was like there was a death in here," Al Martin said of the clubhouse atmosphere after the game in which Kendall was hurt.[14] Kendall's drive and gutsy play had made him "the heart and soul of the team." And even before his injury, for much of the first half of the season, increased offense could not always compensate for faltering starting pitching. Still, the nucleus of the future contender is in place in such players as Kendall (whose ankle, as of spring training 2000, appears to have healed), Kevin Young, Brian Giles, 1999 rookie pitcher Kris Benson, among others—the dream of a new ballpark and a winning team in the year 2001.

I may seem to idealize baseball. But I am acutely aware of its problems: often hostile labor relations, wildly escalating salaries, too many owners and players (and umpires!) who lose sight of the greater good of the game. But that isn't baseball. I think of what the Pirates have meant to generations of my family. I think of Al Martin's fluid grace as he jogged toward his position in left field. I think of his grace off the field as he came to terms with a disappointing season in 1998, and followed with a near career year in 1999.[15] I think of my step-granddaughter Caitlin, whose first word, after "book," was "Bucs." Overriding all the negatives is the simple fact that, in baseball, we find a focus and a context for our capacity to love. How indeed, I ask myself, could we ever let that go?

LAURIE GRAHAM was an editor at Scribners for eighteen years and is the author of *Rebuilding the House*, a memoir, and *Singing the City*, a celebration of Pittsburgh's industrial landscape. She lives in Pittsburgh.

7

AN UNFORGETTABLE TEAM THAT PITTSBURGH FORGOT

CHRIS ELZEY

IN 1979 *THE FISH That Saved Pittsburgh* debuted in cinemas across the country. A light-hearted picture about a struggling pro basketball team turned contender, *Fish* was panned by critics nationwide. "Condensed down to the fifteen minutes or so of actual story line that's in the film," huffed *Variety, Fish* "might make a good half-time featurette" for NBA telecasts. "All it's got going for it is some fancy basketball footwork" by Julius Erving and other NBA stars. The *New York Times* was equally critical: "A record number of athletes and singers and comedians turn up in *The Fish That Saved Pittsburgh,* and *still* this feels like a movie with nothing going on." To the *Washington Post* the basketball movie was "an uninspired sports comedy" based on a "gimmicky premise." No surprise *Fish* floundered at the box office.[1]

Fish's story line is this: A third-rate franchise stuck in a perpetual slump, Pittsburgh's make-believe entry in the NBA (the Pythons) is the laughingstock of the league. Fed up with losing, the players quit—all except for rookie superstar Moses Guthrie (played by Julius Erving). Reasoning that the fate of his beloved Pythons lies with the stars, the club's fourteen-year-old waterboy consults a friendly astrologer (played by Stockard Channing). She instructs him to restock the team with players who, like Moses, have the birth sign Pisces. As only Hollywood could imagine, the Pythons' wacky owner (played by Jonathan Winters) adopts this Age-of-Aquarius plan and inks a bunch of athletic oddballs (all Pisces) to contracts. Feeding off some sort of cosmic energy, Pittsburgh's astrologically souped-up squad (renamed the Pisces) steamrolls the competition and goes on to win the title.

The makers of *Fish* were wise to set the movie in Pittsburgh. How better to convey a deep sense of basketball desperation than to make Pittsburgh the team's hometown? After all, the Iron City never has had much luck with professional basketball. Clubs have come and gone, with as much regularity as barges pulling their loads up the Monongahela. *Fish* invoked memories of these past professional teams—their successes as well as their failures. In no case was this truer than with the Pittsburgh Pipers of the American Basketball Association (ABA).

The Pipers were organized in 1967, one of the ABA's eleven original franchises. The team began slowly, but early season trades brought new players, and with new players the Pipers began to win. Like the fictional Pisces, the Pipers were an assortment of characters out of a Marx Brothers movie, an odd cast of basketball castaways, journeymen, and also-rans. But like their image in film, the Pipers had a superstar—a "Moses Guthrie" whose wizardry on the court foreshadowed the kind of razzle-dazzle Julius Erving would bring to *Fish*'s basketball scenes. With enormous hands (eleven inches long), an immense wingspan (some say a thirty-nine sleeve), and superhuman skill, the Pipers' Connie Hawkins (the Hawk) did things with a basketball others only dreamed of. He was Mr. Play of the Day before instant replay and ESPN.

Yet the Hawk was not the only attraction. Guards Charlie Williams and Charles "Chico" Vaughn and forward Art "Crazy Artie" Heyman excited fans with their talent and amused others with their antics. Their freelance style blended perfectly with the run-and-shoot game of the American Basketball Association. Fast breaking at every opportunity, the Pipers were a schoolyard player's fantasy. Twice they scored 150 points, then an ABA record for the most points in one game. High scores and nonstop action kept fans exhilarated, as if passengers on a rollercoaster. Two winning streaks—one fifteen games, the other twelve—combined to form a league-best fifty-four wins. If the Pipers had had a taller center they could have beaten many NBA teams.

The Pipers, of course, did not play in the NBA. They played in the ABA, the yin to the NBA's yang. Dubbed the "rebel league," the ABA spruced up the pro game with a playground aesthetic that altered the nature of the sport. Rather than playing a plodding, conservative brand of basketball (as the NBA was wont to do in the 1960s), ABA players were more showbiz, cutting loose and strutting their stuff with an eye-opening array of dunk shots, one-on-one play, between-the-legs dribbles, and imaginative playmaking. The league's colorful red, white, and blue ball accentuated the shake-and-bake effect of these schoolyard moves, adding spice to the games. The three-point shot, the ABA's most popular rule, spread the defense and opened up the lane. With fewer defenders in the middle, exciting drives were easier to make. Fans of the young league enjoyed the action of uninhibited, full-court competition. No wonder the ABA called itself the Lively League.

Unfortunately for owners, the Lively League did not beget lively business. But owners knew the risks. Their aim was to hold on long enough until the ABA might merge with the NBA. Such thinking had precedents. A year earlier another start-up league, the American Football League (AFL), had hit it big, merging with its rival, the National Football League (NFL). The AFL/NFL merger inspired ABA promoters. Recalled one investor, "What we tried to do was force a merger, just like the AFL did to the NFL. That was the way we convinced guys to invest in our league. We told them to get in now for less than half of what it costs to buy an NBA team. Then when the two leagues merged, your investment would double in value."[2]

Success depended on a large bank account and steadfast perseverance. Months before the start of the first season, the *New York Times* reported that "each of the eleven [ABA] members has given assurances that it can operate for a minimum of three years, regardless of losses, on budgets of $500,000 a year or more." Investors were sincere. One owner, Art Kim of the Anaheim Amigos, had earlier told the *Times* that unlike the owners of the deceased American Basketball League (ABL), who did "not have the dedication to stick it out," owners of ABA franchises were determined to make the ABA work.[3] Kim and his associates could afford to be persistent. *Sports Illustrated* acknowledged that the ABA had "solid financial backing."[4] Several investors boasted multimillion-dollar fortunes. Among the wealthiest was Kentucky Colonels owner Mamie Gregory, a young Louisville socialite worth more than $50 million. Mamie's mother once possessed the forty-five-carat Hope Diamond, now a permanent Smithsonian exhibit.

But low interest in the new league dampened owners' enthusiasm. Most franchises struggled with attendance, many did not have television contracts, and only a handful had deals with their local radio stations. After the first few months the ABA was averaging fewer than 2,500 fans per game. Two California teams, the Oakland Oaks and Anaheim Amigos, were well on their way to losing large sums of cash. The Oaks wound up almost $750,000 in the red, and the Amigos $500,000 by the end of the first season. It seemed few fans desired to watch players whom *Sports Illustrated* tagged as "the slightly too short and too old, the hoped-for sleepers and the discards."[5]

Still, owners were encouraged. A few franchises actually thrived. The Indiana Pacers, for example, emerged as the ABA's hottest draw. During the first month the Pacers attracted more than 7,000 fans a game. By midseason Indiana was outdrawing a majority of NBA clubs. Other ABA franchises, the Denver Rockets and Kentucky Colonels, also drew large audiences. At the same time, several newspapers were giving the ABA good coverage, printing its standings and box scores next to those of the NBA. Such publicity not only helped legitimize the new league, it brightened investors' spirits. Admitted the skeptical *Sports Illustrated,* "You can count on that red, white and blue ball being around for a while." The *New York Times* concurred, stating, "The A.B.A. seems to be for real."[6]

STRANGE CREW IN A STRANGE NEW LEAGUE

No professional basketball team in Pittsburgh had ever seemed to be for real. There was, for example, the Pittsburgh South Siders. Playing in two regional leagues from 1903 to 1915, the South Siders won a championship in 1907. The next pro club in the Iron City was the 1935 Pittsburgh YMHAers (Young Men's Hebrew Association). A decent team, the YMHAers failed to win a title, and two years later they, too, had departed. The Pittsburgh Pirates of the newly formed National Basketball League (NBL) quickly filled the void. In 1937, their first year, they played well enough for a third-place finish. Competing against such NBL powerhouses as the Akron Firestone Non-Skids and the Oshkosh All-Stars during their second season (the Non-Skids won the league's first two titles and the All-Stars the next three), the Pirates were overmatched. They finished the year last in their division and disbanded before the start of the next season. It was not until seven years later that a team from Pittsburgh was again part of the NBL. The Pittsburgh Raiders were a slapdash organization, and their first season was a catastrophe, the Raiders winning just seven out of thirty games. They folded the following year.

Other teams emerged, then disappeared. In 1946 the Pittsburgh Ironmen were born as one of the first eleven teams of the Basketball Association of America (BAA). The Ironmen ended their one and only season with a woeful 15-45 record. Fifteen years later pro basketball returned to Pittsburgh with the Rens of the American Basketball League (ABL). The Rens had a good first year, but a poor second half of the season eliminated them from playoff contention. The next season the ABL shut down two months into its schedule. With the death of the league, Pittsburgh's latest team was gone. The Rens' lackluster performance epitomized the city's experience with pro basketball. Into this world of low expectations the Pipers were born.[7]

The owner of the Pipers was Gabe Rubin, a "theatrical impresario," according to the *Post-Gazette*.[8] Rubin peddled popular culture, owning several movie theaters in the tri-state area that showed mainstream films. But he also dabbled in schlock. Jim O'Brien, a sportswriter in Pittsburgh during the late 1960s, remembered Rubin also owning a theater named the Nixon that "featured 'adult art films.'" As O'Brien recalled, "I knew the Nixon as a place I wasn't allowed to go as a teenager."[9]

Unlike other original investors, Rubin was not flush with cash. His modest wealth came from his modest business. But the price of joining the new league was just $50,000. Compared to the $1.5 million the NBA was asking for expansion teams at the time, the fee for an ABA franchise was a bargain-basement deal. But there were other costs—salaries, arena rental, travel and advertising expenses—and Rubin took on minority partners to help lighten the load. Personnel decisions and overall team operations, however, remained his responsibility. He owned a majority of the team and also served as the general manager. His dual role upset Pipers coach Vince Cazzetta, who "didn't like some of Rubin's basketball decisions." Cazzetta explained, "I would go into his office and ask him a question, 'Who am I talking to? If you are the owner, you can do anything you want. If you are the GM, I want some input.'" The former coach of the Pipers would later say he fought the team's GM "tooth and nail" over many roster changes.[10]

Meanwhile, the announcement that Pittsburgh was to have yet another pro club met with a mixed response. A few in the media predicted success, but most recalled the difficulties of previous teams. Questions about the viability of Rubin's enterprise circulated freely, and the Pipers' owner was battling skeptics before his club played its first game. "If we win consistently," Rubin prophesied, "we'll draw the fans and make out financially."[11] With no television contract, Rubin was forced to rely on ticket sales as the main source of revenue. Local newspapers calculated that it would take well more than 5,000 fans at games to make a profit, not an easy task given the city's basketball history.

Generally, sports reporters expected the Pipers to put on a show, telling readers that Pittsburgh had a real shot to win the ABA crown. The *Post-Gazette* trumpeted that with "a mixture of three top pro stars" and the team's "flock of recent top-flight college luminaries," the Pipers appeared poised for greatness. Underscoring its approval, the paper added, Pittsburgh's roster "reads like 'Who's Who' of college court circles."[12] *Sports Illustrated* tempered the *Post-Gazette*'s adoration. Most of its praise went to management—the magazine called Rubin a "successful promoter"—and to the state-of-the-art Pittsburgh Civic Arena, "one of the niftiest arenas in the country."[13]

The press wasted no time in heralding Connie Hawkins, a twenty-five-year-old schoolyard superstar of the old Pittsburgh Rens who had not played a single minute of college or NBA ball. He was "the man expected to carry the Pipers." He was "one of the best pro stars in the world." He was capable of "[playing] on par with the Chamberlains, Robertsons, and Russells if ever given the opportunity," the *Post-Gazette* believed. The *Pittsburgh Press* proclaimed that Hawkins's skill was so great that he could "play with anybody," and *Sports Illustrated* termed him a "6'9" all-everything." In its pro basketball preview, *Ebony* hyped that he was "good enough to play in any league."[14]

Hawkins certainly was good enough to play in any league, for his talent was the stuff of players' dreams. But a gambling scandal before the start of his freshman year at Iowa had turned his own dreams into a nightmare. He was accused of acting as a go-between for basketball game fixers interested in meeting top college players. Though Hawkins was later proven innocent of the charges against him, in 1961 Iowa withdrew his scholarship. In addition, the NBA thought suspicion was enough, and the best pro league in the world banned him. Fortunately for Hawkins, 1961 was the year that the American Basketball League was readying itself for the pro sport scene.

The ABL was looking for players, and Hawkins fit the bill. He was young, talented, and eager to show his stuff. ABL officials ignored the NBA's blacklist and welcomed him into their league. As far as the ABL was concerned, Hawk's supposed brush with fixers proved nothing. In the finest American tradition, the league presumed his innocence. He signed a deal with the Pittsburgh Rens for just $6,500. The league was a blessing that offered him basketball salvation.

The mastermind of the ABL was Abe Saperstein, founder and owner of the all-black Harlem Globetrotters. Known as the "clown princes of basketball," Saperstein's Trotters wowed fans everywhere they played. Their amazing skill, vaudevillesque shtick, and gag-filled merrymaking were good fun for all. But a Trotter game was not serious sport. It was a scripted event, patterned after racist imagery of African Americans as simpletons and "happy darkies," utterly content with playing basketball burlesque. In 1961 Saperstein decided to test the waters of no-nonsense basketball competition and launched the ABL. With the money his Trotter team made spoofing and slapsticking racial stereotypes, Saperstein financed the entire league himself.

Hawkins was thankful for the chance to play in the new league, and the ABL was thankful to have him. He was its gem, far and away one of its top players. As a toothpick-slender youth fresh out of New York's ghettos (at 6'8" he weighed only 180 pounds), the nineteen-year-old Hawkins led the ABL in scoring and rebounding, and won the MVP. But when the ABL folded in the fall of 1962, he found himself out of a job. Recognizing Connie's immense talent, Saperstein quickly signed him to play with the Trotters. But Hawkins soon grew tired of the Globetrotter routine, feeling exploited, used for his black skin. He believed the night-in-and-night-out Uncle Tomming against inferior competition to be degrading. In October 1966 he quit Saperstein's team and returned home unemployed to Pittsburgh, where he whiled away the winter months shooting baskets alone in empty gyms and frequenting local bars. With at least half of his prime athletic years behind him, he wondered if any real team in any real league would give him a shot. His life was in shambles. But good fortune again visited: the nascent ABA team in Pittsburgh was in dire need of talented ballplayers. Hawk eagerly took the $15,000 the Pipers were offering and signed a contract.

Rubin's best decision was to acquire Hawkins. Not only was Hawk a great player, he was well known in Pittsburgh's basketball community, given both his Globetrotter and Old Ren experience. His inclusion gave Rubin's team immediate prestige. But Rubin required solid players around Hawkins if the Pipers were to be a championship team. One of them was Charlie Williams. Charlie's main asset was his tremendous speed; he was "lightning quick," remembered Pipers coach Vince Cazzetta, who also coached the 6'1" Williams at Seattle University. During his senior year Williams averaged twenty points a game. The *Post-Gazette* remarked that the speedy Washington state native "was one of the main reasons why the [Seattle] Chieftains were called top-drawer on the West Coast." Like Hawkins, Williams was the kind of player around which coaches built teams.[15]

But like Hawkins, Williams was also damaged goods. In 1965, his senior year, it was alleged that he had neglected to inform authorities of a bookmaker's bribe made to a teammate. His university expelled him, but he later returned to school when investigators dropped the charges. Unfortunately, Williams, whose father was a minister, had been tarnished by the sinful scandal. The NBA barred him from competing. For the next two years he worked as a teacher in Seattle, all the while keeping his basketball skills sharp, hoping some day to get a shot with an NBA squad. His wish almost came true in 1967. Realizing both Williams's talent and box-office appeal with local fans, the NBA's expansion Seattle Supersonics signed him to a one-year contract. But NBA commissioner Walter Kennedy, ever mindful of the league's boycott on Williams, nullified the deal. Williams was crushed. Once again, innocence was no defense in the court of the NBA.

Hawkins and Williams were not the only players who used the

Pipers as a means to resurrect dead careers. Charles "Chico" Vaughn was a steady (when sober) twenty-seven-year-old guard who had spent five years in the NBA with St. Louis and Detroit. While in the NBA Chico's career had steadily deteriorated, quickened by his thirst for alcohol. Vaughn was a proficient scorer, averaging double figures over his NBA tenure. His real talent, however, was on defense. He had quick reflexes, a nose for the ball, and an uncanny knack for intercepting passes. As David Wolf noted in *Foul! The Connie Hawkins Story,* Vaughn had an equally uncanny knack for missing practice. During his first year with the Pipers (and only his sixth as a pro), Chico once told Connie, "I'm getting too ol' to practice. The Chic got to save his strength for the games." Vaughn did whatever he could to avoid practice, Wolf pointed out, and a death in the family seemed a weekly occurrence. Remembered Pipers trainer Alex Medich, "Chico lost four aunts, ten brothers, five sisters that season—and his father died about five times."[16]

Another Piper who salvaged his career was Art Heyman, a 6'5" guard/forward who had earned All-American honors while a collegian at Duke. The *Sporting News* and the Associated Press both voted him the nation's top college player in 1963, and he became the New York Knicks's first draft pick that same year. Expectations ran high for Art. *Sports Illustrated* observed, "Not since Oscar Robertson flashed onto the scene four years ago has the arrival of a player been so eagerly awaited as that of Heyman by his New York fans."[17] Scoring fifteen points a contest in his first year as a pro, Heyman delighted Knicks supporters. His defense, however, disappointed them. Heyman lacked the foot speed to stay with quick guards and the size to defend tall forwards. Consequently, his man, whether a guard or forward, almost always outscored him. Frustrated with Heyman's inability to play good defense, the Knicks traded their former number one draft selection to San Francisco in 1965. From there he went to NBA clubs in Cincinnati and Philadelphia, and then to Boston. Eventually, he found his way to Hartford, playing one season for the semiprofessional Eastern League team. The next season he signed with the ABA New Jersey Americans, where he played two months before being traded to Pittsburgh.

As an ABA pro, Heyman excelled, pumping in eighteen points a game his first year. The "run and gun" nature of the new league masked his deficiencies on defense. But Heyman also excelled at playing the rebel, taking his cues from a 1960s culture that snubbed officialdom. "Coaches would tell me to do something, and I'd say, 'Go f—— yourself,'" he would later tell *Sports Illustrated*. "I didn't respect authority or structure."[18] It was precisely this lack of respect for authority and structure that got him into fights with some unlikely combatants. In one college game against North Carolina, he fought with both an opposing player and a male cheerleader—then socked the Carolina coach in the crotch.[19] So heated was the fray, police had to intervene in the skirmish. Wrote Hawk's biographer David Wolf, "Heyman was in so many fights he almost turned the fieldhouse riot into a varsity sport."[20] No wonder the athletic world labeled him "Crazy Artie."

Heyman liked to think of himself as a "swinger," a role he relished. He hung out with Broadway Joe Namath, owned a restaurant on New York's Upper East Side (*the* place for swinging), and took extra care with his fashion, often sporting a "high, white turtleneck sweater, long sideburns, jazzy sports coat and tight pants," as the *Post-Gazette* noted of the hip and stylish Piper. He mingled with like-minded people, the paper adding, "Art moves around with a swinging crowd." Commenting on his "swing-ability" in an article headlined "Hey, Man—Newest Piper Can Swing," the *Pittsburgh Press* told readers that he owned "a bachelor pad in New York's liveliest, after-dark playground area, the Upper East Side."[21] Heyman seemed to lead a groovy, Hugh Hefner kind of life.

Crazy Artie's offbeat and eccentric personality jibed perfectly with the wackiness of the new league. From the very moment the ABA went public, it gave serious sports fans good reason to be wary. Desperate to ingratiate themselves with the media, ABA officials turned the league's first press conference into part promotional event, part happy hour. "The buffet was loaded with delicacies of every description," Garry Davidson, one of the league's initial investors, recalled, and "whiskey flowed like water." Celebrities rubbed elbows with reporters. Scantily clad waitresses served hors d'oeuvres while cheerleaders in bikini tops and hot pants distributed miniature red, white, and blue basketballs. The league sunk $35,000 into the press conference and in return it received a Playboy party for jetsetters. Sighed investor Davidson, "Everyone had fun, but no one took us seriously. It was a joke, and it made us look ridiculous."[22]

The ABA's first draft contributed to its seriocomic image. Two different teams drafted the same player, other clubs picked players who already had signed with NBA teams, and the New Orleans Buccaneers drafted Olympic pole vaulter Bob Seagren. The Dallas Chaparrals proved completely incompetent when the club's owner picked players not according to ability but rather by alphabetical order. Even when teams did their homework, and believed they had selected good players, they found themselves burned. Sportswriter Terry Pluto recounted in *Loose Balls: The Short, Wild Life of the American Basketball Association* that the Oakland Oaks discovered the mark of their folly at their first press conference. To lighten up the affair, the Oaks decided to have a three-point shooting contest—owner Pat Boone included. With his one-handed set shot, the clean-cut crooner known for his white V-neck sweaters, spiffy white buck shoes, and hit song "Love Letters in the Sand," outshot a pair of Oaks draftees. Oakland closed out their schedule with a seventeen-game losing streak and finished the year with the worst record in the league.[23]

In the ABA the outlandish became the everyday, as Pluto showed in *Loose Balls*. The Denver Rockets traveled in their own plane, a DC-3 circa 1941. A former German air force officer, whom the team nicknamed the "Red Baron," piloted the flying bucket of bolts. The Dallas Chaparrals' mascot was Miss Tall Texan, whose claim to fame was her 6'7" height, "give or take a few inches for my hairdo," as she divulged to a secret few. A New Orleans/Pittsburgh matchup was interrupted for an hour when the arena's lighting cut off—a possum had gotten stuck in the stadium's wiring and short-circuited the electricity. The ABA made its debut on Friday, October 13, 1967, a date that should have tipped off everyone as to what was in store (88).

Action on the court mimicked the zaniness off it. Exactly what was going to happen in an ABA game was anyone's guess. It was roller derby meets the World Wrestling Federation, with a bit of Australian Rules Football thrown in to keep things from becoming too routine. Fights, though, were a regular occurrence, and fans could expect to see a couple of pushing matches every game. The referees seemed to condone this mayhem, turning their heads when elbows started to fly. "You almost had to present your X-rays to get a free throw," *Los Angeles Times* sportswriter Jim Murray penned about the roughhousing in the league's initial season. One contest featured a bench-clearing brawl—in front of thousands of children on Kids' Day. Remembering his first season in the league, all-star forward Mel Daniels told ABA chronicler Terry Pluto, "it was seventy-eight games and seventy-eight fights" (66–67).

But fistfights did not put people in seats. Except for Indiana, Denver, and Kentucky, ABA franchises had to beg fans to watch their games. The Anaheim Amigos, for instance, drew ninety-eight people to one contest, and the crowd for another was so thin that the radio play-by-play could be overheard from any seat in the house. Numbers in Houston fell even lower (eighty-nine to be exact). The Minnesota Muskies especially had difficulties. It was not uncommon for games in Minneapolis to have fewer fans in arena seats than people along the sidelines. One Muskie contest against the Indiana Pacers was so poorly attended, the Pacers' television crew had to convince the thousand or so Muskie supporters to move to one side of the stadium so that viewers in the Hoosier state would think there was a good turnout (63–64).

Unfortunately for the Pipers, Pittsburgh was more like Minneapolis or Anaheim than Indianapolis or Denver. Pro basketball simply had no home in the Steel City. Pittsburghers adored their baseball Pirates and fawned over their football Steelers. Both teams had deep roots, extending back decades. They had proven their loyalty to the city—not so with the Pipers. The only long-established custom of basketball in Pittsburgh was losing and leaving. Why should fans become interested in the sport when its teams shuffled out of town as quickly as they shuffled in? Little surprise that commentators expressed skepticism whenever the Pipers' future was discussed. Not only was there no pro basketball tradition in Pittsburgh, Pittsburghers were not interested in starting one.

Other developments diminished the Pipers' chances for success. In 1967 the Pittsburgh Penguins skated for the first time. The team had a tough year, but Pittsburgh's amiable relationship with its minor league Hornets of the American Hockey League had educated Pittsburghers to the sport, creating a core of hockey devotees, many of whom passed an appreciation on to their children. Penguin fans even formed a booster club that traveled to games as far as Los Angeles, Montreal, and Minneapolis. At midseason the Penguins were drawing 7,000 spectators per game. For one early February contest, the Penguins had a crowd of 12,563, at the time the largest to see an athletic event held in the Civic Arena. As interest in hockey multiplied, it increasingly overshadowed pro basketball. To Pipers player Charlie Williams the city's sporting allegiance was clear: "Pittsburgh was a hockey city."[24]

That Pittsburgh was becoming oversaturated with pro sports was obvious to the *Post-Gazette*. "The entertainment dollar can be split only so many ways," the paper noted. "Inroads of a new game are bound to cut into the receipts of established franchises."[25] The *Post-Gazette* pointed out that debt plagued all but one sport—auto racing, which saw a 25 percent increase in annual profit. In contrast, the 1967 Pittsburgh Phantoms of the National Pro Soccer League had lost $750,000, the Pirates had seen Forbes Field attendance fall by almost 200,000 for the 1967 season, the Steelers were just breaking even, and the Penguins were in the midst of skating on financial thin ice. The paper painted a bleak future for the Pipers.

TOUGH START, FANTASTIC FINISH: THE PIPERS' 1967–68 SEASON

The Pipers, of course, were hoping to prove detractors wrong. It went without saying that the players wanted a healthy, robust franchise, for many had already experienced basketball skid row and knew it was not a friendly place. The Pipers opened the year on the road against the New Jersey Americans, a team they had beaten easily during the exhibition season. For most of the game the Americans led, and it looked as if the Pipers would start off with a loss. But in the closing minutes of the game Pittsburgh narrowed the gap, thanks to some outstanding play by Hawkins. With only seconds remaining, Williams hit two free throws to put the Pipers up by three. The Americans passed the ball inbounds and heaved up a desperation shot, but it was way off the mark, and the Pipers won the first game in franchise history, 110-107. Hawk paced Pittsburgh with thirty-four points.

The following night 5,000 people came to see the Pipers play the Minnesota Muskies in Pittsburgh's home opener. It started out a festive affair, as a ceremony before the game officially welcomed the Pipers to Pittsburgh. Sixteen Scottish dancers entertained the crowd and the twenty-piece Pittsburgh Piper White Heather band serenaded fans with the melodic wail of bagpipes. Music and dancing were the only highlights for the locals, however. Playing sluggishly and committing numerous turnovers in the second half, the Pipers managed just thirty-nine points to the Muskies' fifty-four, and lost, 104-86.

Coach Cazzetta blamed the Pipers' lackluster effort on the tough game against the Americans the previous night, and the early return flight the next day. Newspapers were less forgiving: "Welcome to Losers' Club," a *Post-Gazette* headline screamed in reference to the baseball Pirates' disheartening finish that same year. "It didn't take the Pittsburgh Pipers much time to join Pittsburgh's sad sack sports fraternity for 1967," grumbled Al Abrams, sports editor for the paper. In "only their second game of the season," the Pipers "looked tired and played tired. Even the reputedly great Connie Hawkins must have been tired judging by his off night."[26]

Pittsburgh's first two games anticipated the first third of the season. They exhibited short bursts of competence interspersed with frequent demonstrations of inefficiency. A string of five wins would be followed by losses on the road and a lackadaisical effort at home. To many the Pipers appeared lethargic, confused, even disinterested in their play. As the player expected to carry the team, Hawkins drew the most criticism whenever the Pipers faltered. "Quite often Connie is conning the fans," wisecracked the *Pittsburgh Weekly Sports*. "What really bugs a guy about Hawkins is that here's an athlete endowed with all the physical assets necessary to make it big." But the only thing "he does is go around believing he's the greatest and that the world owes him a living." The sports newspaper suggested "Cazzetta ought to kick him in the pants instead of pampering him."[27] Only Pittsburgh's black paper, the *New Pittsburgh Courier,* tried to understand the reason for Connie's sub-par performances: "He's picked up a lot of bad habits the last couple of years. As a result he is going to be made to look bad unless he gets his game back to where it was when he was in the old American Basketball League."[28]

Two early losses at home proved especially costly. In November the league-leading Indiana Pacers came to town. They were tough, and their rough physical style had lifted them to a 9-2 record. The Pipers battled for three quarters, but faded in the fourth. The Pacers outscored them by eighteen in the final stanza, and won, 100-83. "It was simply a case of poor shooting and giveaways," observed the *Post-Gazette*.[29]

Two weeks later, the Pipers played the New Jersey Americans, a team expected to challenge for the ABA crown but, like the Pipers, one that had yet to find its rhythm. The Americans had only five wins to their name. Still, they were talented, and three NBA veterans on their roster made them a formidable opponent. In the end the referees—not the players—decided the contest. The Americans made fourteen more free throws than the Pipers, and New Jersey defeated Pittsburgh, 114-109.

Sparse crowds further compounded the Pipers' woes. Reported attendance rarely climbed above 1,500—and that was a generous estimate. Of the first nine games played in the Pittsburgh Civic Arena, only the opener drew more than 2,000 people. To entice Pittsburghers to games, management offered season tickets at cut-rate prices and marketed the team in newspapers, stores, and schools. On Ladies' Night, the price of a three-dollar ticket was reduced to fifty cents, and on Students' Night to one dollar. One plan proved particularly effective. Youngsters would receive an allotment of tickets, sell them, and keep a portion of the money. It was a good fund-raising tool for schools and it put fans in the stands.

The youngster-as-ticket-agent scheme drew 7,840 spectators to watch the Pipers play the Houston Mavericks, a young team with the worst record in the league. Motivated by the large turnout, the Pipers jumped out to a fifteen-point advantage and never let up. They crushed the Mavericks, 124-84. For Rubin, the lopsided victory was not the only reason to be happy. The crowd was the largest to date, tantalizing him with the possibility that professional basketball might make it in Pittsburgh after all.

But the Pipers left for a four-game road trip the next day. Without Cazzetta coaching the team—he was back in Pittsburgh recovering from an illness—the Pipers struggled, and wound up 0-4 for the trip. The four straight defeats, which included two in a row to a mediocre Denver Rockets club and another to the Maverick team the Pipers had demolished just four days earlier, lowered Pittsburgh's record to 11-12 (and just 1-8 over the past two weeks). To the players' credit, they had played on five consecutive nights. They were tired and Rubin probably knew it. But that was little consolation. He needed results and fast. For the first time all season his team was below .500. Rubin was convinced that if the Pipers were to make it in such a fickle market as Pittsburgh he would have to do it with a revamped lineup.

A day after the Pipers returned, Rubin traded for "Crazy Artie." Pipers fans were familiar with Heyman's violent and unpredictable behavior. As a member of the Americans earlier in the year, he had gotten into a heated scuffle with his own teammate under the Civic Arena stands. It was exactly this kind of pugnacious behavior that made Rubin think Heyman would be the perfect complement to the easy-going Hawkins. "There's no question that our team lacked muscle," the Pipers' owner said. "Now we have some. And Art also will make the entire team hustle. That's the way he goes all night." Others agreed. "One of the raps against the Pipers," a correspondent for the *Post-Gazette* observed, "was that they lacked a fighter. Now they have one." With such descriptions of Heyman as "a new spirit," "a driving force," a "rough and ready fellow," and "a motivation the Pipers have needed" circulating in local papers, the Pipers seemed ready to break out of their slump.[30]

Stop their skid they surely did, but no one could have imagined the huge payoff resulting from the trade for Heyman. Crazy Artie's hustle and scrappiness inspired his new teammates, and his pinpoint passes set them up for easy scores. He also gave Pittsburgh another scoring threat. With Heyman playing alongside Hawkins, the Pipers now had one of the best tandems in the league. In Heyman's first game for Pittsburgh, Indiana found out just how dynamic the Pipers' duo could be, with Hawkins and Heyman combining for forty-three points. The Pipers slipped past the Pacers, 103-100, and the losing streak was over. A victory over the Denver Rockets followed, and back-to-back wins became six, which turned into twelve. Soon the Pipers were riding the crest of a fifteen-game winning streak, the longest of any ABA club—and the lengthiest of any Pittsburgh pro team since 1909, when the baseball Pirates won sixteen consecutive games.

At first it seemed Pittsburghers hardly noticed the turnaround. Heyman's second game as a Piper saw 698 spectators dot the 13,000-seat Civic Arena. Cazzetta likened the game to playing in "a vacuum." Gradually, however, fans began to respond to the team. With headlines screaming "Pittsburgh Nails Down 6th in Row," "Pipers Rap Muskies for 8th Straight," "Perky Pipers Pick on Amerks, 146-124," "Pipers Rip

Houston for Tenth in Row," and "Pipers Run String to Dozen," readers of the *Post-Gazette*'s sports page could not help but notice the string of victories.[31] Attendance climbed from 698 to 1,037 to 3,032, and then from 3,231 to 3,585. By the streak's twelfth game, 7,240 fans came out to watch Pittsburgh take on Dallas.

The winning streak bolstered players' confidence and momentarily eased management's concern over sluggish ticket sales. For the next two months attendance figures hovered around 3,000. The figure was still 2,000 short of the break-even mark, but it showed that the club had at least made some inroads with fans. Commenting on the increase, one Piper executive confided in the *Post-Gazette,* "It's nothing short of remarkable." The Pipers' newfound energy and the team's sudden ability to draw more fans left many disbelievers red-faced. Optimism about the club's future began to appear more frequently in newspapers. "The Pipers are here to stay," proclaimed a team's spokesman in the *Post-Gazette*. Observed the sports editor for the paper, "Certainly, the picture looks a lot brighter for a team [the Pipers] some people were betting wouldn't survive the first year."[32]

In the Pipers Pittsburgh had a diamond but still, few seemed interested—a shock since the 1960s could hardly be considered the golden age of Pittsburgh pro sports championships. As far as Steel City teams winning titles, the decade was starving time for fans. Capturing the disappointment, the *Post-Gazette* remarked in the fall of 1967, "This city needs a winner badly."[33] To the dismay of many, Iron City pro teams had ignored the call. After being picked to finish atop the National League in 1967, the Pirates' dismal, sixth-place performance that same year left fans dejected and upset. The Steelers, too, were a washout, finishing dead last in the Century Division (4-9-1). And the Penguins seemed they would fare no better, stuck near the bottom of the NHL's Western Division. Yet the city, desperately craving a winner, did not feast on the Pipers. Nothing seemed to move the city from its implacable ennui.

The few Pittsburghers who followed the Pipers were anything but bored. A close division race at season's end with the Minnesota Muskies heightened interest. In the last week of the regular season, Pittsburgh held a three-game advantage with three games to play. The only chance the Muskies stood was if they went 3-0 and the Pipers 0-

3. But when Minnesota lost to Indiana first, the prize fell to Pittsburgh. In the meantime, the Pipers finished strong, winning the rest of their games to wind up 54-24, the top record in the league. Home-court advantage for the playoffs was theirs. Rubin and his players looked forward to the likelihood that postseason play would excite the city. Surely then fans would come out and support the team.

But of the last six regular-season home games, only two had drawn more than 2,500 spectators. After experiencing some mild success at the gate during the fifteen-game win string, the Pipers were now struggling. In a *Pittsburgh Press* article headlined, "Everything But Fans," coach Cazetta expressed frustration: "I don't expect the town to go crazy if we win the playoffs but I do wish I could notice a little feeling, a little enthusiasm." Despite the fact that the Pipers were winning, "it doesn't feel electric in the city," the Pipers' coach said a day after the playoffs had started. "It's almost a feeling like who cares, and I can't get used to this."[34]

The Pipers faced the Indiana Pacers in the first round of the playoffs. During the season, the Pipers had taken six games out of ten from the Pacers, but had lost the last two. Before 2,189 onlookers watching the first game of the best-of-five series, the Hawk punished Indiana's defense for thirty-eight points, leading his team to a 146-127 victory. Five other Pipers scored double digits. Indianapolis was the site of the second game, and the outcome resembled the first. With five Pipers scoring in double figures this time, Pittsburgh ran past the Pacers, 121-108. The series came back to the Iron City for the third game, and the home team did not disappoint the small contingent of 3,141 who attended. A forty-eight-point deluge by the Pipers in the third quarter set up a 133-114 triumph, eliminating the Pacers and advancing Pittsburgh to face the winner of the Minnesota/Kentucky series. Again the Pipers had benefited from a balanced attack, five players hitting eleven or more points. Collecting thirty-four, Williams was Pittsburgh's top scorer.

The Minnesota Muskies had a tough time with the Kentucky Colonels—a surprise to many since Minnesota possessed the second-best record in the league (50-28). ABA followers looked to the Muskies to get rid of the Colonels quickly. Instead, Kentucky dragged the best-of-five series to a final game. The Pipers were not complaining, since it gave them time to heal some nagging injuries. Both Hawkins and Heyman had lower back pains, Williams's hamstring was sore, and center Tom Washington, who was playing with a soft cast over his left wrist, had two bum knees. The longer the Minnesota/Kentucky series lasted, the Pipers figured, the better. By the time Minnesota finally advanced, the Pipers had had a much-needed week off to rest. The Muskies hardly knew what hit them. Pittsburgh cruised past Minnesota in the best-of-seven series, splitting the first two games at home (125-117 and 137-123), and then sweeping the next three (107-99, 117-108 and 114-105). Crowds for the three games in Pittsburgh numbered some 2,800 a game—a sad statement, to be sure, given the fact that the Muskies drew three times as many fans when they hosted the Pipers. And this from a Minnesota franchise almost certain to leave once the season was over.

Awaiting the Pipers in the championship round were the New Orleans Buccaneers, winners of the ABA's Western Division. The Bucs were led by Doug Moe and Larry Brown, heady players who later became NBA coaches. Like Hawkins, Moe had been accused in college of conspiring with gamblers to fix games and subsequently blacklisted by the NBA. He spent the next several seasons languishing in the Italian league. Moe was a good player, especially on defense. He was neither fast nor quick, and he could barely jump over the Sunday *New York Times*. But what he lacked in athleticism he made up for in savvy and hustle, eschewing flamboyance for fundamentals. His "old school" style produced machine-like efficiency. Though somewhat stiff and robot-like, he was still good enough to be named first team, all-ABA. Larry Brown, Moe's teammate, was one of the best point guards in the league. Scrappy and tenacious on defense, the second-team all-pro guard still relied on a two-handed set shot from the perimeter.

To compare the Pipers' style to that of the Bucs' is to compare jazz great Dizzy Gillespie to *American Bandstand* host Dick Clark. Pittsburgh thrived on the freedom of the schoolyard, while New Orleans played more of a structured, team-first kind of game. Virtually every Piper had grown up on a steady diet of playground ball. Hawkins owed his talent to the tutelage he received on New York's blacktops. The freelance style of Vaughn, Williams, and Washington showed that they, too, had apprenticed on the playground. Even Heyman, that Jewish exemplar of "whiteness," played a "black" game, finding that the flair and creativity of a street-ball style prized off-balance shots and whirling drives through the lane, two of his pet plays. If the Bucs were workmen, the Pipers were artistes.

The racial composition of the teams reflected their stylistic difference. Of the Bucs' starting five, only guard Jimmy Jones was black. In fact, New Orleans had only three black players. The Pipers were their mirror image. Heyman was the lone white starter, and, except for three other white players, the rest of the team was black. With the series beginning two weeks after the assassination of Martin Luther King Jr. (the Minnesota series actually had started on April 4, the day King was shot), the racial contrast between the two teams took on added meaning, and the widespread violence that ensued in scores of American cities forced many who followed the series to see it as something more than just innocent competition.

Black Pittsburghers living in the Lower Hill District experienced the unrest caused by King's death firsthand. Most of the rioting in Pittsburgh occurred in the Lower Hill neighborhood. Like other northern ghettos roped off from the American Dream by racism and discriminatory residential patterns, the Hill was one of the most disadvantaged areas in the Steel City. Over 95 percent of Hill residents were black—next to the Homewood-Brushton area, the Hill was Pittsburgh's largest African American community. The Hill District had an unemployment rate of 16 percent, four times higher than Pittsburgh's white, middle-class neighborhoods—and eight times more than upper-income areas like Banksville, Stanton Heights, or nearby Squirrel Hill. Worse yet, one out of three families in the Lower Hill District eked out a living on incomes below the poverty level. In Lawrenceville, one of the city's most deprived white neighborhoods, just one out of twenty families lacked sufficient resources to be considered below the poverty line. No wonder the mood on the Hill was volatile.[35]

The ruthless slaying of King sparked this tinderbox of discontent. On the first night of rioting, fires set by arsonists lit up the sky, engulfing the downtown area in smoke. Groups of young vandals prowled the Hill's streets and alleyways, plundering shops and stores and shattering windows of businesses. By the second night of rioting, no fewer than thirty-five fire bombings had rocked the area. The following day the *Post-Gazette* reported that from the time the rioting had started a total of 950 arrests had been made. In addition, six residents had suffered gunshot wounds.[36] Responding to the disorder, Gov. Raymond P. Shafer shut down liquor stores, placed restrictions on gasoline sales, and declared a state of emergency. Thousands of National Guardsmen poured into the city (one was Pipers reserve guard Steve Vacendak), and a curfew imposed by Mayor Joseph Barr prohibited residents from leaving their homes after dark. But in the troubled Hill District angry residents ignored the mayor's directive. "There must [have been] more than 1,000 persons running wild on the Hill," a police spokesman declared on the second night of the curfew. Pipers player Charlie Williams, who lived in the Hill District, remembered hearing that rioters were going "to come down to the Civic Arena" and destroy the stadium.[37] The presence of armed troops surrounding the arena, however, deterred the mobs. The Pipers' home court escaped the nearby ransacking unscathed.

The lawlessness, the vandalism, the looting—all served to highlight the strained race relations in the city. The fear was that the destructive force of the riots would provoke a white backlash, which in turn would incite black rioters to commit more violence. Newspapers urged for cooler heads to prevail. In an editorial four days after the first night of rioting, the *Post-Gazette* told readers, "The looters and vandals and arsonists represent only an infinitesimal portion of the total Negro population. . . . Most black people do not turn to criminal acts to get revenge." When looking for a cause for the violence, the paper added, white residents "should avoid blanket condemnation based on skin color." The *Pittsburgh Press* echoed the *Post-Gazette*'s remarks, editorializing that the riots "reflected only the primitive behavior of a very small percentage of the Negro community." The individuals responsible for the havoc were "not representative of the black race."[38]

Given the overlap of the playoffs with King's assassination and the riots that followed, it seems odd that Pittsburgh's sportswriters abstained from commenting on issues of race in the series. Instead, journalists lashed out at readers for shunning the Pipers, "one of the best kept secrets of all time in this city." The *Post-Gazette* called the home crowd of 2,665 that witnessed Hawkins score thirty-nine points in a 120-112 victory over the Bucs in the first game of the series "a sad reflection on a club that has won eight of nine tough playoff games." The Pipers "deserve better treatment," the paper told readers. To Pipers owner Gabe Rubin, the reason for the small playoff audiences was clear: The "riots that took place in the Hill District" had scared fans away.[39]

Cazzetta's immediate concern was not the inability of his team to attract ticket buyers but rather the health of the players. Williams's hamstring ached, Heyman's left arch throbbed, and Washington's jaw was wired shut, a souvenir from a blow he had taken to the face in the Minnesota series. Adding to his misery was a reinjured wrist. Vaughn joined the ranks of the Pipers' walking wounded, having sustained a deep gash over his left eye during game 1. The injury had swelled overnight and was sure to reduce his productivity for the second contest. Drawing the most attention from New Orleans defenders, Hawk experienced the usual bumps and bruises. Though banged up, he would play.

Hobbled by injuries and slowed by aches and pains, the Pipers in game 2 were unable to get their fast break in gear. Their troubles worsened when Hawkins fouled out in the third quarter and Heyman was not able to pick up the slack. The soreness in his left arch greatly curtailed his scoring. He managed just two points in twenty-three minutes of play. The small Civic Arena crowd of 3,877 was restless. With most of his starting five either in foul trouble or injured, Cazzetta was forced to go deep into his bench. The second team kept the game close, but the Bucs' starters held off the Pipers' reserves to win, 109-100. New Orleans now had home-court advantage.

The Bucs hosted games 3 and 4. The change of venue gave the Pipers a few days to recuperate and a chance for bruises to heal. New Orleans's home court was the 7,000-seat Loyola University Field House, a tight little stadium with extra-cozy confines. When full, its capacity crowd seemed to hover over and spill onto the court. Three times during the regular season the Pipers had lost in that fieldhouse. Yet the setback in Pittsburgh had proven to them that the home-court advantage was overstated. To win in New Orleans was to return the favor. With guarded optimism the Pipers arrived in New Orleans for game 3.

A near-capacity crowd was on hand. The Pipers jumped out to an early eight-point lead, and stretched it to thirteen when Vaughn nailed a three-pointer with two minutes left in the first period. But then the Bucs started to make their shots. New Orleans chipped the thirteen-point margin to ten by halftime, and there the Pipers' lead remained until the start of the final quarter. That Pittsburgh was ahead by ten with only one quarter to play was an impressive feat, especially since Hawkins had scored just thirteen. Vaughn's hot hand (he finished with twenty-seven) helped compensate for Hawk's cool shooting. But in the fourth quarter Vaughn, too, started to cool down. Meanwhile, the Bucs stayed hot. With 1:30 left, New Orleans took a 102-101 lead—its first in the game. The rest was all Bucs, and they won, 109-101. New Orleans had outscored Pittsburgh by eighteen points in the fourth quarter. "Pipers Blow It, Trail in Series," boomed a *Post-Gazette* headline the next day.[40] The Bucs were again on top, two games to one.

Fans in the Crescent City were an unruly bunch, and they did almost anything to throw the Pipers off their game—stomping, booing, hissing, raising Cain. To one Pittsburgh reporter, the New Orleans faithful were not just hooligans but slobs: Bucs supporters used "the court as a wishing well and wastebasket by throwing pennies, paper cups, and half-eaten candy bars." Another Iron City journalist described them as a "mob" and "vociferous buffs," whose madcap rowdyism "left [others in attendance] thinking that the Mardi Gras was still on."[41] It seemed Bucs fans would stop at nothing to ensure a victory for their team.

According to Hawk's biographer David Wolf, Connie personally felt the malevolence of the New Orleans crowd. Warming up before the fourth game, Hawkins heard racial slurs hurled in his direction. "Nice shot, nigger," a man blurted after Connie made a dunk. "Hey, nigger, way to go, nigger," the voice repeated. Showing his racism, another man chimed, "Yeah, nigger, nice shot." Enraged, Hawkins tried to locate the men. He scanned the crowd and moved off the floor, fists balled. Fortunately Hawkins' teammate Leroy Wright saw the ugly scene about to unfold. He intercepted Connie and told him to cool it.[42] Obliging Wright, Hawk channeled his indignation into the game. He started out fast and finished the half with nineteen points. Despite his efforts, Pittsburgh trailed, 52-47. But the Pipers, inspired by the Hawk's determination, would come back, and eventually snatch victory with a 106-105 overtime win. Hawkins had had a monstrous night—forty-seven points and thirteen rebounds. Tied at two games apiece, the Pipers regained their confidence and recaptured home-court advantage.

The conduct of Bucs fans shocked Hawkins and his teammates, for a line separating tolerable courtside behavior and hate-mongering had been crossed. To utter such racist remarks as the country still grieved the death of its great civil rights leader demonstrated the lengths some white Americans would go to preserve a racial caste system. The words and actions of a few Bucs' faithful suggested indifference, even satisfaction, over the country's tragic loss. It was an affront to the memory of Martin Luther King Jr. and everything he represented, a sad reminder that bigotry still was deeply entrenched in American society.

It went without saying that the Pipers were happy to be leaving New Orleans. But they knew that in order to win the title, one more game would be played in the Big Easy. Yet that was the least of their worries. After two hard-fought games played on consecutive nights, the Pipers came away more hobbled than ever. In addition to the pain of Heyman's arch, Williams's hamstring, and Washington's jaw and left wrist, Vaughn had injured his groin, and the Hawk his right knee, partially tearing the right medial tendon. For the Pipers Connie's injury was the most serious. Although the injury was not career-threatening, it was serious enough to list his status as questionable for game 5.

Without the Hawk in uniform, many believed the Pipers stood little chance. And with other key Pittsburgh players banged up, prospects indeed looked bleak. As if the gloom cast by the injuries was not enough, the Bucs suffered only some minor cuts and scrapes. News that Hawkins would sit out game 5 lifted New Orleans's spirits. Confident and healthy were the Bucs, and most observers assumed that the game would be a rout. But the Hawkins-less Pipers countered the Bucs' sureness with superb play from Williams, Heyman, and Vaughn, the trio scoring eighty-one points for the game. In the end, the Pipers made six more field goals but fifteen fewer foul shots than the Bucs. New Orleans eked by, 111-108, and reclaimed control of the series, three games to two.

Unlike the Bucs, the Pipers could not rely on their fans to pull them through rough spots in games. The *Post-Gazette* made this point abundantly clear, admonishing readers who avoided Pipers games. The paper reminded readers that game 5 of the series, the most important professional basketball game in the city's history, had drawn so few fans as to leave 9,000 seats in the Civic Arena empty. "Once again," bemoaned the *Post-Gazette,* "a crowd of only 3,347 showed up. This is disheartening for Rubin, Cazzetta, and all of the players."[43] Rubin reproduced the paper's disgust, exclaiming that Hawkins was more of a celebrity in New Orleans than in Pittsburgh: "When Connie Hawkins walks down the street in the Iron City, nobody asks him for an autograph. At least ten kids asked Connie for his signature when we were in New Orleans the past week."[44] Not much hope existed in Piperville for the Piper five.

The Pipers, however, remained positive. "Sure, we are down a game," Cazzetta declared, "but we can bounce back." Perhaps Cazzetta's optimism was a means to mask the fear that the Pipers would lose the series. There certainly was not much reason for cheer. The Bucs were in command, Hawkins was hurt, and game 6 was back in New Orleans. But Connie knew that for his team to have a chance he had to stay upbeat. "I've been talking to the boys," Hawkins told a reporter, "and they want nothing more than to win these next two games. It's pride with us." There was no need for panic, assured the Piper star, "all we have to do is give them the fast treatment and they won't catch us."[45] The "fast treatment" was the fast break, *the* basic component of the Pipers' game. Cazzetta later called it a "hurry-up, early offense," and praised it for being the engine behind the Pipers' success. "We will bring the title to Pittsburgh to show the fans they have a top club," Hawkins proclaimed.[46]

To predict victory was not to procure it. A game still had to be played—with or without the Hawk. In front of a noisy crowd shoehorned into the Loyola Field House, both teams warmed up. Visibly wincing, Hawkins gimped through lay-ups. The knee was sore, and it pained him to jump and crouch into a defensive stance. Nevertheless, he would try to play. With his knee heavily bandaged, he started the game slowly, but soon discovered that the more he ran, the better the knee felt. Before long he was showing flashes of his healthy self, notching nine points in the first quarter. Other Pipers, however, were having a rough time. Williams forced shots, Heyman could not stop all-ABAer Moe from scoring, and Vaughn was a nonfactor, scoring just two points, five for the entire game. Except for Piper reserve Jim Jarvis, who scored thirteen, the rest of the team seemed more injured than Hawkins. Nothing was going their way. The Bucs, in contrast, were on a roll, and took a 72-59 lead into the locker room at the half. A basket by Moe at the beginning of the third quarter added two more to New Orleans's lead, and 7,200 sweaty fans sensed a championship. Victory champagne was chilling on ice in the New Orleans locker room.

All at once Hawk started to soar. He sailed, skyed, and wheeled and dealed. He drained shots from every angle on the floor. He even flew in for some spectacular Michael Jordanesque floaters that would have made the future Chicago Bull proud. It was as if his knee injury never had occurred. Rowdy Bucs fans watched helplessly as their club's double-digit lead dwindled. Momentum was on the side of the Pipers. Hawkins's foul-line jumper late in the third quarter (his twelfth and thirteenth points of the period) evened the score and silenced the antsy crowd. A last-ditch run by New Orleans bore no fruit, and the Pipers won the thriller, 118-112. Williams had tossed in twenty-three points, and Heyman twenty. But the true star was Connie. He finished with forty-one points and twelve rebounds, stunning the Bucs and casting a pall over the fieldhouse.

Hawkins's grit amazed the respective coaches. Watching his star player single-handedly defeat the Bucs on one leg, Cazzetta was convinced that Hawkins was "the greatest basketball player in the world." A flabbergasted New Orleans coach Babe McCarthy could only exclaim, "That's the best I've ever seen him play."[47] Such comments were kind praise. But for Hawkins, individual recognition was not as sweet as knowing that his team had escaped with a victory. The Pipers were still alive, and, more important, there would be a game 7—in Pittsburgh.

In this series the theory of the home-court advantage had been an illusion. Of three games in Pittsburgh, the Pipers had lost two. Scant fan support helped contribute to this irregularity. The *Post-Gazette* hoped to rectify the situation by issuing numerous calls for Pittsburghers to get behind their team, announcing two days before the Bucs and Pipers were to meet that "this is the local roundball fans' last shot to support the city's only pro team winner." Previewing the Pipers/Bucs matchup on the day of the final contest, the newspaper rephrased Paine's revolutionary call: "Now is the time for all good basketball buffs to come to the aid of the Pipers." Pittsburgh's ABA team "would like to have a large gathering of area rooters on hand to change the tune."[48]

The tune changed: 11,457 people thronged the Civic Arena for the finale. For once, the din from a sellout crowd could be heard echoing throughout Pittsburgh's home arena. The crowd was so large that the starting time had to be delayed for half an hour to give fans enough time to find their seats. Williams recalled that he and his teammates "couldn't believe all the fans in the stands."[49] In the Pipers' locker room, players and Cazzetta ached to begin. They knew the importance of the game, and the enormous turnout served to heighten the significance of it. Crazy Artie threw up four times before the opening tip.[50] Hawkins nervously massaged his right knee. Cazzetta displayed his usual poker face, concealing his nervousness and excitement.

Game 7 belonged to the Pipers. The Hawk swooped in for breakaway dunks, Vaughn harassed the Bucs' guards on defense, and Heyman scored off several drives and pull-up jump shots. But it was Williams who inflicted the most damage, torching the Bucs for fourteen first-quarter points, and seven more in the second. The basket seemed twice its normal size to the home team. A flurry of three straight three-pointers by Vaughn halfway through the third period lifted the Pipers' advantage to twenty-one. But in the fourth quarter the Bucs responded with a run of their own, forcing Pittsburgh into several turnovers, converting turnovers to points. With three minutes left in the game, the Pipers' twenty-one-point margin had shriveled to a paltry five. "I was a little nervous there," owner Rubin would later admit in reference to his team's slippage.[51] But when leading scorer Doug Moe was ejected a minute later for disputing a call with the officials, New Orleans's comeback was over, and the Pipers beat the Bucs, 122-113, capturing the first ABA crown.

The Civic Arena overflowed with jubilation. Hundreds of fans streamed onto the floor, smiling, celebrating, whooping it up. Williams, who paced the Pipers with thirty-five points, remembered that center

"Tom Washington was so happy that he just broke down and cried."[52] In Pittsburgh's locker room, boisterous laughter and shouts of glee filled everyone's ears, as the hollow pop, pop, pop of champagne bottles uncorked cracked the air. For a bunch of NBA blacklistees, has beens, or never weres it felt good. They had not won an NBA championship, but they had proven to the city that they were a championship team. The hearts and minds of Pittsburghers were theirs at least for one evening. "Pipers Win ABA Title, 122-113," hollered a *Pittsburgh-Press* sports-page masthead the following day.[53] With the news, the entire city now knew it had had a winner right at its doorstep.

What was to become of the Pipers only Rubin precisely knew. Fans assumed that he would move the franchise since the Pipers had done so poorly at the gate. Newspapers refused to confront the inevitable. There would be headlines: "Pipers Plan to Go Again"; "Pipers to Stay in Pittsburgh"; "Rubin Denies Moving Pipers." Rubin was equivocal. He told the *Post-Gazette* that he "would like to stay in Pittsburgh and will if it is economically possible." The *Sporting News* did its part to allay the fears of Pipers fans, remarking, "Despite the poor response to a winning team, Rubin is not anxious to relocate." Three weeks later brought additional good news. Rubin said that his first year as owner was "rewarding in many ways."[54] Maybe, just maybe, Pipers fans hoped, the club would stay.

The truth was that two weeks after the ABA finals Rubin already had some offers from outside investors. The only real option Rubin had to recoup the previous season's losses—which came close to $350,000—was to sell the team, but the proposals so far had been unsatisfactory. With half-hearted interest he continued to pursue the possibility of remaining in Pittsburgh. But with no television or radio contract, and limited sponsorship deals in the offing, the likelihood of the Pipers staying indeed seemed dim. The clincher came when Rubin learned that because of league scheduling he was unable to move the dates of several Pipers games from Tuesday and Friday nights to Saturday night and Sunday afternoon. Most local high schools played their games on Tuesday and Friday evenings. In late June he sold 85 percent of his share in the club to Minneapolis businessman and lawyer William Erickson. The deal stipulated that the Pipers would move to

Minnesota and replace the Muskies, who had bolted for the warm Florida sunshine to become the Miami Floridians. Following in the footsteps of their pro basketball predecessors, the Pipers left Pittsburgh.

That a good Muskie team had failed to draw a decent gate did not deter Erickson from bringing the Pipers to the Twin Cities. He was enthusiastic about his venture, and he had the league's backing. Not all of the Pipers would be coming, however. The team's new board of directors had turned down Cazzetta's request for a higher salary. Cazzetta had asked for the extra money as a means to help defray moving expenses to Minnesota for him and his family. Upset at being snubbed, Cazzetta, the ABA's Coach of the Year, left the Pipers. To fill his position Erickson hired Jim Harding, a former college coach and fiery disciplinarian who made Bobby Knight look like a nursery school teacher. "If I find a griper [on my team]," the Pipers' new coach told the *Sporting News* a month and a half into the season, "he will be dealt with accordingly. And [players are] going to play my way, or not play at all."[55]

Harding's coaching philosophy was militaristic: break players down to build them up—and scream and cuss and yell any time an error was made. Fear and punishment, doled out in verbal abuse and wind sprints, were his motivational tools. Not surprisingly, players loathed his practices. Charlie Williams would later say Harding's training camp "was brutal, absolutely brutal. We didn't have double sessions, we had triple sessions." And "we always went full tilt."[56] To make matters worse, Harding refused to rest his starters during games, often playing them a full forty-eight minutes. Pushed to such extremes, the Pipers wore down in the latter half of the year (at the mid-season All-Star break the Pipers stood 20-12 and atop their division). The reigning ABA champs finished their second season an underachieving 36-42, fourth in the five-team Eastern Conference.

The Pipers quickly discovered that Minnesota was not the land of 10,000 lakes but rather one gigantic mountain of debt. Management spent money as if it had an endless supply. Costs exceeded revenue, and expenditures depleted what little income the team could generate. Just to balance his books Erickson had to average some 6,000 more people a game than had come to Muskies contests the previous year. Instead his team fell 5,000 short, and by the end of the season the

Minnesota Pipers were, according to the *New York Times,* $772,000 in debt.[57] Combined with the hefty bill incurred while in Pittsburgh, the club now owed over $1 million. Lacking the funds necessary to settle his account with Rubin, in June the cash-strapped Erickson forfeited his claim to the team. Rubin was once again in charge of the Pipers. Two months later he brought the Pipers *back* to the Steel City, where they became the Pittsburgh Condors.

The Hawk, however, would not be returning. Instead, he went to Phoenix, signing a multiyear contract with the NBA Phoenix Suns. A whopping $6-million-dollar damage lawsuit brought against the NBA by Hawkins forced the league to the bargaining table. In the out-of-court settlement NBA officials granted the Hawk permission to compete in their league as well as compensatory damages totaling $600,000. It was a defining moment in sport history. Connie was not only the "first player to sue a major league and gain both a contract and damages," noted David Wolf in a 1969 issue of *Life,* "he [was] also the first basketball player named in a betting scandal to use the courts to clear his name." Hawkins was indeed fortunate to have cleared his name, since it meant that he would not have to play for the Condors. Former ABA guard Steve Jones remembered that the Condors were so awful and mismanaged that more than one player "did jokes saying that if Pittsburgh wasn't basketball's end of the world, you could see it from there."[58] The Condors' combined, three-year record was a dismal 90-162, poor enough for two second-to-last-place finishes and one dead last. Three years after they returned to Pittsburgh, the Condors went bust, ending big-league basketball in the Steel City for good.

It was to the misfortune of basketball fans that the Pipers left Pittsburgh after that inaugural season. Rather than being the start of something great, the move to Minnesota signaled the beginning of the end for pro basketball in the Iron City. If the team had stayed in Pittsburgh and acquired a true center of NBA caliber, the Pipers could have won more ABA titles. Fan support most surely would have increased, and the club might have changed the city's attitude toward professional basketball.

This scenario, of course, is just speculation, a pipe(r) dream, so to speak. People make decisions without the benefit of hindsight, and one would assume if Rubin had had a chance to peer into the future and see the dismantling of his club, he would have opted to keep the team in town. Perhaps the NBA eventually would have added the Pipers, as it did in 1976 with some other old ABA clubs (San Antonio, Indianapolis, Denver, and New Jersey). Today, the only thing that fans remember about the Pipers is not that they brought the city a title but rather that they left the Steel City. As one of only three local teams that won championships in the 1960s (the Hornets of the American Hockey League and the 1960 baseball Pirates were the others), the Pipers achieved something that should not be forgotten. Sadly, Pittsburgh has done just that, forgetting the one brief moment when basketball outshone all other sports. It has forgotten, too, an unforgettable season that culminated in an unforgettable championship for an unforgettable team. The Pipers were the first ABA champs. Their feat should be remembered.

After playing six years of professional basketball in Luxembourg, Australia, Belarus, and Poland, Chris Elzey returned to the United States to pursue a graduate degree in American Studies. He is currently a Ph.D. candidate at Purdue University.

8

HOW A NEW YORKER CAME TO LOVE THE PENGUINS

BROOKS D. SIMPSON

WHY THE PENGUINS? Why 1990? I was not a native of the Pittsburgh area; indeed, I had only visited it three times prior to the start of the 1990–91 season. The first time, in the fall of 1986, I took advantage of the opportunity to give a paper at a conference in downtown Pittsburgh to join my fiancée, with plans to meet her grandmother before embarking on an excursion through western Pennsylvania. After giving my paper in the morning, I walked through downtown Pittsburgh and then out toward the Civic Arena, commonly known as "the Igloo" because of the shape of its white dome. Although the Pens were in town that night, Jean and I did not go to the game. Nor did we linger any longer during our second visit in the summer of 1987, when we made the grand tour of my prospective in-laws, or our final visit in 1990, as we prepared to make the move to Arizona. My wife's family hailed from the Pittsburgh area, but none of them showed any interest in the Penguins, although my new grandmother-in-law rooted for the Steelers and the Pirates. If I linked my in-laws in any way with hockey, it was because Jean had attended Haverford, just outside Philadelphia (home of the memorable chant, "Kill, Quakers, kill!"), and her family lived just outside of Hershey, home of the Hershey Bears, then an affiliate of the much-despised (in my world) Philadelphia Flyers. Jean's bemused expression when I recited the litany of Flyers crimes against humanity was balanced by the fact that as a field hockey player, she could follow its cousin on ice, and never more than when we attended an Islander-Capitals game in Landover in the spring of 1987. Surrounded by over 18,000 rabid Caps fans, she taunted the Caps' captain, Rod Langway, accusing him of dirty play and commenting on how stupid it was for someone to play without a helmet. Impressed with her passion, I was also thankful that we were not in Madison Square Garden, where speaking ill of a Ranger player has been known to bring on a riot.

Nor could one say that I had ever displayed any fondness for the Penguins. In my mind, they had long been a mediocre team (or worse), with nondescript light blue jerseys that appeared to be pale replicas of New York Ranger uniforms. Joining the NHL as part of the league's doubling in size following the 1966–67 season, the Pens hoped to build on a frail foundation of a hockey tradition. From 1925–26 to 1929–30, the Pittsburgh Pirates had been terrorized by the National Hockey League; however, the minor-league Hornets had enjoyed success in the American Hockey League. What made the franchise distinctive was its home arena, complete with retractable roof—although hockey under the stars was not to be. With Red Sullivan as the team's first coach and veteran winger Andy Bathgate as its first name player (acquired through the league-wide expansion draft), the team had a distinct Ranger flavor. Unfortunately, those Rangers had struggled to make the playoffs, and so did the Penguins, who did not taste postseason play until the 1969–70 season, when they finished in second place and prevailed over the Oakland Seals before losing to the St. Louis Blues in the West Division finals. The glory was short-lived. The league took over management of the team after owner Donald Parsons decided he could no longer afford to lose money; it looked to be a omen of things to come when the team's mascot, a real penguin, died. Far more tragic was the fate of rookie sensation Michel Brière: an off-season automobile accident left him in a coma from which he never emerged. His death would loom over the franchise for years to come.

Over the years, the uniforms changed, but the Pens remained more or less hapless. In the team's first seven years of existence, it never finished a season with a winning record and had only two playoff appearances to its credit. Only in 1975 did the Pens first assume a role of importance in my consciousness, when that year's playoffs proved pivotal for my rooting allegiances. As a boy I had been a Rangers fan, and had even attended a hockey camp that featured Ranger stars Rod Gilbert and Brad Park. Every season the Rangers showed great promise; every playoff something would go wrong, and they would fall short in their quest to win their first Stanley Cup since 1940. Complicating matters was the arrival of the New York Islanders in 1972. The team played its home games at Nassau Veterans Memorial Coliseum, only a short drive from home; it was easy to get good seats and to get my father to take me to games. We never again ventured into Madison Square Garden. However, the infant Isles were a disaster on the ice in their inaugural year, followed by a second season of below-par play. Thus it was somewhat of a surprise when they jelled into a competitive force their third season, earning a playoff spot opposite the Rangers. It was time to choose. Putting aside years of frustration with the Rangers, I cheered on the new kids on the block, and they rewarded me by beating the Rangers in overtime of the deciding contest. Their next opponent: the Pittsburgh Penguins.

The Penguins of that year were a team that was emerging in its own right. Led by wingers Jean Pronovost, Rick Kehoe, and rookie scoring sensation Pierre Larouche, they had finished third in their division, with a record just a shade better than the Islanders (and a point total that would stand as the team's best for nearly two decades); among the team's other players was former Ranger Vic Hadfield. The Pens ripped through the Islanders for three straight wins, leading me to conclude that a change of teams had not led to a change in playoff fortunes. After all, only one team—the 1942 Toronto Maple Leafs—had rallied from a 3-0 deficit to win a best-of-seven playoff series. But I was in for a surprise—and Pens fans were in for a shock. With Glenn "Chico" Resch replacing a then still-developing Billy Smith in goal, the Islanders reeled off three straight wins, forcing a deciding seventh game in the Igloo. A third-period goal by Islander captain Ed Westfall completed the miracle comeback as the Isles held on to win, 1-0. Westfall, after his days on the ice, moved to the Islander broadcast booth and claimed that Pittsburgh hockey people would identify him as "the guy who almost put this franchise out of business."

By now the Penguins' struggles were becoming noticeable. The cross-state rival Philadelphia Flyers claimed a second consecutive Stanley Cup championship that spring, besting the Buffalo Sabres, who had entered the league in 1970—the fourth season of the Penguins' existence. Other members of the original six expansion teams had enjoyed some success; in contrast, the Pens found themselves playing in a division with the legendary Montreal Canadiens, who were about to embark on a string of four consecutive championships. And the organization went bankrupt that June, with the IRS padlocking team offices at the Civic Arena. A new ownership group, led by Wren Blair, who had previously worked with the Minnesota North Stars, offered some hope. Pronovost and Larouche banged in more than fifty goals apiece in 1975–76; along with Syl Apps, they were three of the league's top ten scorers. The following year saw the scoring subside, but the team still made the playoffs for the third year in a row, and seemed ready to assume its place beside the Steelers and the Pirates as part of the Steel City's sports success story—an impression reinforced by the team's decision to adopt black and gold as the new team colors. Even a poor performance in 1977–78 proved but an interruption, for the team, despite mediocre regular season performances, reeled off another four consecutive postseason appearances; however, they never proved to be much of a playoff threat, winning one series and putting up a valiant fight before losing to St. Louis in the first round of the 1981 playoffs.

The Penguins might have improved on that record had they experienced stability off the ice. The embarrassment of bankruptcy was followed by the short tenure of Blair and his associates. In 1977 Edward J. DeBartolo secured a third of the franchise, and the following year he took over. In 1981 he also assumed control of the Civic Arena. Perhaps now the pieces were in place to start building something that mattered.

What was almost death for the Penguins in 1975 was the birth of something special on Long Island. The two teams would not meet again in the postseason until 1982; by that time much had changed. Fueled by the arrival of sensational young talent and shrewd management and coaching, the Islanders developed into a powerhouse. However, playoff stumbles against Toronto in 1978 and—of all people—the now-hated Rangers in 1979 brought back nightmares of playoffs past. Was I ever to see my team skate around the ice holding the Stanley Cup aloft? Yes, I would, thanks to Bob Nystrom's overtime goal in game six of the 1980 playoffs (against the also-hated Flyers). The Islanders repeated again as champions the following year, and entered the 1982 playoffs against the Pens determined to win a third consecutive cup, the one that would mark them as a dynasty.

The Penguin team they encountered that year in the best-of-five preliminary round had just joined the Patrick Division, filled with perennial contenders for the Cup. It was a fair team, losing a few more games than it won each year; their 75-point season in 1981–82 (31 wins, 36 losses, 10 ties) was no match for the Islanders' league-leading record of 54-16-10 for 118 points, including a string of fifteen consecutive wins. That the Penguins had broken the streak with a 4-3 win on February 21 was forgotten; that star Islander winger Mike Bossy has suffered a knee injury in the season's last game—also against Pittsburgh—was dismissed as inconsequential, especially after the Islanders rolled over the Pens in the first two games by a combined score of 15-3. Then it was the Penguins' turn to mount an improbable comeback. Goaltender Michel Dion held the New Yorkers to one goal in game 3, won by Pittsburgh in overtime on a Rick Kehoe goal. Watching the game on television, I could not escape the feeling that there was more to come. I was right; the Pens then smashed the Islanders in game 4, forcing a deciding fifth game on Long Island that would be played on the eleventh anniversary of Michel Brière's death.

April 13, 1982, will always stand out in my memory as one of the most exciting nights I have ever experienced as a hockey fan. Three playoff series had come down to a final contest, and in each case a major upset was possible. The scoring machine known as the Edmonton Oilers found itself battling the Los Angeles Kings; the legendary Montreal Canadiens were trying to fend off the challenge of the upstart Quebec Nordiques in what amounted to a blood feud; and here were my Islanders looking to stop the Penguins' fantasy of dethroning the champions. Like the Islanders themselves, I was more afraid of losing than I was looking forward to winning. Lose to the Pens? Can you spell "choke"? That I was finishing my income taxes that night only added to the anxiety as I watched the game.

After a scoreless first period marked by my adding up the numbers on my 1040, Nystrom opened the scoring in the second period. Ah, I thought, it was all a momentary scare—the Isles would prevail. The sense of relief lasted about a minute, for the Pens quickly tied it up. Five minutes later they scored again; just over two minutes later they added a third goal off the stick of Penguins' defenseman Randy Carlyle. At the end of two periods, the Pens led, 3-1; Dion had stopped all but one of the Islanders' twenty-five shots on goal.

The Islanders were done. No one could convince me otherwise. As the third period opened, I paced back and forth, watching as Dion stopped shot after shot. Once more a hot goalie was carrying an inferior team; once more a superior team was pressing too hard. Nor were the Isles alone: Montreal was struggling, and Edmonton was in trouble. For nearly thirteen minutes of play the agony continued; then Carlyle took a penalty, putting the Islanders on the power play, something that was almost lethal in normal times, although it had misfired in four previous attempts. They were not to be denied this time, as defenseman Mike McEwen fired a rebound past the fallen Dion.

It was 3-2. Just over five minutes remained. I couldn't stand it.

Desperately, the Islanders pressed for the tying goal. With just over two minutes to go, they dumped the puck into the Pens' zone. Carlyle—who would win the Norris Trophy as the league's best defenseman—spun to gather it. As he did, he tried to keep an eye on the onrushing Islander forechecker, John Tonelli. The puck bounced over Carlyle's stick; in one motion Tonelli blasted it past a stunned Dion. 3-3.

It was a reprieve, but whether Tonelli's goal meant salvation was still in abeyance as the teams headed to overtime. It was wide open, end-to-end action, and several times the Pens almost scored. As the game clock ticked pass six minutes, Tonelli broke loose on a breakaway. Dion stopped the shot, but neither he nor Carlyle could control the rebound. On his knees, Nystrom dug out the puck; Tonelli pounced on it. 4-3, Islanders.

It was a night of upsets and near-upsets. Quebec brought down Montreal in overtime; the arrogant Oilers were humbled by the Kings.

And that night the Pittsburgh Penguins came closer than any other team to defeating the New York Islanders during the Islanders' string of four consecutive Stanley Cups. But the Pens could not build upon the promise of 1982. Instead, they collapsed. They would miss the playoffs for six consecutive seasons; they would dip to a league-low record of thirty-eight points in 1983–84. But misfortune brought with it opportunity, for the Pens' last-place finish entitled them to the first pick in the 1984 amateur draft, and they chose a young man named Mario Lemieux.

Rumor had it that the Pens had eased up in the latter part of the 1983–84 season to insure that they would have the top pick in the 1984 draft. Everyone assumed that Lemieux would be that pick. Hailing from Montreal, he had shredded the Quebec Major Junior Hockey League with 247 goals and 562 points in 200 games over three seasons—including totals of 133 goals, 149 assists, and 282 points in his final year (to which he added another 52 points in fourteen postseason contests). He played for Laval—Mike Bossy's junior squad—and he appeared ready to carry on the scoring tradition established by the Islander winger and Montreal's Guy Lafleur. What made Lemieux different, however, was the grace with which he moved—at 6'4" and 200 pounds, no less—and how he used his reach to deke out goalies and deposit pucks into wide-open nets. At first the French-speaking rookie appeared shy and withdrawn as he struggled with English, but his performance on the ice—starting with a goal on his opening shift in the league against the Boston Bruins—was astonishing. At the mid-season All-Star game he secured the Most Valuable Player trophy after tallying twice and adding an assist; he finished the year with exactly 100 points and the Calder Trophy as rookie of the year. However, the Pens still finished in last place in their division. The following season saw them climb to fifth place (Lemieux notched 141 points); they did not move up the following campaign, and in 1987–88 the team slipped back into last, despite Lemieux's league-leading 168 points and his first Hart Trophy as Most Valuable Player.

I was too busy watching the Islanders win two more championships and nearly win a fifth to pay much attention to events in Pittsburgh. Even as the Islanders started their slow decline, I did not find the Penguins impressive, an impression reinforced when I saw them lose to the Islanders one winter evening at Nassau Coliseum. Young

Lemieux had immense talent, to be sure, and wingers fortunate enough to be placed on his line enjoyed career years that they could never replicate without him. Still, the center seemed selfish and self-absorbed, and his offensive production did not automatically make the Pens a playoff team. Even the addition of Paul Coffey, the game's premier offensive defenseman, in 1987 did not noticeably change the ultimate result, for whatever the Pens achieved offensively, they gave away defensively. True, in 1988–89 they finally made the playoffs and even won the first round against the Rangers, but a loss to the Flyers in the division final ended whatever dreams the Pens had of postseason glory. Once more Lemieux put up amazing numbers (85 goals and 114 assists); this time he was joined by lumbering winger Rob Brown (with 49 goals) and Coffey (with 113 points); in a single playoff contest he scored five times and added three assists in a 10-7 victory. But by now the numbers appeared to be as meaningless as they were impressive. If opponents could weather the Lemieux storm, they could then take advantage of the thin Pens lineup to counterpunch; neither Lemieux, Brown, nor Coffey was strong defensively. Indeed, the Pens looked to be little more than a pale imitation of the Edmonton Oilers of the early 1980s, a team that matured into a championship unit only when it learned that it was as important to stop the other team from scoring as it was to score. True, Lemieux could turn his wingers into stars, but he could not lift the club by himself, and he could do nothing about the horrid yellow jerseys the team sometimes wore, a color scheme that proved painful to watch on television. And he was capable of sensational performances in All-Star games (in 1990, playing in front of the home crowd at the Civic Arena, he scored four goals) and his prodigious scoring (a forty-six-game point streak). And without Lemieux (out with what would become a chronic back problem), the team stumbled, especially in the 1989–90 season, when it collapsed down the stretch. Although Lemieux returned for the team's last game, the Pens, needing a tie to clinch a playoff spot, fell in overtime to the Buffalo Sabres when defenseman Uwe Krupp fired in a shot from the blue line. Who snuck in the playoffs as a result? The Islanders.

Little did I know at the time how the juxtaposition of these two teams was to become even more meaningful for me. For as the Penguins started to improve, the Islanders eroded. The cornerstones of the championship teams retired—Bossy in 1988 after a year devoted to rehabilitation; Denis Potvin, whose hard hits and hard shots from the blueline had made him one of the league's best two-way defensemen, also in 1988; Billy Smith, the goalie who swung a mean stick, in 1989. By 1990 only center Bryan Trottier was left from the 1980 team that had commenced the run of four straight championships. They were not easily replaced. Sure, the Isles had a dandy dashing center in Pat LaFontaine, and center and team captain Brent Sutter was respected around the league for his all-around play, but elsewhere the decline was obvious. Islander wingers treated the puck like a hot potato; the team's defense was erratic at best. Only a combination of LaFontaine's heroics and Lemieux's injury had led to the 1990 playoff spot, for the previous year the Isles had failed to make the playoffs. Whatever magic had gone into building the team was now gone; rumors persisted that ownership was not interested in investing in a winner.

And then the Islanders released Trottier, marking the occasion by issuing a fax from the team office. That the team chose to treat a man and a player long identified as the heart and soul of the Islanders this way was simply astonishing. True, Trottier was no longer the dominant player he had once been. He had won the Calder Trophy (rookie of the year); the Art Ross Trophy (league's leading scorer); the Hart Trophy (league's most valuable player); the Conn Smythe Trophy (1980 playoffs MVP). He was one of the league's leading playoff performers, having once recorded points in twenty-seven straight games over three seasons—one of the few scoring records not held by Wayne Gretzky. But he had struggled the past two seasons, and his scoring totals in 1989–90 were embarrassingly low. Had it not been for his impressive skills at winning faceoffs and playing two-way hockey, as well as his leadership qualities, he would have been let go long ago; as it was, people wondered whether in cutting Trottier the team was also cutting expenses.

Fan allegiance is a strange thing. There are folks who believe in blind loyalty to a single franchise, win or lose. It's almost as if they root more for the uniforms than for the players who wear them. I count my friends who are die-hard Cub fans as belonging to this group. And, of course, there is the pressure to root for the hometown team. Geography determined my interest in the Rangers and the Islanders, but now I was on the move. Having spent the Islander dynasty years in the hockey haven that is Madison, Wisconsin, I had since moved, first to Tennessee, then to South Carolina; now as I heard of Trottier's release, Jean and I were readying to move to Arizona. To a large extent the Islanders of 1990 were no longer "my" Islanders. My sister still cheered on LaFontaine, and my mother proclaimed her support for winger Patrick Flatley (who had played for Wisconsin during my time there—and was obviously too afraid to enter one of my history classes). But for me, someone who had followed Trottier from his rookie year of 1975–76, something was gone.

Trottier's play embodied values that I had respected when I had played hockey. Play both ends of the ice; hit hard but fair; take as much joy in making a good pass to set up a goal as in scoring a goal; play to win. Trottier with the puck was a joy to behold, for he controlled the tempo of the game as he sought out his teammates, muscled off opponents, and did all the little things needed to prevail. In an age where Gretzky's magic mesmerized viewers, the more discerning fan noticed that Trottier was just as effective in his quiet way, and that, unlike Gretzky, he could excel at both ends of the ice.

And now he was gone. And the way in which he left the Islanders snapped something within me. No, it was not that the team had been coarse in how it was done (although it was); nor was I naive enough to think that loyalty counted for much in professional sports. But it was clear from the way in which Islander management handled the situation that it was giving the brushoff to fans. General manager Bill Torrey, who had once extolled Trottier's virtues, now rested content with the remark that it was time to give young forwards Tom Fitzgerald and Rob DiMaio a chance to develop. Sure. In the following season DiMaio played exactly one game for the Islanders; Fitzgerald suited up for forty-one contests, tallying a total of ten points. The Islanders' problems at center in the wake of Trottier's departure caused them to trade for Ray Ferraro, a fine player, but one who cost them the services of defenseman Doug Crossman, who had been the team's only real offensive threat from the blueline. Trottier's release was a cost-cutting measure, plain and simple. It suggested that management was not willing to expend the resources necessary to rebuild the team. Fan support might be appreciated, but it would go unrewarded. In short, if Trottier was going to be a free agent, maybe I should become one, too.

I mulled my choice of allegiance carefully. What if Trottier signed with the Rangers or Flyers? Could I overcome years of despising both teams? And what if he became an Oiler? Arrgh! Indeed, I had thought for some time that two teams who could have benefited from his services were the up-and-coming Los Angeles Kings and Detroit Red Wings. In each case Trottier would not be expected to shoulder the entire load of leading a new team; instead, he would add depth and skill. This was not a case of jumping on a bandwagon, for the Wings had finished out of the playoffs on 1989–90, and the Kings were not much better. But each franchise looked promising, appeared to be well managed, and contained on its roster some players I had long admired.

On July 20, 1990, Bryan Trottier made his choice. He signed a contract with the Pittsburgh Penguins. I confess that I had not contemplated the prospect of rooting for the Pens, and it was not an automatic assumption that I would do so. But there were some factors that made it an appealing prospect. First, among his new teammates was another newcomer, Joe Mullen. Mullen and his brother Brian were New Yorkers who had made it to the NHL. They had been affiliated with the Rangers as stickboys; Mullen's choice of number 7 was a clear tribute to Gilbert, who, like Mullen, was a right-winger (Brian, at the time a member of the Rangers, wore number 19, as did Ranger center Jean Ratelle). Mullen had come to the Penguins four days after general manager Craig Patrick had hired as coach none other than Bob Johnson, who had coached at Wisconsin during my first three years there; his assistant coach, Tom Osenton, and I had gone to school together in New Hampshire (one of his players had been Brian Mullen). Those personal associations aside, Johnson had been most impressive as a promoter of hockey in the United States and as the coach of the Calgary Flames: it had been his Flames that had stopped the Oilers' bid for a third straight championship in 1986.

Johnson was known for his exuberance, especially his trademark saying, "It's a great day for hockey!" Just as important was his ability to teach as well as to inspire his players—something the Pens had lacked behind the bench, and something that a young team sorely needed. That was the lesson Patrick had taken from his tenure as Pittsburgh's coach during the previous season when he assessed his talent and the team's prospects. To help him in that task, Patrick named Scotty Bowman director of player recruitment and development. Bowman came to the team with a strong reputation as an excellent coach and general manager with St. Louis, Montreal, and Buffalo; he had directed the Montreal club to five Stanley Cups in the 1970s.

I began to think that I might find the Penguins to be an interesting team after all. I already enjoyed a link to the team through marriage; I had always enjoyed watching Paul Coffey bring the puck up, wheeling and darting through the opposition so quickly (even as I knew he was a defensive liability). And owner Edward J. DeBartelo seemed to be committed to winning, unlike Islander management. But some old feelings die hard. I still harbored reservations about Mario Lemieux. Yes, he had great tools and wonderful talent as an attacker, but I wondered whether he had the other skills necessary to lead and to win. Like Trottier, he had the Calder, Ross, and Hart awards on his mantel; but there was no Conn Smythe for playoff MVP. Still no one could doubt his talent with the puck, as in a New Year's Eve game where he scored in every possible way (shorthanded, even-strength, power play, penalty shot, and empty net). The back troubles that had sidelined him during the 1989–90 season, however, persisted. Nine days before the Pens signed Trottier, Lemieux underwent surgery to repair a herniated disk. At first it looked as if he would be ready to take to the ice, perhaps in training camp; the appearance of an infection pushed back the timetable for months. Perhaps that was why Patrick had signed Trottier in the first place . . . just in case.

I was not overly impressed with some of the other Penguins. Goaltender Tom Barrasso, acquired by the Pens in 1989, had shown little of the promise that made him a sensation during his first two years in Buffalo; I knew next to nothing about wingers Kevin Stevens and Mark Recchi or center John Cullen, three young players with offensive promise; another winger, Rob Brown, merely feasted on Mario's leftovers. Center Randy Gilhen was at least generous enough to surrender number 19 to Trottier. And who was this kid Jaromir Jagr? In short, Trottier's decision to join the Pens may have tipped the scales in my struggle over team allegiance for the 1990–91 season, but I was not convinced that I had latched on to a team of destiny at just the right moment.

After an opening-night win at Washington, the Pens returned home to confront the New Jersey Devils. I anxiously awaited to see the highlights on television that evening, and I was not disappointed. Trottier scored twice in the third period as the Pens won, 7-4. Perhaps there was hope after all. Making my switch all the sweeter was news from Long Island that LaFontaine, who had come to the same conclusion I had about Islander management, was holding out for a new contract. Without LaFontaine the team crumbled, and even his return could not undo the damage.

Yet it was not exactly easy being a Penguins fan that year. Lemieux missed fifty-four games due to his ailing back—something that was starting to become a familiar theme in his career. In his absence it was up to other players to pick up the slack. Essential to the team's offensive success was a line centered by Cullen, flanked on the left by Stevens and on the right by Recchi; Coffey moved the puck skillfully from the backline. Jagr chipped in with twenty-seven goals. Mullen and Trottier missed stretches with injuries, but it was becoming evident that the team as a whole was scoring more and allowing fewer goals. Still, much had to be done if the Penguins were to go anywhere.

Patrick had added veteran experience to the Pens during the off-season, but he was far from finished. Several early-season swaps brought new spare parts in the form of winger Scott Young and defender Gordie Roberts; Jiri Hrdina, obtained from Calgary, would help the rookie (and fellow Czech) Jagr adjust to life in America. A midseason deal bolstered the blueline with the addition of Larry Murphy, an offensive-minded defenseman, and Peter Taglianetti. However, the most daring deal involved giving up something to get something else. Patrick dealt Cullen (who at the time had ninety-four points), defenseman Zarley Zalapski, and minor league forward Jeff Parker to the Hartford Whalers in exchange for centerman Ron Francis and defensemen Ulf Samuelsson and Grant Jennings. With Lemieux ready to play, Cullen was out of place; Zalapski was filled with potential but it was not clear whether he would develop. Francis's offensive numbers had dipped since his days as the featured player in the Hartford lineup, but he might thrive playing behind Lemieux, while Trottier anchored the checking line. Samuelsson was big, hit hard, and played dirty (although teammates never admitted that), giving the Pens a physical presence in defense that they lacked. The deals appeared to help. The Penguins claimed the Patrick Division championship (their first division title), but a 41-33-6 record was not exactly heart-stopping.

At first glance the improvements appeared to fall short of success as the Pens struggled in their opening round confrontation against the New Jersey Devils. After the two teams split the first two games (Pittsburgh's win came on a Jagr overtime goal), the Devils grabbed two of the next three games to take a 3-2 series lead. To make matters worse, Tom Barrasso was injured in the sixth game; however, backup Frank Pietrangelo stepped in and the Pens won 4-3 before returning to Pittsburgh, where the Pens took the series with a 4-0 win. It was on to face the Washington Capitals. Once more the Pens dropped the series opener, and, to make matters worse, Paul Coffey broke his jaw. Still, with Barrasso back in net, the Pens rallied and won four straight games to advance to the conference finals. Not since 1970 had they been this close to the Stanley Cup. It was a good question whether they would get any closer, for their opponents were the Boston Bruins—and the Pens had struggled at Boston Garden.

Once more the Pens fell behind in a playoff series, losing the first two games in Boston. The Bruins, who had made it to the previous year's championship round, seemed prepared to make a return visit. But then the Pens, led by Samuelsson and Stevens, started hitting everything in sight. Bruins winger Cam Neely crumpled to the ice, a victim of one of Samuelsson's hits. The Bruins soon followed, as they lost four straight games to the Pens—who had survived the loss of Coffey. It would be on to the finals to face the Minnesota North Stars.

Although Minnesota was a hotbed for high school and college hockey, the North Stars had struggled there and, aside from two strong playoff runs in the early 1980s topped by an appearance against my Islanders in 1981, they had done little to distinguish themselves. Even now the club was in financial trouble, and there were rumors that it would soon relocate. Thus it seemed appropriate that they would confront the Penguins in 1991, with the winner claiming its first-ever Stanley Cup championship. True to form, the Pens lost the opening game, 5-4, but then in game 2 Lemieux took charge. Late in the second period, with Pittsburgh nursing a one-goal lead, Lemieux broke through at center ice, split a pair of Minnesota defenders with a beautiful move, beating the goalie with a backhander as he was falling. It was a memorable example of his magnificent skill with the puck; it became even more important a reminder of his value after Lemieux's back gave out as he was lacing up his skates prior to game 3, which Minnesota won with number 66 on the sidelines.

Lemieux and the Pens returned ready for business in game 4. Stevens, Francis, and then Mario popped in pucks in rapid succession in the first period, but it was Trottier's goal that proved decisive in a 5-3 victory at Minnesota. Back in Pittsburgh, Lemieux was at the center of the Pens offense, scoring once and setting up two other goals as the Pens built up a 4-0 lead, then prevailed, 6-4. Game 6 provided no such excitement. At the tail end of a power play in the first period, Trottier won a faceoff and helped set up Ulf Samuelsson for the game's first goal; Lemieux then tallied a shorthanded marker (and set up three more scores) as the Pens coasted to an 8-0 victory and their first Stanley Cup.

There was no doubt that Lemieux was the star of the show, with sixteen goals and twenty-eight assists; there was also no doubt that it was the building of a team around a superstar that had set the stage for a championship. Francis had provided steadiness and critical two-way play as he found new joy; Stevens and Recchi continued to put pressure on opposition goalies; Larry Murphy filled in when Coffey went down with a broken jaw; goalie Barrasso finally lived up to his promise as a skilled netminder. Mullen had scored twice in the final game, a taste of the skill he could provide; and Trottier was in the middle of it all, his offensive skills slipping but his two-way play evident as ever. When the team brought the Stanley Cup back to Pittsburgh for an outside celebration, it was Trottier who told the happy fans, "Enjoy it, Pittsburgh. Enjoy it, baby."

It's one thing to win a championship, and another to defend it. Whether the Pens would be able to repeat was unclear as they came to Phoenix in 1991 to play in an exhibition game against the Los Angeles Kings. Among those who did not dress for the game was Trottier, who now, in his position as president of the NHL Players' Association, was engaged in negotiations to prevent a strike. Although the game resulted in a tie, the Pens moved the puck with confidence; one still worried whether they were so freewheeling as to offer too many opportunities to the opposition.

But then perhaps hockey was not uppermost in the minds of the players at that moment. As they prepared to report to training camp to defend their championship, they learned some devastating news: Bob Johnson was diagnosed with brain cancer. For weeks the ceremony of raising the championship banners was put on hold, as the team hoped against hope for Johnson's return. Finally, it became evident that the coach was slipping away. On October 19 the banners went up; just over a month later, on November 26, Johnson died at his home in Colorado Springs. However, his presence remained with the team for the rest of the season. The next evening, as the Pens took to the ice to play the New Jersey Devils, everyone noted that just outside the bluelines "It's a great day for hockey" was emblazoned on the ice surface; the Pens wore patches in Johnson's memory bearing his nickname, "Badger."

Johnson's tragic death overshadowed other pressing problems as the Pens entered the 1991–92 season. Troublesome contract negotiations with Mark Recchi, Kevin Stevens, and Ron Francis highlighted the possibility that management could not afford to keep the team together—and DeBartelo was looking for a buyer. Eventually Recchi signed and the Pens matched an offer sheet presented to Stevens by the Bruins; Francis did not come to terms until the season was underway. There was talk of trouble between the NHL's Players' Association (with Trottier as president) and the owners. And the team had to get used to a new coach, for on October 1 Scotty Bowman returned to the bench.

Over the years Bowman had gained a reputation as a no-nonsense coach who sometimes was unsparing of his players' feelings and did not hesitate to give additional ice time to key players. The contrast with Johnson was evident; the impact on team chemistry was yet to be seen. Several early season contests suggested that the team was relying on its ample offensive talent to win shootouts, a brand of play that was exciting in the regular season but rarely led to prevailing in the playoffs. Moreover, preliminary reports that leaked out prior to the sale of the team to a group of investors led by Howard Baldwin and Morris Belzburg suggested that the first order of business would be shaving the payroll, perhaps by selling players.

The Pens stumbled through the first fourth of the season as players wrestled with the loss of a beloved coach, adjusted to Bowman, pondered issues of payroll and ownership, and struggled to emerge from a championship hangover. Then the team streaked, first up, then down, as Lemieux's back acted up again; even the presence of five Pens on the All-Star roster (Lemieux, Stevens, Jagr, Coffey, and Trottier—a good case could have been made for Mullen as well) could not conceal the team's troubles.

The season was filled with notable individual performances. Lemieux secured his third scoring title with 44 goals and 87 assists while missing sixteen games due to injury. Jagr picked up his game in his second year in the league, and before long wags noted that reshuffling "Jaromir" produced "Mario Jr." Murphy demonstrated sufficient offensive talent at the blueline to render Coffey and his huge contract expendable. Francis blossomed as a second-line center, playing sound hockey at both ends of the ice. Stevens skated fast, hit hard, and had a deadly shot: he finished with 54 goals and was runner-up to Lemieux in the scoring race. Joe Mullen still had his scoring touch, including back-to-back four-goal games; Trottier showed flashes of his former offensive brilliance when he took Lemieux's spot, and his leadership became even more evident when some players became disgruntled with Bowman.

The friction between players and coach was part of a larger dip in team fortunes; at times it looked as if the Pens would find it difficult merely to make the playoffs. Once more Patrick decided to engineer a trade. Coffey headed to Los Angeles and Mark Recchi packed his bags for Philadelphia; among the players Pittsburgh received in return were bruising winger Rick Tocchet, lanky defenseman Kjell Samuelsson, and backup goalie Ken Wregget. The trade made the team bigger and tougher at the sacrifice of some scoring and speed. Before long the team record inched past mediocrity; they fought off none other than the Islanders and then crept into third place, ahead of New Jersey, by season's end—although that was delayed by a player strike that began on April 1 and lasted ten days—with NHLPA president Trottier among the key players in reaching a settlement.

Because of their third-place division finish, the Pens opened the 1992 playoffs on the road against second-place Washington. Once again the Pens lost the opener, just as they had in each series in 1991; they then fell behind, 2-0, as Washington's close-checking style and hot goalie Don Beaupre shut down the Pittsburgh forwards. Lemieux put on quite a performance in game 3, scoring three times and setting up three more goals in a 6-4 win. Washington's Dino Ciccarelli returned the favor in game 4, knocking home four goals in a 7-2 Capitals win. The Pens were one loss away from elimination. In normal circumstances, that's not exactly an ideal position. However—and here my experiences as an Islander fan held me in good stead—perhaps the Pens had the Caps just where they wanted them. Washington had demonstrated in the past that they found it difficult to close out a series. Against the Islanders they had taken a 2-0 lead in a best-of-five round in 1985, only to lose the next three; two years later, they were in front, three games to one, before the Isles roared back to win the next three. Now it was Pittsburgh's turn. A solid two-way team effort resulted in a game 5 win, 5-2; Lemieux exploded again with a five-point performance to lead the Pens to victory in game 6, 6-4; and then the Pens shut down the Caps and squeezed out a 3-1 win in the deciding seventh game.

Next on the schedule were the New York Rangers, who possessed the league's best regular-season record. That in itself irritated me—after all, I still despised the Rangers, Flyers, and Oilers from my days as an Islander fan—but worse still was the fact that the New Yorkers were led by former Edmonton Oiler Mark Messier, who had played a key role in derailing the Islanders' "Drive for Five" back in 1984. One did not have to like him (especially his tendency to resort to cheap shots followed by displays of injured innocence) to respect his leadership ability. Messier had taken Manhattan by storm when he arrived in the Big Apple in October; he led a quality lineup into the playoffs. Perhaps this year the Rangers would break their fifty-two-year-old drought that fans across the league commemorated by shouting, "1940! 1940!"

For once the Pens decided to take an opening game, played in Madison Square Garden, grabbing a three-goal lead and then holding on for a 4-2 win. However, the team's fortunes appeared to disintegrate in the next contest. As Lemieux handled the puck during a Penguin power play, Ranger forward Adam Graves delivered a two-handed chop with his stick, breaking a bone in Mario's hand. Lemieux was soon joined in the trainer's room by Joe Mullen, who blew out his left knee and was lost for the playoffs. Taking advantage of the stunned Pens, the Rangers took game 2 . . . and then game 3, 6-5 in overtime.

Without Mullen—it was clear he would not return that season—and Lemieux—doctors said it would take at least a month for the hand to heal—it looked as if the Pens faced a nearly impossible task (even though Messier had also missed the last two games). The league decided to suspend Graves for four games, but that was small compensation. Trottier donned the captain's *C;* the rest of the team readied itself to battle back without their superstar. What seemed almost impossible became even more difficult in game 4, as the Rangers worked hard to grab a two-goal lead that looked insurmountable with ten minutes to go in the third period. That all changed when Ron Francis scored from center ice to cut the margin to one, the puck bouncing wildly off Ranger goalie Mike Richter's glove and into the net. Digger Troy Loney then tied up the contest less than two minutes later. In overtime Messier coughed up the puck to Murphy, who fed Francis for the game winner. Jagr's two goals—one on a penalty shot—led the Pens to victory in game 5; Pittsburgh then closed out the Rangers in the next contest, a 5-1 win. It was a remarkable performance without Lemieux; curiously, the Rangers lost every game that Messier played and won the two he sat out. Francis and Jagr led the way while Barrasso played a steady game in net.

After two thrilling and dramatic series, the conference finals proved to be anticlimactic. Jagr scored the winner in a game 1 overtime triumph; Lemieux returned to the lineup and got three points in a game 2 win. The Bruins didn't have a chance, as Barrasso's solid netminding continued and the Pens swept through the final two games at Boston Garden. Most remarkable was a shorthanded effort by Lemieux, who broke through center, pushed the puck through the legs of Boston rear guard Ray Bourque (one of the best to ever play the position), rushed past the startled Bruin, gathered the puck, and wristed it over goalie Andy Moog's glove.

Only the Chicago Blackhawks stood in the way of a second Stanley Cup for Pittsburgh. Led by center Jeremy Roenick and goalie Ed Belfour, the Hawks promised to put up a fight. And so they did in game 1, jumping out to a 4-1 lead. This time Jagr joined Lemieux in the spotlight. After Tocchet deflected a shot home to cut the lead to 4-2, Lemieux banked the puck onto the net off Belfour's leg pads; then Jagr took the puck through virtually the entire Chicago team and tied the score. It looked as if the game was headed for overtime when Lemieux broke by defenseman Steve Smith. Aware that to let number 66 get away was tantamount to conceding defeat, Smith hooked him. Up went the referee's arm: Smith went to the penalty box. On the ensuing faceoff, Francis directed the puck back to Murphy, who drove it on net. Belfour kicked at the puck; it went to Lemieux, who banged in the rebound for a 5-4 win with a dozen seconds left.

Pittsburgh also prevailed in the second contest, 3-1, with Lemieux again netting the winning goal. It was then on to Chicago, where Pittsburgh won game 3, 1-0, and then survived a high-scoring contest in game 4. The teams exchanged goal for goal in a 3-3 first period. Tocchet and Roenick traded goals in the second; but in the third period the Penguins slowly built a lead on tallies by Murphy and Francis. Only the goaltending of Blackhawk backup goalie Dominik Hasek prevented a runaway victory (and gave hockey fans a taste of what Hasek would do in later years). Roenick cut the margin to one, but the Blackhawks could not get any closer; their final chance was snuffed out when Trottier blocked a blast from Chicago defenseman Chris Chelios as time expired. Pittsburgh had retained its hold on the Stanley Cup in a four-game sweep—and eleven consecutive victories.

Lemieux, who recorded sixteen goals and thirty-four points in only fifteen games, secured his second Conn Smythe trophy as the playoffs' most valuable player. However, Mario pointed to Barrasso's goaltending as a key to the repeat win. Others recalled Francis's heroics at critical moments, especially in the Ranger series, and the scoring punch provided by Stevens and Jagr. Players marveled as Trottier once more danced around the ice with the Cup held high—and chuckled at his more spectacular performance several days later at Three Rivers Stadium, where he took advantage of a damp tarpaulin to waterslide with the chalice. But one name remained on everyone's mind. "Thanks to Bob Johnson's vision, all of this is possible," Bowman told the Three Rivers crowd. "The coach of the Pittsburgh Penguins will always be Bob Johnson."

And yet if Johnson was the coach of the Pens, Lemieux was clearly the captain. He had grown as a player, and not just because of his artistry with the puck. His willingness to overcome injury, his desire to play defense, his ability to express himself (overcoming an early shyness complicated by the fact that English was his second language) all contributed to the overall picture. One wondered what Lemieux could do if he had not been hampered by injuries.

By the beginning of the 1992–93 season, people were whispering about the possibility of a Penguins dynasty. After all, not since the Islanders had any team clicked off three consecutive Cups (not even Edmonton). This time the Pens dominated in the regular season. Stevens, Jagr, Mullen, and Francis proved strong offensively, as did a raft of up-and-coming forwards. Barrasso found himself defending the net in front of a solid if not spectacular corps of defensemen. But it looked as if this would be the year that Lemieux would mount a challenge to Wayne Gretzky's season scoring records.

And then it happened. Lemieux was stopped again, not by an on-ice opponent, but by his health. This time, however, it was not a hockey-related injury, but cancer—specifically Hodgkin's disease. In mid-January 1993 doctors removed an enlarged lymph node from his neck; Lemieux then commenced radiation treatment. Sure, it was caught early; sure, the prognosis was positive; but for Lemieux, who had served as honorary chairman of the Pittsburgh Cancer Institute and who had witnessed cancer in his own family, it was clearly a moment to take stock. Forgotten for the moment was his 104 points amassed so far in an effort to surpass Gretzky's scoring records; during the next several weeks Buffalo's Pat LaFontaine took over the lead in the scoring race. But Lemieux was not yet done. On March 2, he took his last radiation treatment, then scored a goal and set up another in a 5-4 loss at Philadelphia. He was not content simply with coming back; he wanted to beat out LaFontaine for the scoring title. And so he did—in part with back-to-back four-goal games and 42 points in his final fourteen contests. It was an amazing story—and it only added to Lemieux's legendary status. That he had won two consecutive scoring championships while missing forty games was remarkable enough; that he had battled back from cancer and overcame the impact of energy-draining treatments was even more astonishing.

The Penguins cruised into the 1993 playoffs. They had ended the regular season by running off a string of consecutive victories that shattered the Islanders' record set back in 1982 (a streak snapped by Pittsburgh). The team added to its record of consecutive playoff victories in its opening game against first-round foe New Jersey, then stumbled before dispatching the Devils. Their next opponent? The Islanders. The New Yorkers had scrambled through the regular season, mounting a late drive to snatch third place; then they made their way past the Washington Capitals in six games, including three consecutive wins in overtime. However, their series-clinching win was marred when the Capitals' Dale Hunter felled Islander center Pierre Turgeon with a vicious crosscheck as Turgeon was celebrating a score off a steal. Whatever chance the Islanders had of defeating the Penguins appeared to go down with Turgeon, the team's leading scorer: a separated shoulder would keep him out of action.

With everything going their way, the Penguins took to the ice at the Igloo in game 1 ready to continue their march to a third consecutive Stanley Cup. Minutes later, however, trouble appeared when Lemieux's back acted up after colliding with an Islander forward. As Mario left the ice, he took something with him—the Penguins' edge. Realizing that the ice surface was now level again, the Islanders took advantage of lethargic play by the Pens and netted two shorthanded goals on the way to a 3-2 win. Rallying without Lemieux, the Pens, led by Barrasso's twenty-six saves, roared back to take the second game, 3-0; with Lemieux gingerly skating, they captured the third game at New York—but it was evident that they were in for a battle. That became evident in the fourth contest, in which each team scored four times in a seesaw third period of a topsy-turvsy 6-5 Islander win. Once more the Pens proved sloppy with the man advantage, as Tom Fitzgerald netted two shorthanded markers while killing off a single penalty.

If the Penguins were a bit bewildered by this turn of events—and feeling a tad uncomfortable at playing the role of the favored team—it did not show in the fifth game, which they won convincingly, 6-3. Surely now the killer instinct would kick in; since 1991 they had failed to win only once in ten tries to close out an opponent. But the Islanders stood their ground in a tough 7-5 win in the sixth game, forcing the series back to Pittsburgh for a deciding seventh contest.

The series had been as tough on me as it was on the two teams. Like most Penguin fans, I had expected the team to coast through the first two rounds, an expectation rendered all the more reasonable by

Turgeon's absence. But one could not but be moved by the gutsy Islander performance against the champs coming on the heels of the cliffhanger series against Washington. Nor had I ever rooted against the Islanders in the playoffs. Nor did I do so now. Instead, I just watched, stunned at what was unfolding. So, it seemed, were the Penguins. Lemieux looked shocked when Islander rookie defenseman Darius Kasparaitis began hitting everything in sight, including the league's leading scorer. No one was on the Pens' bench to calm them down, to restore the team's composure, to steady shaky players. Perhaps Trottier could have done that—but he was now working in the Islanders' front office. Surely he recalled what it felt like to encounter this situation: he had in 1982, when it was the Islanders who were dumbfounded and the Penguins who were bracing to upset the two-time defending Stanley Cup champions who had ripped through the regular season and established a new consecutive win streak.

As in 1975 and 1982, the deciding game of this Penguin-Islander confrontation proved memorable. Turgeon dressed for the game, but he was not a factor. Neither was Kevin Stevens, who smashed face first into the ice after colliding with Islander defenseman Rich Pilon. The injury left the Pens with a queasy feeling; so did Lemieux's muffed attempt to convert on a breakaway, a gaff that stood in sharp contrast to his ability to deke out goalies and bury the puck the previous two years. The two teams traded goals in the second period, before wingers David Volek and Benoit Hogue gave the Isles a 3-1 lead midway through the third period.

Was this 1982 all over again? If it was, then it was time for the Pens to commence their bid for hockey greatness some eleven years, one month, and one day after that memorable April 13. Obviously Ron Francis had read the script. He brought the Pens to within one with just under four minutes left; then, with Barrasso out for a sixth attacker, he fired the puck toward the Islander net. Rick Tocchet deflected it into the net behind Islander goalie Glenn Healy. The clock showed a minute left; the game was tied.

I admit that my spirits sank a bit when Tocchet scored. I don't know why. After all, I had lived and died with the Pens for two years; these Islanders held on to the team's past greatness by the thread of captain Pat Flatley's jersey (Flatley had been a rookie on the 1984 playoff team).

No such qualms disturbed my wife, who remained a defiant Pittsburgher (even if she was born in Boston). But there was something I didn't like about this version of the Penguins. They had become a bit haughty, a tad too overconfident, a little too self-assured. The hunger to win was gone, replaced by an expectation of winning. In contrast, the Islanders of the 1980s, however calmly confident they were of their ability, were spurred on by the belief that they were not accorded the respect they deserved and by a fear of losing that they transmitted to their fans, including me. There was fear on the faces of the Penguins, but it was a fear born of confusion and panic, not determined desperation. Still, they had fired sixteen pucks at Healy during the last twenty minutes, and two of them had landed in the net. If the Pens were going to shed the Islander jinx, it would be now.

Momentum in overtime is a strange thing. One team may appear ready to close out the contest; another may be holding on in sheer terror. Still, players on both teams know that a bad bounce, a missed assignment, a goalie screened for a moment, and it's all over. A mad scramble had ended the 1982 thriller, but it was not to be this time. Instead, a Penguin breakdown resulted in a 3-on-1 Islander dash down the ice. Center Ray Ferraro, who had notched two consecutive overtime winners against Washington (and probably should have been credited with a third that was awarded to Brian Mullen [Joe's brother]), fed winger David Volek on his right; Volek cranked and slapped at the puck. Tom Barrasso never moved. The Igloo fell silent. 4-3, New York.

Volek's goal ended more than the Pens' bid for a third straight championship and a claim to rank alongside hockey's dynasty teams. It also signaled the beginning of the end for the team's glory days. That was not evident at first. Surely the Pens had missed a great opportunity to repeat. Had they gotten past the Islanders, all that remained were three third-place teams (Montreal, Los Angeles, and Toronto) and a possible confrontation in the finals against Wayne Gretzky's Kings (Gretzky and Lemieux never faced off against each other in playoff competition). The following year, the Pens put together another solid season. Efforts to shake up the club's lineup proved abortive: the Pens essentially undid a deal whereby they had acquired colorful Los Angeles King Marty McSorley, sending him back to the Left Coast in exchange for two forwards (including Shawn McEachern, who had been part of the original trade). Trottier returned as an assistant coach and player, although his contribution was limited by injury and evidence that perhaps it was time for him to stay behind the bench.

National telecasts made much of Trottier's reunion with fellow veterans Ron Francis and Joe Mullen, which inadvertently highlighted the team's inability to inject new talent into the lineup. One reason for Trottier's return may have been Lemieux's deteriorating health: he played in only twenty-two games as he battled the effects of his treatment for Hodgkin's disease. Still, the Pens copped the division championship—and then fell apart in the playoffs, losing to the Washington Capitals in six games as Caps coach Jim Schoenfeld devised a defensive scheme that stifled Lemieux, Stevens, Tocchet, Jagr, Francis, and company. That was depressing enough: even worse was the fact that the New York Rangers, after steamrolling over the Islanders, took advantage of Pittsburgh's absence to make their way through the Eastern Conference, running over Washington and hanging on against New Jersey before claiming the franchise's first Stanley Cup in fifty-four years in seven games over Vancouver.

Perhaps the Pens benefited from the strike-shortened 1995 campaign, for it gave aging players some respite. Still, Lemieux sat out the season to devote all his time and energy to battling his cancer; Barrasso was also lost due to injury; and Stevens was gone, sent to Los Angeles in yet another trade that brought high-scoring and light-checking winger Luc Robatille east. Francis and Jagr formed a powerful combination as the Pens started strong before leveling off; Jagr, who in Mario's absence was developing into a dominant player, won the scoring title: Francis laid claim to the Selke and Lady Byng trophies (defensive forward and sportsmanship). However, after defeating Washington (again after being down three games to one), the Pens bowed to the eventual champions, the New Jersey Devils, in five. The whole shortened year went by like a blur for me, in part because I was teaching in the Netherlands that spring and found it difficult to keep track of what was happening.

Compared to the team's record of futility through most of the 1980s, the Pens' post-championship playoff performances in the 1990s were encouraging. Still, in the shadow of two championships, it looked as if the team was simply not realizing its potential. Perhaps Lemieux's return would bring back the glory days. Skating alongside Francis and Jagr for much of the season, Mario was indeed remarkable. He bested Jagr for the scoring championship with 69 goals and 161 points, won another MVP award, and scored his five-hundredth goal (against the Islanders). Jagr finished as runner-up in the scoring race, while Francis came in fourth; together the three players combined to register 429 points. But Stevens was gone in a trade to Boston; so was Tocchet, who was now in Los Angeles (eventually the former teammates would be traded for each other). More important, everyone knew from past experience that whatever happened during the regular season paled in contrast to the annual playoff struggle. The highlight of the first-round encounter with Washington was a four-overtime thriller won by the Pens' Petr Nedved; among the minor memories was a shouting match between Caps coach Schoenfeld and Pens' assistant Trottier. Even more rewarding was a second-round romp over the Rangers.

In contrast to the Pens of the early 1990s, this squad put all its eggs in one basket (albeit a big basket). Lemieux, Jagr, Francis, and Nedved provided the offense; other forwards struggled to keep the opposition in check. The blueline corps was not especially distinguished, and while the returning Barrasso teamed with Ken Wregget to stop pucks, once in a while the tandem would slip. Moreover, there was a sense that time was running out for Lemieux. His recurring back problems were aggravated by the punishment he suffered every night from opposing players; he complained that the game was being destroyed by the clutch and grab tactics employed by less talented players to handcuff skilled skaters and stickhandlers. The Pens' real problem, however, was the team's lack of depth up front and a less-than-intimidating defensive corps. These weaknesses became evident when the Pens played the upstart Florida Panthers in the conference finals. Florida goalie John Vanbiesbrouck almost single-handedly stopped the Pens' offense; once more the home crowd at the Igloo witnessed a series-ending defeat in game seven, a 3-1 Panther victory. Lemieux and Jagr were held to a goal apiece, and Mario credited the Panthers' determined defensive play with holding him in check—but part of the problem was that Ron Francis was sidelined for the series, allowing the Panthers to concentrate on Lemieux and Jagr. In a series in which every goal counted, the Pens could not score enough of them.

In many ways, the loss to the Panthers marked a divide in my relationship with the Pens. While several mainstays of the championship squads remained, others had vanished. It was hard to follow the team when one had to rely on national telecasts from ESPN and Fox. And one sensed that Lemieux's days were numbered, and that while he might continue to play, he had seen his last chance at the Cup vanish against Florida. Perhaps he knew as much, for rumors of his impending retirement circulated throughout the press. But even more important was the fact that Phoenix was about to acquire its own hockey team. The Winnipeg Jets, unable to make ends meet despite a solid base of loyal fans, were looking for a new home after a proposed move to Minnesota collapsed. Aware of the crowds that had attended neutral ice games at America West Arena in the early 1990s on the heels of the annual preseason exhibition tilts, NHL commissioner Gary Bettman drew on his old NBA connections in contacting Jerry Colangelo of the Phoenix Suns. Shortly thereafter it was announced that the Phoenix Coyotes would start play with the 1996–97 season.

With a new team in town, it was only a matter of time before old allegiances begin to fray. After all, in these days of free agent players and franchises on the move, to retain a lifelong loyalty seems a little bit old-fashioned (although I've remained a Yankee fan). Besides, the very things that had drawn me to the Penguins were now fading away; 1996–97 proved to be the last year Joe Mullen and Bryan Trottier saw service with the Pens. Mullen retired, having scored 500 goals; Trottier moved on to other coaching opportunities. The year also proved to be Mario Lemieux's last campaign. Ron Francis was approaching the end of his contract, and recurring ownership problems made it unlikely that he would re-sign with the club. Still, old attachments die slowly. I made sure that the whole family would get to see what proved to be Lemieux's only regular-season appearance in Phoenix. In a game that saw its share of ties and lead changes, it was left to Mario to save a point for Pittsburgh when he set up the tying goal as regulation drew to a close. He could still move the puck with confidence (witness his three assists); however, his teammates, aside from Francis and Jagr, were no longer the talented group they once were. That became evident to even the most casual observer when the Flyers terminated the Penguins in the postseason in five games.

Lemieux led the league in scoring his final season, but even he admitted that he was not quite the player he had once been. The eight-time All-Star now had six scoring championships to go along with three league MVP awards and his two Stanley Cup rings; he finished with 613 goals and 881 assists for 1,494 points, averaging just over two points a game—even better that Gretzky. But it wasn't enough. Part of the problem was that the Penguins were no longer the balanced team they once were. Placing Francis and Jagr alongside Mario made for some great moments, but the tactic also laid bare the Pens' weak supporting cast. General manager Craig Patrick scrambled to build and rebuild, making trade after trade, but he could not repeat his earlier feats of magic. Part of the problem was the team's slumping financial situation. Keeping together the team of the early 1990s had proven costly, and the team was still paying off players no longer on the roster as part of deferred-compensation packages. Could the team afford to re-sign Francis? Could it keep Jagr? Would it stay in Pittsburgh? All pressing questions, to be sure, but my mind was now elsewhere, as I pondered the fortunes of another team whose very presence in the Southwest was testament both to hockey's growing popularity and its troubled existence in Canada.

It's been several years since I drifted away from the Penguins. I'm not alone. Francis did indeed depart for the Carolina Hurricanes—who had once been his old team, the Hartford Whalers—where he soon was reunited with Paul Coffey, whose smooth skating no longer conceals his defensive liabilities. Trottier works behind the bench of the Colorado Avalanche. Kevin Stevens is a shadow of his former self with the New York Rangers; Larry Murphy went to Detroit, where he picked up two more Stanley Cup rings under Scotty Bowman. Other members of the championship teams still skate for other teams or have embraced retirement.

Yet, out here in the Valley of the Sun, as my daughters Rebecca and Emily howl for their Coyotes, one can still see signs of the past. Rich Tocchet served two years with the Coyotes until a late-season trade in 2000 sent him back to Philadelphia, his first team; he stood out for his leadership and hard-nosed play. Jeremy Roenick, the former Blackhawk who was a subject of controversy in the 1992 finals, now whirls and spins at America West Arena; Travis Green, a member of the 1993 Islander team that brought the Penguins' bid for a dynasty to a crashing halt, centers another line, occasionally skating with another member of that Islander squad, Benoit Hogue. Keith Tkachuk fills the role of the power forward framed in part by Stevens—and he's from Massachusetts, too. Defenseman J. J. Daigneault played on the Pens team that nearly reached the finals in 1996, while general manager Bobby Smith was on the 1991 North Stars team that lost to the Pens in the finals. Battles over arena conditions, the impact of economics (revenue streams, free agency, and such), player holdouts, contract disputes, new ownership, even whispers of a franchise shift should funding for a new rink fall through (Scottsdale voters have just approved the building of a new facility) all remind us that its no longer simply a game, if it ever was.

But the Coyotes are far from alone, as I am reminded every time I think back to the two teams who crossed paths at critical times for some two decades. The New York Islanders frittered away what they had gained in 1993; once one of the best-managed teams in sport, it is now one of the worst, a league laughingstock desperate for a new owner and a new building. Fan loyalty may be touching, but it should not be a one-way street based upon an insane attachment to a team that seems to care little for its fans. It is perhaps no coincidence that the management group that controls Nassau Veterans Memorial Coliseum also oversees the Pittsburgh Civic Arena, where the Penguins found themselves throttled by the terms of occupancy and the cost of maintaining a team. For the Pens had mortgaged the future to pay for the present in the early 1990s; several players (including Tocchet) awaited payments from the team. It looked as if the Pens were about to vanish forever. Perhaps the team would be relocated; perhaps the league would dissolve it (which raised eyebrows—where would Jaromir Jagr, still one of the game's top forwards and the scoring champion in the 1998–99 season, end up?). The Penguins had barely survived earlier ownership problems, which had plagued the franchise since its arrival back in 1967. Would it finally collapse?

Not if Mario Lemieux had anything to say about it. If Ed Westfall's goal back in 1975 had nearly destroyed the franchise, Lemieux had saved it, then brought it to the promised land. Upon his retirement he had been elected to the Hall of Fame, which waived the usual three-year waiting requirements. Joining him at the induction ceremonies were two other people with Penguin connections—Bryan Trottier and Glen Sather, who had spent part of his journeyman career as a left winger wearing the blue and black. But the occasional golf tournament did not satisfy Lemieux. Concerned about the state of his old team (which still owed him a substantial amount of money), Lemieux became active, first in efforts to keep the team in Pittsburgh, and then in putting together a deal to buy it. On the eve of the 1999–2000 season, the player became an owner as a group assembled by Lemieux renegotiated leases and rents and assumed operations of the team.

Whether Lemieux the owner proves as successful as Lemieux the player was in saving the Pittsburgh Penguins remains an open question. The key will be to see if he can gather around him the same sort of team that he led to two Stanley Cups. I wouldn't bet against him. After all, in the first year under his ownership, the Pens broke even financially as they enjoyed some success on the ice. An injury-plagued Jagr still led the league in scoring, and the Pens advanced to the second round of the playoffs, succumbing to the cross-state rival Flyers after a surprisingly easy first-round defeat of the Washington Capitals. Mario's magic may yet save the franchise again.

BROOKS D. SIMPSON is professor of history and humanities at Arizona State University and author, most recently, of *Ulysses S. Grant: Triumph over Adversity, 1822-1865.*

(Above) The Pittsburgh Steelers of 1966, hoping for the best but probably expecting more of the same. Frank Lambert is #46. Big Daddy Lipscomb and John Henry Johnson had both retired by 1966, but Brady Keys #26, Ray Mansfield #73, and Marv Woodson #47 were still playing their hearts out. *(Pittsburgh Steelers.)*

(Right) Frank Lambert is the only Steeler to make the transition to teaching history at a Big Ten University. For two years he experienced the exhilaration and sheer fun of playing the game in Pittsburgh. *(Courtesy of Frank Lambert.)*

New league, new ball, and one of the greatest players in the world. But not even Connie Hawkins and an ABA championship could fill the seats with fans. (*Copyright* The Sporting News.)

Bryan Trottier was a stand-out for the Penguins. Here he plays against the Chicago Black Hawks in the 1992 Stanley Cup Final series.
(*Pittsburgh Penguins.*)

The Pirates Lumber Company—Manny Sanguillen, Rennie Stennett, Richie Hebner, Al Oliver, Richie Zisk, Willie Stargell, and Dave Parker. They hit with power, ran with grace, and played with joy and pride. (*Pittsburgh Pirates.*)

Dock Ellis' smile was as quick as his fastball, and both brought joy to Pirate fans in the Age of Disco. Few players were as consistently interesting and quotable as Ellis. (*Pittsburgh Pirates.*)

Roberto Clemente could do it all—hit, hit with power, run the bases, and field. He swung a bat like a whip and threw the ball on a rope. Private and proud, he was often misunderstood but never ignored. (*Pittsburgh Pirates.*)

Tony Dorsett during his senior season at Hopewell Township High School, on his way to a 264-yard game against Sharon High. From Hopewell, Dorsett went to the University of Pittsburgh, the Dallas Cowboys, and the record books. (*Richard "Butch" Ross.*)

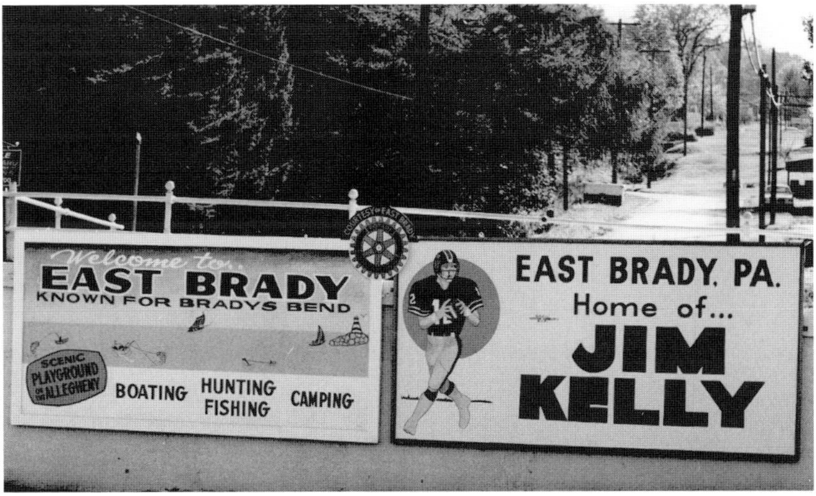

East Brady had quarterback Jim Kelly, but other towns throughout western Pennsylvania had their own local heroes who went on to become stars in college and professional football. *(Leroy Andre.)*

The game is only part of the fun during football season. Here, the tailgate parties are in full swing in the Three Rivers Stadium parking lot prior to the Steelers-Browns kickoff. *(Joel Levinson, from* Pittsburgh Moments.*)*

With his hair slicked back like Harry Greb's, nose flattened like Jack Dempsey's, and broad shoulders, young Art Rooney appeared like a 1920s boxer. In fact, he was an outstanding fighter.
(*Pittsburgh Steelers.*)

Sport was always part of Rooney's life, as much a part of him as the smell of cigar smoke. He was to Pittsburgh sport what the Empire State Building is to New York City.
(*Pittsburgh Steelers.*)

9

BASEBALL IN THE AGE OF DISCO

RACE, RESPECT, AND THE PITTSBURGH PIRATES

ARAM GOUDSOUZIAN

IT WAS JUST ANOTHER routine day for the 1979 Pittsburgh Pirates, a typical clubhouse mood. Hours before an August game in the midst of a pennant race, loud disco music screamed out of the stereo. Rookie catcher Steve Nicosia snuck up on pitcher Bert Blyleven and threw a bucket of water in his face. Phil Garner and Don Robinson wrestled on the floor, while Ed Ott stalked Tim Foli with a bat. Jim Rooker threw a white sheet over his head, cut holes for his eyes, and wrote "KKK" on his forehead. With a fungo bat wrapped in newspaper and set on fire, he paraded around the locker room, finally poking at an unsuspecting Manny Sanguillen. The black Panamanian, who had bent over to pick up a sock, let out a howl. He promptly clubbed Rooker with a ukelele.

In the corner sat Willie Stargell, dressed in jeans, sandals, and a silk shirt unbuttoned to the waist, white ten-gallon hat atop his head. The man they called "Pops"—a loose and jovial team leader, massive home-run hitter, and highly public figure for the black community—leaned back in his chair and surveyed the atmosphere that defined his team as much as their on-field achievements. "There go those Pirates," he smiled. "They're at it again."[1]

The Pirates would win the World Series that year, a capstone on a decade of impressive success: world championships in 1971 and 1979, Eastern Division titles on four other occasions. Yet their legacy, as the raucous locker-room scene indicated, extended beyond victories and championships. Throughout the decade the Pirates put forth an image of interracial cooperation, a meritocratic melting pot of Latins, whites, and American blacks. They developed genuine friendships across racial lines, even comfortably teasing each other about their heritages. In large part this freedom existed due to the excellence of the team's racial minorities. Black players—Roberto Clemente, Willie Stargell, Manny Sanguillen, Al Oliver, Dock Ellis, John Candelaria, Dave Parker—formed the core of the Pirates' on-field talent. Moreover, the black players epitomized an ethic that defined not just the Pirates or baseball, but also illuminated an important trend in modern American sports: an emphasis on spectacular performance, style, masculine pride, and individualism.

This trend originated in black culture. Out of a rich tradition of slave-era folktales, spirituals, and work songs, black Americans forged a consciousness of community and resistance to white authority. In the twentieth century this ethic found expression in proud, visible, individual voices. The blues of Ma Rainey and Robert Johnson voiced the common joys and grievances of black cultural life. On city streets young black men played "the Dozens," trading insults in a safe forum and establishing respect through their verbal facility. A new series of mythical black heroes, more aggressive and individual than the old trickster heroes, emerged within black folktales: "ba-ad niggers" like the legendary Stagolee provided a type of catharsis and self-respect for angry blacks in a racist world, while "hard moral men" like the famed John Henry defeated whites on their own terms. Professional boxing provided dramatic, real-life examples of these ideals. Jack Johnson, heavyweight champion in the early twentieth century, flaunted authority by sleeping with white women, dressing in fancy clothes, and driving flashy cars. Joe Louis, heavyweight champion during the Depression, accepted white standards of behavior but similarly destroyed all challengers.[2]

Baseball, too, had its expressions of black consciousness, especially in Pittsburgh. Segregated from all-white organized baseball in the first half of the twentieth century, the Negro Leagues developed a less conservative, more frenetic style that black Americans recognized as their own. Gus Greenlee's Pittsburgh Crawfords and Cum Posey's Homestead Grays were important black cultural institutions and boasted some of the game's finest talent: Oscar Charleston, Judy Johnson, the quicksilver "Cool Papa" Bell, the powerful slugger Josh Gibson, the outrageous pitcher Satchel Paige. But black baseball heroes could not vault into the national consciousness until Jackie Robinson's reintegration of baseball with the Brooklyn Dodgers in 1947. At the expense of the Negro Leagues, players like Robinson and Willie Mays became national icons.[3]

Alas, following the initial courageous step of racial integration, baseball reverted to its conservative nature. Few teams hurried to follow the Dodgers' lead, and the Boston Red Sox did not even integrate their squad until 1959. During the social upheavals of the 1960s, the sport remained remarkably undisturbed. The St. Louis Cardinals, led by proud black players Bob Gibson, Bill White, and Curt Flood, did win two World Series during the decade. But clearer expressions of black style came in basketball, where athletic stars like Wilt Chamberlain, Bill Russell, and Oscar Robertson revolutionized the game. The boxer Muhammad Ali merged sport with political life as he captured the heavyweight title in 1963, proclaiming, "I am the greatest!" His conversion to Islam and refusal to enter the Vietnam War infuriated many Americans and reflected his defiant insistence on individualism. By the time track athletes Tommie Smith and John Carlos celebrated Black Power on the medal stand with raised fists at the 1968 Olympic Games in Mexico City, social protest and black sport had become inextricably intertwined.[4]

The fracturing of the civil rights movement in the 1970s transformed the relationship between sports and racial politics, just as baseball began a new era, what writer John Parrish called "its postreligious phase." Shedding the imagery of an idyllic pastime, baseball consciously marketed itself as entertainment for the television age. Trying to appeal to a broader public, major league baseball expanded by four teams in 1969. To the dismay of purists and the delight of casual fans, the sport endorsed high-scoring, home-run filled contests by lowering pitching mounds and in 1973 adding the designated hitter in the American League. New multipurpose, artificial turf stadiums and colorful, even garish uniforms reflected owners' and marketers' growing determination to draw in fans with a wide, if shallow net. "We're more sophisticated in promoting our product," explained Milwaukee Brewers general manager Harry Dalton in 1979. "We're utilizing marketing techniques, expanding our advertising, taking surveys, emphasizing group sales." The players, too, recognized their own value as entertainers. Curt Flood's initial challenge of the reserve clause and the 1975 arbitration ruling granting free agency redefined players' relationship with management. "It used to be that the general manager and the manager provided a father figure for us players," noted Willie Stargell in 1973. "Players are becoming more like independent contractors and we're getting more equality with the club people."[5]

Black players played a vital role in baseball's maturation as a modern marketing enterprise. This role reflected the changing relationship between sports and American racial politics. From Jackie Robinson to Curt Flood to Roberto Clemente, certain blacks had managed to combine dramatic athletic talents with an outspoken political awareness. Robinson's Brooklyn Dodgers embodied the ideals of integration in the 1950s. Flood's St. Louis Cardinals reflected the aggressive pursuit of individual rights for blacks in the 1960s. But the Pittsburgh Pirates of the 1970s were sport's finest example of the decade's marriage between black politics and popular culture. In the wake of the civil rights movement stood a generation of proud, black cultural icons. On the silver screen, movies like *Shaft* and *Superfly* portrayed cool, defiant, sexually charged black men. Black singers like Marvin Gaye and James Brown paralleled this style in music—"Say it loud," sang Brown, "I'm black and I'm proud."[6] In sports, the Pirates reinforced this ethic with their aggressive black masculinity. Despite the different attitudes and approaches of the team's black stars, their dramatic athletic feats, interracial camaraderie, immersion in black style, concern for the black community, and awareness of racist double standards all reflected an insistence on acting and being treated like a man.

No player was more spectacular, more proud, or more outspoken than Roberto Clemente. A star since the late 1950s, his last years defined the Pirate ethic and set a standard for later Pirates. Clemente played baseball as if his masculinity was on trial: on and off the field he demanded to be noticed and appreciated. A devastating line-drive hitter and breathtaking rightfielder, he brought a level of showmanship to the game that could irk opponents and fans. One columnist described his approach as "doing something the hard way when it could be done the easy way merely because the hard way is prettier. Clemente swings extra hard and spins around for effect. He makes basket catches. He heaves high, hard throws from the outfield that cause certain sensitive souls to gnash their teeth." He often charged at a fly ball, dropped into a slide, and caught the ball inches from the ground in spectacular fashion. It was unnecessary, but a testament to Clemente's special talents. As his teammate Dock Ellis admired, "You have to be *good,* to be a hot dog."[7]

In the twilight of his long and productive career, Clemente still insisted on giving the fans an exceptional performance. During a mid-June game in 1971 at the Houston Astrodome, with two outs and a man on first base in the eighth inning, he preserved a 1-0 victory by stealing a home run from the powerful hitter Bob Watson. Clemente snared the ball ten feet in the air, crashing into a concrete wall. Somehow holding on for the third out, he suffered a bruised ankle, gashed knee, and swollen elbow for his trouble. The Astros fans gave him a standing ovation. Demanding the same appreciation on a national stage, Clemente visibly chafed at that summer's All-Star game when the Detroit Tigers' Mickey Lolich tried to pitch around him. It was the eighth inning, and Tiger Stadium was still buzzing over Reggie Jackson's mammoth 520-foot home run innings earlier. After two pitches outside the strike zone, Clemente stepped out of the batter's box, dropped his bat to the ground, and gestured at Lolich to pitch him a strike. Lolich demurred, flinging a fastball high and away from Clemente. The proud Puerto Rican stubbornly lunged at it, muscling the ball into the upper deck in center field and displaying his talents to the entire country.[8]

In that year's World Series, as the Pirates upset the heavily favored Baltimore Orioles in seven games, Clemente achieved the national notoriety denied him in the past. Part of his prominence centered around a public controversy with Oriole leader Frank Robinson, after Clemente complained about the condition of the outfield in Memorial Stadium. "Tell him to watch the way I play right field," boasted Robinson, "or buy a ticket and sit in the stands." A defiant Clemente scoffed at Robinson's remarks, adding, "In Puerto Rico, when I am a boy, I play without shoes. I am a professional. I can play anywhere." He proved it during the series: against a pitching staff that included four twenty-game winners, he batted .414 and hit safely in every game, despite playing the first contest with a severe case of food poisoning. He fielded with his usual passion and flair. The writer Roger Angell described the remarkable performance as "throwing and running and hitting at something close to the level of perfection, playing to win but also playing the game almost as if it were a form of punishment for everyone else on the field."[9]

He easily won the series' Most Valuable Player award. "Now everyone knows the way Roberto Clemente plays," he proclaimed. "They saw me in the World Series." His pride was doubly stoked by the memory of the 1960 World Series, when the Pirates won but a young Clemente chafed at his eighth-place finish in that series' MVP balloting. He left the victorious clubhouse prematurely, offending some teammates. This time, as an undisputed team leader, he enjoyed the celebration. As champagne poured and teammates hollered, he displayed the incongruous combination of dignity and individual pride that defined him. Speaking with a television reporter but addressing his parents, he said, "En el dia mas grande de mi vida, les pido sus bendiciones." ("On the proudest day of my life, I ask for your blessing"). To sportswriter Dick Young, he exulted, "Nobody does anything better than me in baseball."[10]

All aspects of Clemente's unique personality—his intense drive for success, his aloof personality, his hypersensitivity to slights—revolved around his demand for personal respect. That demand sometimes alienated fans, opponents, and teammates. He stayed away from his teammates' late-night revelry, instead choosing to rest for the next day's game. He sometimes skipped batting or outfield practice, with management's permission. Unlike most players, he answered media questions honestly, especially about injuries, and developed an unfortunate reputation as a hypochondriac. He sat out with pulled muscles, tension headaches, a nervous stomach, an inflamed tendon in the heel, malaria, a strained instep, bone chips in his elbow, a curved spine, hematoma of the thigh, unaligned discs in the neck and back, severe food poisoning, and insomnia. But Clemente felt he owed the fans his best performance—if he could not play his best, he could not achieve the respect he felt was his due. For that same reason he demanded management's special attention in the clubhouse. "They know it is not the special treatment he really craves," explained one sportswriter, "but that he wants the freedom to be able to demand special treatment. . . . Just the freedom is enough."[11]

Clemente's insistence on respect extended beyond personal concerns to larger matters of racism, especially for Latin players. He complained that star Latins like himself, Juan Marichal, and Felipe and Matty Alou never received endorsement contracts. More often, he boiled at the general double standard imposed upon blacks and Latins by the media. "How come you sportswriters always bring up negative things about the Black and Spanish players?" he once asked. Writers emphasized his injuries or showmanship, or his teammates' outspokenness. "But, when you talk about the white players, it's most nice things, you say. Like you say, so and so, he has a pretty wife, and nice kids. He sells stocks during the off-season. But with the non-white player it's why don't you like the coach? Or something else that's controversial." Again, he insisted upon respect. "I'm a man first and a baseball player, next. Treat me that way."[12]

Clemente tried to help others achieve this respect. Despite his remoteness, his teammates acknowledged him as a leader, especially his fellow Latins—when he traveled to Puerto Rico to help the Pirates sign John Candelaria, Clemente favored the young pitcher by speaking in Spanish across the negotiating table to make sure Candelaria received a fair contract. This admirable concern for his fellow man ultimately led to his tragic death. On December 31, 1972, a plane carrying relief supplies for Nicaraguan earthquake victims crashed in the Gulf of Mexico. Clemente, the organizer of the mission, was on board. As Puerto Rico wept and Clemente's wife received sacks of condolences, writers and teammates paid homage to their proud and misunderstood teammate. The Baseball Hall of Fame suspended its usual five-year waiting period and enshrined Clemente. In an appropriate touch of statistical trivia, he finished his career with exactly 3,000 hits.[13]

That hitting proficiency was the mark of the Pirates. *Sports Illustrated* called the 1972 combination of Willie Stargell, Al Oliver, Manny Sanguillen, and Roberto Clemente "Four Murderers in a Row." These devastating hitters, the magazine surmised, must strike fear in the hearts of pitchers: "Sinewy, determined men wielding clubs stride endlessly to the plate—grinning hideously no doubt in anticipation of ridiculing the pitcher, deminking his wife and impoverishing his children." Young hitters like Richie Zisk, Rennie Stennett, and Dave Parker complemented them. The players took an obvious joy in their aggressive, free-swinging style. When once asked why he always swung at the first pitch, Manny Sanguillen exclaimed, "Because it makes me feel good!" Even after Clemente's death, the Pirates remained a powerful team with impressive depth. In September 1975 they beat the Chicago Cubs, 22-0. Stennett tied a major league record for a nine-inning game by smacking seven hits.[14]

The Pirates' reputation as hard-swinging, flamboyant, powerful hitters earned the team a national following. National League president Chub Feeney reported in 1975 that the Pirates would draw over 1.5 million fans on the road that year; rival clubs begged the league to schedule at least one weekend series against the Pirates. "People like to see those bombers from Pittsburgh," explained Feeney. "The fans love seeing Oliver and Stargell and Parker and Hebner and Zisk and Sanguillen swinging for the downs. They root for the pitchers to strike them out, but they're not too disappointed when one of the Pirates hits a home run."[15]

This reliance on powerful hitting sometimes cost the Pirates. In the midst of a disappointing 1973 season, bullpen coach Dave Ricketts argued that "over the years, Pittsburgh has been a hitter's team. We have not learned to function as a whole team. We don't hit or run or bunt." The players' aggressive insistence on swinging at first pitches periodically sabotaged their efforts. In 1975, one of a few seasons that the Pirates ranked last in drawing walks, San Diego pitcher Randy Jones shut them out with only seventy pitches. Yet in an age of artificial turf, lower mounds, closer fences, and narrower strike zones, the Pirates' formula generally worked both for competitive and marketing purposes. Baseball now favored high-scoring, home-run hitting, crowd-pleasing slugfests. Willie Stargell in particular satisfied this need for athletic entertainment. His power inspired legend—manager Danny Murtaugh claimed that even when his back was turned, he could tell when Stargell was batting by the distinctively loud crack of the bat.

By the end of the decade, Stargell had hit four balls into Three Rivers Stadium's stratospheric upper deck. Before anyone else ever hit a home run completely out of Dodger Stadium, Stargell had done it twice.[16]

The Pirates bolstered their slugging reputation with the move to Three Rivers Stadium and its compact, symmetrical outfield. Stargell anticipated the 1970 move out of cavernous Forbes Field "like a kid on Christmas Eve who couldn't wait to open his presents." His wife, Dolores, after charting his hits from 1969, predicted he would have hit twenty-two additional home runs in the new stadium. Three Rivers' other features reflected baseball's transition away from its image as a rural pastime. The stadium boasted an all-purpose Tartan turf surface, moving grandstands that accommodated football spectators, brightly colored orange, yellow, and red seats, a 274- by 30-foot computerized scoreboard, and a four-tiered glass-enclosed dining room called the Allegheny Club. Fans dutifully responded to the electronic message board's pleas for vocal support. Popular rock music blared over the loudspeakers. By the end of the decade, a mascot called the "Pirate Parrot" patrolled the field while the club added more promotions and giveaways. In a bow to the television age, Three Rivers even hosted the first World Series night game in 1971. The city put itself on display, as the downtown Golden Triangle shone with the lights of every office window. The *Sporting News* reported on not just the game, but the television image itself: "NBC's cameras caught the downtown scene beautifully from vantage points high in the stadium. TV viewers enjoyed the results of some excellent camera work both inside and outside the stadium." Three Rivers and the Pittsburgh area had become an enormous television studio.[17]

The Pirates' television-friendly image included a newer, flashier fashion statement. Concurrent with the move to Three Rivers, the team adopted modern polyester, double-knit uniforms with tight, form-fitting pullover jerseys, tailored pants with an elastic drawstring, and garish mustard-colored caps. The team name blared in gold, gothic script. They continued to innovate in 1976, when all major league teams adopted commemorative pillbox caps, with raised sides and a flat top, in honor of the bicentennial. The Pirates insisted on making their cap, ringed by three gold stripes and bearing a scripted *P,* a permanent fixture. Teased by the media for looking like "a softball team from the corner tavern" or "enormous hornets," the team reveled in their sartorial distinction. By 1979 the Pirates dressed in either yellow or white jerseys, yellow or black caps, and yellow or black pants—enough for sixty-four possible combinations of modern baseball fashion.[18]

Off the field the Pirates' black players also dressed in the latest modern styles. The media sometimes fixated on their outfits. Stargell, Ellis, Dave Cash, and Bob Veale donned accouterments such as see-through shirts, planter-style straw hats, enormous floppy caps, big gold and silver belts, glistening polyester bell-bottom pants, black mink coats, and suits in leather or crushed velvet. Some players sported long sideburns, Fu Manchu mustaches, and Afro haircuts. Like the on-field uniforms, these styles brought attention to the Pirates and identified them as modern men attuned to the importance of visual images. Yet their own personal clothes, and the media attention they generated, further suggested the close ties between modern American cultural life and black fashion. Stargell and Ellis, not white players like Bill Mazeroski or Bob Robertson, embodied the Pirate image.[19]

The national identification of the Pirates with black style and achievement was reinforced on September 1, 1971, during a routine late-season game against the Philadelphia Phillies. That night manager Danny Murtaugh posted the lineup: Rennie Stennett (second base), Gene Clines (center field), Roberto Clemente (right field), Willie Stargell (left field), Manny Sanguillen (catcher), Dave Cash (third base), Al Oliver (first base), Jackie Hernandez (shortstop), and Dock Ellis (pitcher). For the first time ever, a major league baseball team started a game with nine blacks. They generally fielded at least five or six black starters anyway, and that night regular white starters Bob Robertson and Richie Hebner were nursing injuries. But the milestone also spoke to the Pirates' racially progressive organizational culture. Unlike many other teams, the Pirates developed black pitchers and catchers—the so-called thinking man's positions. Outstanding catchers and pitchers like Sanguillen, Ellis, and Veale rose through the Pirates' farm system and demonstrated the ability of black players to perform at these crucial positions.

The all-black lineup eventually merited a brief mention in national sports publications such as *Sports Illustrated* and the *Sporting News,* but at the time some players did not even realize it. Around the third inning, Cash turned to fellow infielder Oliver and smiled, "Hey Scoop, we got all brothers out there." Only then did Oliver look around him and laugh, "We sure do!" Most of the players joked about it, with some blacks teasing, "Hey, all you white guys, you can take a rest tonight." To the media, they emphasized their color-blind outlook. Stargell insisted that the racial composition of the lineup "doesn't make a difference on this team." Luke Walker, the white pitcher who relieved Ellis and won the game, professed, "All I saw on the field were eight men and myself. I think all the guys feel the same way." When a reporter asked Murtaugh if he realized his lineup had nine blacks, Murtaugh replied, "I thought I had nine *Pirates* out there on the field."[20]

The Pirates celebrated their diversity—their locker-room banter included constant teasing about ethnic heritage and physical slapstick interaction. In a nation divided by race, the Pirates tried to defuse that tension through humor. It was a unique atmosphere, based on the Pirates' black and Latin majority. When white pitcher and former Houston Astro Jerry Reuss arrived for the first time in the Pirates clubhouse, he could not believe the smiles and playful shoves that accompanied insults like "nigger" and "Dago." "You use the big N!" he gaped. "Anybody who said nigger in Houston would have gotten himself killed." Unlike most every other team, the racial minorities were not just isolated stars in white-dominated clubhouses. The Pirates had black and Latin pitchers, catchers, and role players. White Pirates could not simply ignore their black teammates or fail to confront the issue of race.[21]

The Pirates' style extended beyond the field or their dress. Once locker rooms were tombs where players and coaches dispensed tired clichés to bored sportswriters. The Pirates, however, boasted what *Sports Illustrated* called "the loudest, trashiest-mouthed, loosest, most uproarious dressing room in baseball." In the early 1970s a visitor to the clubhouse might find Dock Ellis imitating Clemente, limping around, rubbing his neck, and complaining in a Latin accent, "Oh, I not like I used to be. I a little bit of an old man now." Later in the decade, one might find Phil Garner and Dave Parker insulting each other, their family, and their ancestors. During one of Danny Murtaugh's managerial stints, he might be holding court with his coaches, cracking self-effacing jokes from his own rocking chair. At any time, one could be certain to find tape flying through the air, wrestling matches, and music ranging from country to rhythm and blues to oldies to disco. *Sports Illustrated* marveled, "One thinks that Evel Knievel, Huey P. Newton, Tennessee Williams and Charo could move in, and the Pirates would work them into its mix."[22]

The Pirates genuinely appreciated each other's company and made connections across racial lines through jocular insults and a relaxed clubhouse atmosphere, fulfilling their public image as sporting ambassadors of racial tolerance and cooperation. But the team was not a colorblind utopia. Just as the clubhouse barbs indicated a convivial and open atmosphere, they also suggested that the players classified themselves and identified each other along racial lines. Black and Latin players in particular kept a sharp lookout for racial discrimination and insisted on being treated with proper dignity.

This demand for respect was undoubtedly forged by minor league experiences. Willie Stargell, by nature a man of peaceful compromise, found his patience tested by a minor league stint in the South. "In the small towns where I played, people treated me like a dog," he remembered. "I lived on back porches in fold-up beds. Other blacks I saw worked in the fields all day until white people came to cart them off." One night in Plainview, Texas, a man pointed a shotgun at his temple and threatened, "Nigger, if you play in that game tonight, I'll blow your brains out." Stargell claimed that he survived these experiences by ignoring them. "I played the role," he wrote. "I saw the racial route as just another obstacle to be stepped over." The more confrontational Dock Ellis chafed at the same indignities. While playing in upstate New York, a fan kept teasing him and calling him "Stepin Fetchit." Ellis charged into the stands with a leaded bat.[23]

Most blacks on the Pirates fell somewhere between Stargell and Ellis on the political spectrum of race relations. But they all shared the common experiences of public humiliation and racism that any well-traveled black man might. As members of the civil rights generation, they knew firsthand the indignities of entrenched racism. As athletes in a competitive sport, they were keenly aware of unfair advantages based on race. And as Pittsburgh Pirates in the 1970s they excelled in a cultural arena dominated by dynamic, masculine black men. Race shaped their relationships with white teammates, concerns for the black community, and grievances with Pirates management.

Black Pirates commonly griped about a perceived racial double standard. The team had problems filling Three Rivers Stadium throughout the decade, and some reporters speculated that the cause lay in the lack of white stars. Outspoken black players felt management followed policies designed to promote white players at the expense of blacks. In 1973, for instance, Manny Sanguillen replaced the martyred Roberto Clemente in right field, despite his catching skill and lack of outfield experience. Gene Clines, an able black outfielder, interpreted the move as a chance to get "some blond hair and blue eyes on the diamond," as a white catcher would undoubtedly take Sanguillen's position behind the plate. Willie Stargell consoled the displaced Clines throughout the season. Clines wanted to be traded and felt he was a victim of discrimination. "He didn't even have a chance to try out for right field in spring training," Stargell complained. "They just gave it to Manny so they could have the Great White Hope behind the plate. The Pirates are afraid to field an all-black team. They don't put the nine best men on the field, because of the fans."[24]

Al Oliver agreed. Despite the powerful hitter's growing comfort at first base, he found himself displaced by Bob Robertson, a white player with mediocre fielding skills. A disenchanted Oliver moved to the outfield, grumbling that "on the Pirates, it is always blacks fighting blacks for a job." Management, he believed, protected Robertson at first base and Richie Hebner at third. Indeed, Oliver only moved back to first base after Robertson left the team. The lack of respect infuriated Oliver. "It's a pride thing," argued Oliver's wife, Donna. "Robertson flops out, and they send Al out there for two years to learn a new position and he learns it and the boy flops out, so Al comes back to first base. That's enough to insult anybody."[25]

In most cases, players measured respect in dollars and cents. In the aftermath of his move to the outfield, Oliver demanded a higher salary, proclaiming that "before I go between the white lines, I'll get the amount of money I want and feel I deserve. If I don't, I will sit it out and try some other occupation." The ballplayers linked material comfort to their own pride and masculinity. "Al Oliver has so many high standards," explained teammate Dock Ellis. "He wants to portray an image: being super, super-style." The home runs, the fame, and the cool demeanor needed the quantified respect of management. As Oliver stated, "My main goal in life is for people to respect me, not as Al Oliver the ballplayer, but as Al Oliver the person. I have pride in myself."[26]

The same motivations drove Willie Stargell. "I want to be an individual," he reflected in the midst of his 1973 contract talks. "As a ballplayer, I'm not looked at as a man. I am just another star with no liberty." His production and importance to the team equaled that of any major league player, including Henry Aaron and Joe Torre. But Stargell earned less, and it rankled him: "I don't feel right in their company. They carry a certain confidence that I can't. I need money to be with Aaron and the others man to man. When I'm in their presence, I know I am not in that class, even though I feel I belong." Money reflected masculinity: the more richly compensated received more respect from their organizations. Stargell further realized that the respect derived from a large contract could erode racism. In an angrier moment, he explained that whatever a man's skin color "you can damn near demand respect, or command it if you got the money." He called it the "green Jesus."[27]

If the Pirates' players had their druthers, most of their comments on contract negotiations and racist management would never have reached the public. But in mid-decade, authors Bob Adelman and Susan Hall compiled a collection of informal Pirate interviews from the 1973 season and published them under the title *Out of Left Field: Willie Stargell and the Pittsburgh Pirates*. The book exposed the seamier underside of professional baseball: the bickering, the expletive-laced locker-room banter, the racial resentment, and the players' personal lives. Stargell and his teammates had figured the book would be a traditional, positive account of the team, not an exposé in the mold of Jim Bouton's highly controversial 1970 account of life in the major leagues. Instead, this *Ball Four* of Pittsburgh recorded the Pirates' views on race and baseball.

Out of Left Field also exposed two particularly embarrassing aspects of the players' lives: their sexual infidelity and drug use. "I like to get together with someone," explained the married Stargell, "because it breaks up the monotony of road trips and you can slowly unwind after a game. I need the relaxation." He did not regret his actions as long as his home life remained "smooth." "I do know," he qualified, "that if my wife fooled around while I was on the road, I would kill her!" Adelman and Hall also interviewed female "groupies" who slept with famous ballplayers. One named Gayle said, "They could be the ugliest men in creation, but because they got a name for themselves, the girls will screw them, so ballplayers take advantage of girls in every city."

These revelations may have stained the players' image, but the admission of rampant drug use also humiliated the Pirate front office. Dock Ellis revealed the mutual secret: "One thing management knows about and don't discuss is our little pick-me-ups. Whole team is on pills. I have taken about fifteen at one time. . . . Management doesn't look because they think it helps the gate. Keeps us winning. Keeps the fans coming."[28]

The claims of racial discrimination, the demands for financial respect, and even the sexual and narcotic escapades marked a transition toward a more modern baseball ethic. Previous generations undoubtedly experienced the same disgruntlements and dalliances, but never in such a visible fashion. The increased acceptance of showboating, the encouragement of home-run hitting, and the new uniforms and stadiums all signaled the incorporation of baseball into a national entertainment culture. The revelations of books like *Ball Four* and *Out of Left Field* reminded fans that their national pastime also included the flip side to that culture. Baseball players dealt with issues like money, personal temptation, and racism in a very public arena.

Throughout this transition, the Pirates' image remained fixed to the team's black stars—men with extremely different personalities and political philosophies, but linked by mutual investment in their black identity. Their pride, their concerns, and their emphasis on masculinity spoke to an attitude beyond the color-blind aphorisms they fed the public. Shades of Roberto Clemente's supreme confidence and his demands for dignity were revealed in his Pirate teammates. "As far as hitting a baseball," once proclaimed Al Oliver, "I'm the best. Nobody hits the ball as hard and as consistently as I do." It was a statement Clemente himself might have made.[29]

No Pirate felt the death of Clemente more than friend and teammate Manny Sanguillen. The two had made an incongruous pair: Clemente aloof and sensitive, Sanguillen smiling and ebullient. "The Smiling Panamanian," as broadcaster Bob Prince dubbed him, brought a splash of color onto the field. He ran the bases with arms akimbo, dashing with exceptional speed for a catcher. At bat he swung freely at pitches above his head or in the dirt, consistently managing to pound line drives into the outfield. Behind the plate he brought an uncontained enthusiasm to the game, always chattering and laughing. His natural effervescence entertained the public and brought a light spirit to the game.[30]

Unfortunately, Sanguillen suffered from the same lack of recognition that Clemente so detested. The publication *Black Sports* reported in 1972 that major league players voted him the league's best catcher over Cincinnati star Johnny Bench, 420-157, even though Bench received most of the public's adoration and All-Star votes. Sanguillen realized the hypocrisy, though unlike Clemente he rarely complained. He did share Clemente's concern for helping poor Latin Americans. He almost joined Clemente's fatal flight to Nicaragua and volunteered as a diver with the search party to look for Clemente's body. When Pirate manager Bill Virdon asked him to replace Clemente in right field, Sanguillen complied for the sake of the team but never felt comfortable. "I feel like maybe I should play left field," he surmised, through his thick accent. "Right field is Roberto's job. I feel strange down there because he's my great friend and I watched him play there." Clemente and Sanguillen shared an emotional bond based on their humanitarian concern and black Latin identity.[31]

Few others came so close to Clemente. Yet the clubhouse respected his ability and leadership, even someone as different from him as the young, brash, extroverted, and comical Dock Ellis. In Clemente's last years Ellis would sometimes urge the venerable leader to join the team on social occasions. "We going to get down together, *everybody,*" Ellis would proclaim. The players enjoyed seeing the normally tense Clemente relax with them, and the elder statesman appreciated the goodwill of his younger teammates. Ellis also fought the notion that Clemente did not identify with the struggles of American blacks. Some members of Pittsburgh's black community had the impression that the inhibited and solitary Clemente stayed apart from black issues. Clemente was Puerto Rican, Ellis insisted, but "he was as *black* as you can *get*. He was into it."[32]

Though polar opposites in temperament and approach to the game, Ellis shared Clemente's notions of masculine pride, public performance, and individualism. For outrageous deeds and outspokenness, no baseball player—perhaps no one on earth—matched Dock Ellis. In May of 1970, for instance, Ellis forgot that he was pitching the first game of a doubleheader in San Diego. The night before, he drove to Los Angeles, called a girlfriend, and spent the night dropping LSD. He awoke from an hour of sleep at about ten in the morning, took another half tab of LSD, and drove back to San Diego. In the clubhouse he tried to perk himself up with Dexamyl and Benzadrine. It worked. That night Ellis pitched the only no-hitter of his career.[33]

Poet and essayist Donald Hall once wrote that if Ellis "were a fictional character, he would be inconsistent and unrealistic." Bob Adelman and Susan Hall caught Ellis during a rain delay yammering in a stream-of-consciousness chatter that illustrated his pride, camaraderie, and utter absurdity. He mocked the other team ("Look at that left-handed peep-out-of-ass hitter"), teased his teammates ("Get Willie up off his feet. Going to take him twenty minutes to warm up"), idly bragged about himself ("I am going to leave this club. See where they end up at. Wouldn't have no color whatsoever on the team"), and flashed to his off-field exploits ("Can't think of nothing but sex in the dugout"). On another instance, Ellis revealed his plans for a game where he was not scheduled to pitch: "This afternoon, I've got me a chickadero in the stands, but I am supposed to keep the pitching record. Going to get myself kicked out of the game by vamping the umpire. Then I'll go in the stands." A few innings later he berated the umpire: "You going to tell me to shut up? You ain't no school teacher. You the principal for the day? You supposed to umpire the game." The umpire ejected him, and he summarily departed for the stands.[34]

Despite his open and extroverted personality, Ellis sometimes felt alienated because of his political attitudes—what he described as "the racial separateness, the 'heavy black thing.'" Although he forged friendships with white teammates like Bob Robertson and Bob Miller, Ellis's stubborn defiance and candid pronouncements could rankle management and fans. He felt the Pirates delayed his entrance to the major leagues because the team already had so many black players. He complained about coming to the ballpark on days he would not pitch. In 1972 a Cincinnati security guard singled out the flamboyant Ellis when he tried to enter the stadium, spraying him with mace after Ellis swore at him and brushed him aside. In 1973 Ellis spent a game in the dugout wearing a huge size 9 cap covering hair festooned with curlers. In 1974 he insisted before a game that he would hit every batter he faced that day. He proceeded to plunk, in succession, Cincinnati Reds Pete Rose, Joe Morgan, and Dan Driessen. Manager Bill Virdon pulled him only after Tony Perez walked on four pitches, spending the whole at-bat dancing around Ellis's beanballs.[35]

"I am free," he once proclaimed after a defiant return from a three-week suspension. "I'm not owned by the team." Young, black, and proud, Ellis translated his rights as an equal human being into an insistence on dramatic individual actions both on and off the field. Since he performed his job, he saw no reason to accept arbitrary authority. He nonchalantly dismissed any suggestion that his actions clashed with team goals. "Virdon used to say I should take the other guys into consideration," he explained. "But I don't deal with other guys. I deal with me. . . . I pitch. I win. I'm free."[36]

Ellis's outspoken nature and acute sensitivity to any suggestion of exploitation or racism attracted writers from across the country. After an outstanding first half of the season in 1971, Ellis suspected he would not start the All-Star game against Oakland's black pitcher Vida Blue. "I doubt very seriously if they'll start a brother from the American League and a brother from the National," he publicly announced. Sportswriters roundly criticized Ellis and celebrated baseball's egalitarianism when manager Sparky Anderson named Ellis the starter. None of the media accepted baseball's existing racism, and no one dared suggest that Ellis's comments actually may have influenced Anderson's decision. Yet if Ellis needed any vindication, it came in a letter from Jackie Robinson. "I appreciate your courage and honesty," wrote the black baseball pioneer. "In my opinion progress for today's players will come from this type of dedication." Robinson, who would die the following year, added, "When I met you I was left with the feeling that self-respect was very important."[37]

That same year the Pirates ran a promotion where three players signed autographs before Sunday home games. The organization set up booths with chain-link wire to protect the players. Although the team voted unanimously to participate in the promotion, Ellis abstained from the vote and refused to fulfill the duty. Management twice fined him one hundred dollars, and Ellis hardly quelled the public uproar with his imperious explanation: "I just don't want to be part of the autograph booth. I'm here to pitch." But Ellis actually objected to the dehumanizing nature of the fenced-in booth. "I'm not going to be in a cage," he privately explained. "I'm no monkey in a cage." His demand for respect may have been abrupt and impolitic, but the next year the Pirates set up long, open tables for autographs guarded by security officers. Ellis gladly took part.[38]

Ellis ignited another controversy in 1975 when a Pittsburgh reporter asked him about the team's dwindling attendance. "Too many black ballplayers," he responded, earning him headlines in the Pittsburgh newspapers. He failed to understand the brouhaha—"I been saying that for eight years," he laughed. But the true uproar arrived in August of that season when he refused Danny Murtaugh's request to warm up in the bullpen. Ellis had pitched the day before and considered the request unreasonable. Murtaugh, who had already butted heads with Ellis over a potential move to the bullpen, seemed to expect the refusal and suspended him the next day. Then, at a team meeting where everyone expected Ellis to apologize, he spoke his mind, accusing Murtaugh of making panicky decisions and implying that general manager Joe Brown had hurt Richie Zisk's performance by not settling a contract dispute. Trying to rally the team, he urged them to ignore management and play as a team. But lacking the filter between thought process and verbal expression, he also urged them to overcome their own weaknesses. "We all know Hebner's got cement hands . . ." he began. At that point the crinkled Murtaugh could take no more, rising to his feet and challenging Ellis to fight.[39]

The Pirates suspended Ellis for thirty days without pay. As the national media indignantly scolded him, Ellis received scathing hate mail from white fans. One man wrote:

> I see where you are pulling a tantrum and refusing to pitch—you black son of a bitch. You are lucky to be able to play ball, when

> the best you could probably do at any other job would be one hundred dollars a month—but—the league is full of stupid, black bastards trying to show that a nigger is as good as, or better than, anyone else.
>
> I suppose like all the other niggers you wear those carnival type clothes too—big hats, the whole bit. You must all look like a lot of clowns in the circus! RIGHT ON!

Another added: "You were brought up in a TAR PAPER SHACK. Now nothing's too good for you. You're just a street nigger that never became civilized. Hope they fire your black ass."[40]

Some people did defend Ellis. A group of young black children held up pro-Ellis signs outside Three Rivers Stadium during his suspension. Teammate Al Oliver insisted to the press that players owned the right to speak their mind and act as individuals. Ellis criticized those who defended management, wondering "how they can look their sons in the eye and say 'I am a man.'" Stargell, the leader and conciliator, publicly stated that Ellis had good intentions but should recognize his error and apologize. Ellis did eventually express regret, after the Pirates dropped his suspension in the wake of a protest from the Players' Association. The organization then traded him to the New York Yankees that off-season. But for all of Ellis's excesses and bombast, he always defended his right of individual expression. After the incident ended, Stargell had to admit, "It took a man to do what Dock did."[41]

Dave Parker assumed the same prerogatives for expressing his masculine individuality. Combined with his phenomenal physical talents, his braggadocio and sense of style placed him at the center of baseball's modern culture in the late 1970s. "I'm wall-to-wall and treetop tall," he would boom before games. "Two things are for sure. The sun's gonna shine, and I'm going three for four." "The Cobra," as he was known, stood 6'5", weighed 235 pounds, hit with astounding power, possessed a cannon throwing arm, and ran the bases as fast as any Pirate. "Every team needs a foundation, and I'm it," he proclaimed in September 1978. Flexing his upper body, he insisted, "Just look at me. They ought to pay me just to walk around here."[42]

Entering the 1979 season Parker seemed poised to fully accept his status as baseball's leading man. He had just won back-to-back batting championships and Gold Glove awards. The MVP of the 1978 season, he hit thirty home runs, batted in 117 runs, averaged .334, and had a .585 slugging average. He had fully recovered from a collision with New York Mets catcher Joe Stearns in June 1978 that had fractured his cheekbone. The cover of *Sports Illustrated*'s baseball preview issue asked "Who's Best?" Parker, towering over Boston Red Sox slugger Jim Rice, answered the question with a confident smile and an upraised finger. The magazine marveled at his self-assurance. "There's only one thing bigger than me," crowed Parker, "and that's my ego." Parker's preposterous pronouncements received ample backing from his spectacular play—clearly, he was the game's most proficient all-around player.[43]

But Parker generated enormous resentment from baseball's white establishment and fan base. No team even drafted the phenomenal physical talent until the fourteenth round, in large part due to his reputation for arguing with coaches—he was labeled a "militant." Reaching the peak of his game, Parker frequently and loudly complained that he was drastically underpaid. With the help of pioneer "super-agent" Tom Reich, Parker signed a five-year, five-million-dollar contract extension. Headlines around the country marveled at the broken financial barrier: Parker was the first player to earn a million dollars in one year.[44]

Pittsburgh, a city with steel-mill roots and a working-class population, hardly appreciated the contract. Parker received death threats, hate mail, prank telephone calls, and boos from the crowd. During a "Bat Day" promotion in June 1979, Parker dropped a fly ball in the seventh inning. Two innings later a fan tossed a bat that bounced directly in front of him. The next year, someone in the outfield bleachers threw a transistor battery that just missed his head and continued another 200 feet. Part of the resentment could be ascribed to Parker's decline in production, but a significant portion stemmed from his unapologetic image as a proud man ensconced in black style. Along with his public boasts, Parker drove a brown Mercedes with brown bearskin upholstery and wore a diamond-studded gold necklace spelling "COBRA." In the tradition of black folk culture's "ba-ad nigger," Parker rejected white expectations of humility and modesty; his flaunting of brash individualism invited racist condemnation. As his teammate

Stargell later reflected, "The baseball world wasn't ready for a million-dollar-a-year black baseball player."[45]

Of all the Pirates, Willie Stargell most assumed Clemente's leadership mantle. A huge, easygoing man that teammates first called "Gentle Ben," then "Sugar Bear," and finally "Pops," Stargell enjoyed a long career with the Pirates and embodied the team's public image. In 1979, as the Pirates charged toward their final pennant of the decade, Parker considered Stargell's role: "He means a tremendous amount to everyone on this ball club. He's our leader, our stabilizer, and for me, my baseball father." Stargell grew into this more complete leadership role very uneasily. The team named him captain in 1973 after Clemente died, but Stargell's softspoken amiability failed to motivate his teammates like the reclusive but passionate Clemente. Dock Ellis emphasized Stargell's distinct individual personality: "Man, there's no way Willie wants to be captain. He don't wanna go talking to players for his manager. He's his own man."[46]

But Stargell's charisma and lightheartedness came to suit perfectly a team with such diverse ethnic heritages. Unlike some of his more outspoken teammates, he displayed a keen media savvy. In 1969 he declared all Sundays "Ladies' Days." "If the boys couldn't get me to sign between Monday and Saturday," he later laughed, "then they wouldn't be able to get my autograph at all." The press enjoyed such stunts and appreciated Stargell's magnetism. In 1979 the *New York Times* admired how Stargell avoided "the tension and sullen inwardness that envelop so many players today." Of course, Stargell also treaded lightly on issues of racial discrimination. Although he often discussed racism in private, complaining about the lack of endorsement opportunities for black athletes in publications like *Ebony* and *Black Sports,* he was the chief promoter of the Pirates' image of interracial cooperation. "It really doesn't make a difference to me what color you are, you're just a guy to me," he told *Sports Illustrated*. "I know some black so-called friends who are dogs."[47]

Although he advocated a color-blind approach to baseball, Stargell displayed a particular awareness for the black community. "I think the black ball player should be responsible to the black community," he told *Ebony*. "He should be visible to the kids in the ghetto." Stargell often spoke to youth groups in the off-season, encouraging them to avoid urban pitfalls like drug use and crime. He also headed the Black Athletes Foundation, a Pittsburgh-based group dedicated to fighting sickle-cell anemia. Joined by teammates like Dock Ellis and Mudcat Grant, as well as basketball stars like Connie Hawkins, the group raised money and lobbied politicians for increased research funding. He also established the Willie Stargell Foundation, a fundraising organization for education, medicine, and relief aid. He even started a successful business in Pittsburgh's black-dominated Hill district, Willie's Stargell's Chicken on the Hill. As a publicity stunt, Stargell promised free chicken to all the customers in line when he hit a home run, prompting broadcaster Bob Prince to develop a catch phrase: "Spread some chicken on the Hill, Will."[48]

Stargell spread plenty of free chicken with his towering home-run blasts, although his production declined in 1976 and 1977 due to injuries and his wife's (successful) bout with a blood clot in her brain. But rather than retire at age thirty-seven, he returned and enjoyed two of the finest years in his career. Now fully comfortable with his leadership role and at the helm of the loosest, most outrageous group of players in Pirates history, Stargell again assumed the mantle of media darling and champion of interracial acceptance. In 1979 he started two gimmicks that the public embraced. First he began awarding "Stargell Stars," gold stickers that symbolized Stargell's appreciation of a job well done. With mock formality, he handed them not only to players but also bat boys, trainers, coaches, office personnel, and fans. With the fans' endorsement, the players decorated their caps with the stars. Second, Stargell asked the team's publicity director to play Sister Sledge's song "We Are Family" during the seventh-inning stretch of home games. Like the Pirates themselves, the disco beat reflected the centrality of black style in the national popular culture. Stargell happily emphasized that the song promoted the same message of unity and pride that he felt the Pirates embodied. As the Pirates marched to the 1979 pennant, Pittsburgh adopted "We Are Family" as their song, a musical celebration suggesting the finest the city had to offer for athletic excellence and racial diversity.[49]

With stars on their caps and disco music pulsating through their veins, the Pirates danced toward the 1979 division title and a date with their greatest rivals, the Cincinnati Reds. Needing extra innings to edge out the Reds in the first two games, the Pirates returned to a rain-soaked Three Rivers Stadium hoping to clinch the pennant. Behind a towering blast by Willie Stargell that Reds manager John McNamara claimed traveled "somewhere into the ionosphere," the Pirates cruised to a 6-1 lead by the seventh-inning stretch. "We Are Family" once again blared over the loudspeakers. In celebration the players' wives jumped from their seats onto a platform behind home plate, gyrating and high-kicking to the loud rhythm. Waving banners and laughing, hugging each other and dancing, the ladies received criticism from some of the media. But it was a fitting tribute for the Pirates—a gregarious, uproarious, notorious bunch in the midst of a "disco-inferno season."[50]

The upcoming World Series threw an intense national spotlight upon the Pittsburgh team. Once again facing the Baltimore Orioles, their World Series opponents from 1971, the series highlighted the characteristics that defined the Pirates' public image: their spirit of interracial cooperation, their embodiment of modern baseball style in a television age, and the leadership of a proud, powerful, black man. While 1971 had been Roberto Clemente's year, 1979 belonged to Willie Stargell.

He had been with the Pirates since 1962. He had hit over 450 home runs in his career, and at age thirty-eight he still led the team in that category. He was the link to the past, an active reminder of Pirate tradition. Stargell reflected on this legacy. Roberto Clemente, he believed, "had started something with his winning, driving attitude. Whatever contribution I've made has been merely an extension of what he started." He preached the importance of a relaxed attitude, of playing the game for fun. Old teammates like Dock Ellis and Al Oliver may have left, but Dave Parker and John Candelaria now filled in, supplying the bragging and teasing. The media continued to highlight the team's diversity and clubhouse antics—Roger Angell likened it to "an overcrowded city block in some ethnically confused but exuberant neighborhood." As the World Series approached, Stargell visibly represented this motley group. "Willie's approval is a must concerning the Pirates," wrote *Sports Illustrated* on the eve of the series. "Some superstars are referred to as *my* man or *the* man, but to one and all Stargell is simply *a* man—the consummate encomium."[51]

The Pirates would need Stargell's leadership as they fell behind the Orioles three games to one in a sloppy, cold Series. In a mid-October freezing rain, Pirates and Orioles shivered through fielding errors on the waterlogged playing surface, while commissioner Bowie Kuhn stubbornly smiled from the stands, refusing to don an overcoat, yet wearing flannel pajamas under his clothes. No World Series had ever so dramatically illustrated that the teams played baseball not for the fans in attendance, but for television. Sportswriter Phil Musick dubbed it "The Roone Arledge World Series," after the ABC television producer. "Three Rivers Stadium," added *Maclean's,* "is as much a TV studio as it is a ball park. It looked good Friday night, the banks of lights erasing shadows, 50,848 chilled patrons taking 'noise' and 'applause' cues from the scoreboard like prime-time veterans."[52]

The schedule accommodated the viewers at the expense of the players. The five games played on weekdays did not begin until after 8:30, to accommodate the largest possible television audience. The Saturday game began less than twelve hours after the Friday game ended, due to an ABC college football broadcast later that day. But the Sunday game did not begin until late that afternoon to avoid a ratings conflict with professional football. With the high scoring and frequent commercial breaks, the opening game took three hours and 18 minutes. The Sunday game took three hours and 48 minutes. Beyond a doubt, the league recognized baseball's status as yet another entertainment choice for the American consumer and tailored the World Series to appease the broadest segment of the American public.[53]

In the face of the grueling weather, scheduling vagaries, and, most important, the Orioles' superior play, Stargell remained cool. "All we need is three one-day winning streaks," he calmly pronounced. Matching a feat performed by only three previous world champions, the Pirates recovered from the deficit and won the World Series. In the tradition of the decade's great Pirates teams, they combined strong pitching with spectacular hitting, batting a collective .323. Stargell, naturally, led the comeback. In the seventh game, with his team down 1-0 in the sixth inning, Stargell belted a two-run home run and scored the winning run in an ultimate 4-1 victory. He had twelve hits in the series, including four in the final game and three home runs. Capping a string of awards that included the Most Valuable Player of the National League Championship Series and co-MVP of the National League, he was named World Series MVP.[54]

But the 1979 World Series was not just a recognition of his baseball talent—it was a forum for the canonization of Willie Stargell. "Stargell Takes Spot Next to Mom and Flag," proclaimed a headline in the *Pittsburgh Post-Gazette*. He had become more than a baseball player: "He began to transcend the playing field, to become a revered father figure." The *New York Times* speculated on Stargell's popularity had he played in New York City. National magazines placed Stargell at the center of their World Series coverage. *Sports Illustrated* named him, along with Pittsburgh Steelers quarterback Terry Bradshaw, as Sportsman of the Year. The Smithsonian Institution displayed his uniform. He had crossed the line between "prominence and pre-eminence" and had become, in the words of one writer, "a full-blown national celebrity," in league with such other black superstars as Julius Erving, Reggie Jackson, and O.J. Simpson. In his sweet, almost corny insistence on the Pirate family, his leadership in the locker room, and his heroics on the field, Willie Stargell both reflected an ethic of black culture that had existed on the team throughout the decade, and had projected his message to a broad interracial American audience. He was a "hard moral man," disco-style.[55]

Thrust into the national spotlight, Stargell reflected on his own upbringing. In the interview room following the World Series triumph, he called his sister to join him on the platform. Her presence brought back a flood of memories from his poor childhood in Alameda, California, where he learned to play baseball hitting rocks with a stick and living on "wish sandwiches" ("That's when you have two pieces of bread and you wish you had some meat to put in between"). The victory also allowed him to expound on his team's family concept. "We took that song 'We Are Family' and identified with it. We weren't trying to be sassy or fancy. We're just a ballclub that is a family in our clubhouse. And that's why we won the World Series, that's why we came from behind." "I hope the world can learn from this," he later added. "As men coming together that's it. From all points of the country, all states, blacks, whites, Latins coming together for a common cause."[56]

Eight years earlier, during the 1971 World Series, Stargell had performed poorly, batting only .208 and driving in one run. Yet he remained unruffled throughout that travail, explaining his lack of histrionics by nodding toward his four-year-old son and saying, "There's a time in life when a man has to decide if he's going to *be* a man." This same self-assurance and maturity drew legions of admirers during the triumphant 1979 campaign. But Stargell's explanation also reflected on the larger issues of race relations and masculinity with the Pirates during the 1970s. The Pirates' black stars possessed various personalities and political philosophies, but all guided their public and private actions by the quest to achieve proper respect. Roberto Clemente's demands for recognition, Al Oliver's frustration with his salary and position, Dock Ellis's refusal to sign autographs in a cage, Dave Parker's gleaming gold necklace, Willie Stargell's pleas for interracial cooperation—all spoke to their positions as proud, black, male athletes in an entertainment culture. In different but interconnected ways, they all insisted on being treated with the respect due every man.[57]

Aram Goudsouzian is a scholar of sport and film history and is currently writing a biography of Sidney Poitier.

10

COAL, STEEL, AND GRIDIRON

HIGH SCHOOL FOOTBALL IN THE PITTSBURGH AREA

PAUL J. ZBIEK

"GREAT FOOTBALL country," once exclaimed Joe Namath, one of the many gridiron legends from the steel and coal towns of southwestern Pennsylvania.[1] Although "Broadway Joe" was never known for understatement, his quotation may be just that. The region has produced some of football's true greats, over one hundred of whom have played in the National Football League (NFL).

At one time or another, almost all of the major college powers have concentrated recruiting efforts in southwestern Pennsylvania's hills and valleys. The region's almost mythical devotion to the game originates on high school playing fields, once referred to by former University of Pittsburgh coach Johnny Majors as "the bedrock of high school football."[2] Scholastic football, a part of southwestern Pennsylvania society for over a century, is an integral part of the region's psyche.

In 1892 Pittsburgh (and the surrounding area) was in the midst of transformation. This steel- and coal-producing center played a major role in America's dramatic post–Civil War industrial expansion. Large-scale urbanization resulted, and a wide variety of cultural and socioeconomic groups had to learn to live and work together. The rapid growth, coupled with a diverse social structure, often resulted in conflict, as witnessed in the violence of the Homestead Strike in July of 1892.[3]

With the turbulence that year the establishment of the first public-school football teams at Pittsburgh High and New Castle High seemed rather unimportant, but in reality a major phenomenon was born.[4] The result, as many have claimed, was southwestern Pennsylvania's superiority in scholastic football, leading to the region's national recognition as a training ground for athletes who established the popularity of college and professional football.

FOOTBALL AND THE COMMUNITY

Football was more than just sport to the people and towns of southwestern Pennsylvania. It was a means of community identification, where pride in one's hometown was directly linked to the success of the high school football team. Football also helped to break down ethnic and class barriers. For the children of Eastern and Southern European immigrants and Southern African Americans, football was a means of assimilation into contemporary American life.

Interscholastic football created some negative situations as well. Community pride often developed into parochialism, as football-based local rivalries precluded regional cooperation. And the importance of high school football sometimes relegated education to a secondary status. Despite these drawbacks, however, there is no doubt that the sport has played a major role in the history of southwestern Pennsylvania.[5]

The establishment and development of high school football in southwestern Pennsylvania was linked to three major occurrences in American history: industrialization, educational reform, and the rise of popular spectator sports. Each played a vital role in why the sport became so important to southwestern Pennsylvanians.

THE STEEL CITY

Although Pittsburgh was already an iron-making center prior to the Civil War, the need for wartime armaments hastened the city's industrial growth. Following the war, new technology allowed Pittsburgh to add steel manufacturing to its ironmaking heritage. By 1900 half of the world's iron and two-thirds of the nation's steel came from the Pittsburgh area. Many surrounding communities became "steel towns," while others mined the coal necessary to fuel the giant furnaces in the mills. As steel became the key ingredient in America's massive industrial expansion, Pittsburgh grew expeditiously. With a population of fewer than 50,000 prior to the Civil War, the city grew to 321,616 in 1900, with comparable growth in the surrounding communities.[6]

The region's original settlers, Scotch-Irish and English, were followed by Germans, Welsh, Scots, and Irish in the first half of the nineteenth century. The late-nineteenth-century migration saw large numbers of Poles, Slovaks, Italians, Greeks, Ukrainians, Hungarians, Croats, Slovenians, and Serbs come to the Pittsburgh area. An influx of African Americans from the mid-South arrived in the early 1900s. These diverse groups were not only divided by culture and ethnic neighborhoods, but also by a stratified employment structure. Generally speaking, members of the established ethnic groups held the management and skilled labor positions, while the recent arrivals toiled at the unskilled jobs. People were more likely to identify with their ethnic group than with a geographic community.[7]

EDUCATION

The second major phenomenon to influence the development of high school football was educational reform. Industrial expansion and political democratization increased the need and demand for public secondary education. In the mid-nineteenth century, public high schools were being established throughout the Commonwealth. New Castle and Monongahela City founded the first public schools in southwestern Pennsylvania in 1854, followed by Pittsburgh (1855), Washington (1856), Latrobe (1859), Sewickley (1862), and Butler and Allegheny (1868). The Pennsylvania Constitution of 1873 made clear provisions for the support of secondary education and by 1900 at least a dozen other cities and boroughs chartered public high schools in southwestern Pennsylvania. With the new century, additional cities and boroughs established secondary schools, while legislation in 1895 and 1901 encouraged rural townships to create central high schools. In 1900 Pennsylvania had at least 300 secondary schools, with over 27,000 students, which was only 6 percent of those eligible for enrollment.[8]

While many affluent children attended private preparatory schools, high schools now attracted children of the rising middle class. In southwestern Pennsylvania the offspring of mill and mine supervisors and skilled workers, almost exclusively from Anglo, Celtic, or German descent, were most likely to attend. Since the children of the immigrant mill- and mineworkers were expected to find employment upon reaching adolescence, it was rare to see any attend secondary school. Rural families often discouraged their children from pursuing an education since it took them away from farm work.

Despite the small enrollment and shortage of community and state funding, students often built strong bonds in these schools. The upwardly mobile nature of the student body made them emulate the extracurricular activities of colleges and prep schools.[9]

SPECTATOR SPORTS

The shifting of America from a rural to urban culture played an important role in the rise of popular spectator sports. Although the upper class had long enjoyed organized sporting competition, by the late 1800s a growing middle class also had the time and money for leisure activities. Although the laboring class worked long hours for little pay, many still had more time and money than farmers did. The proximity of life in the cities made entertainment more accessible and the closing of the frontier brought forth the need for an "artificial frontier," where people could test their strength and character through organized sport.

Oftentimes sport had class distinctions. Boxing was seen as a working-class activity, while baseball was enjoyed by both the workers and the middle class. Such activities as rowing and sailing were solely the domain of the upper class. Football, however, was able to span all classes and ethnic groups. Since it was first played on the elite campuses of Harvard, Yale, and Princeton, it became acceptable to the upper class, but soon the middle class brought the sport to the new high schools.

The hard-fought style of the game also appealed to the laborers in the mines, mills, and factories. While they did not represent an academic institution, they organized clubs or simply held impromptu games near their places of work. Even though the children of immigrants were discouraged or forbidden to play football, it was not uncommon for young boys take part in informal games.[10]

With industrialization, education, and the rise of spectator sports in America, the specific conditions of southwestern Pennsylvania contributed to football's tremendous popularity in the region. Pittsburgh, and the surrounding communities, had the wide cross-section of social classes that embraced the game. An upper class that had gained wealth and affluence in steel and related industries attended elite prep schools and colleges where they saw football as a contest of gentlemen, where one could demonstrate "manliness." The growing middle class, ingrained with Protestant values of hard work and competition, found high school football to be a recreational outlet for these ideals. For the children of immigrant and migrant laborers, seeking to assimilate to a new culture, football was a way to show their "Americanness."

The geographic conditions of southwestern Pennsylvania were conducive for the development of football. The compact nature of towns, so often centered around a steel mill or coal mine, made it easy for young men to form tight-knit social and athletic bounds. However, unlike urban areas, there was usually some open space near the mills or mines that could be used for football. Since sections of the city and surrounding towns were often separated by geographic barriers, such as hills or waterways, an insular effect often occurred. This intracommunity parochialism manifested itself into fierce intercommunity rivalries that were played out on the football fields.[11]

THE BEGINNINGS OF HIGH SCHOOL FOOTBALL

Of all the sports gaining popularity in the late 1800s, football was the logical choice as the first extracurricular sport adopted by the new high schools. Boxing was seen as too rowdy for the scholastic scene, and baseball season occurred primarily when school was out of session. Although schools were encouraged to incorporate gymnastics and exercise programs, these were more for physical training than interscholastic athletics. Basketball would soon gain popularity, but the game was created in 1891 and would take a few more years to find its place in scholastic sport.

The first interscholastic football in Pennsylvania was played between the prep schools of the Philadelphia area. In 1887 the Interacademic League became the first organized conference of secondary schools in the state. Kiskiminetas Springs School (commonly known as Kiski School) recorded the first game played by a secondary-level team in southwestern Pennsylvania. In 1890 they were defeated by Indiana (Pennsylvania) Normal School by a score of 30-0. Kiski School did not play another game until 1892 when they defeated Pittsburgh High School, 12-0. In that same year New Castle High School began its storied football history with a loss to Rayen High School of Youngstown, Ohio, and Park Institute defeated Allegheny High School. Pittsburgh, New Castle, and Allegheny thus became the first public high schools in Pennsylvania to field teams. Also in 1892 two other private preparatory schools, East Liberty Academy and Shadyside Academy, began competition. These humble beginnings gave little indication of the future of scholastic football in southwestern Pennsylvania.[12]

The history of southwestern Pennsylvania high school football can be divided into five eras. The formative years (early 1890s–1906) were a time of unorganized, student-directed programs. With the formation of the Western Pennsylvania Interscholastic Athletic League (WPIAL) in 1906, the second era began. From that date until the early 1920s, there was increasing expansion and public interest in the sport. The third era, from the 1920s to the mid-1940s, saw the sport reach nearly every public school in southwestern Pennsylvania and the participation of the children of the "New Immigrants." During the fourth era, from the mid-1940s through the 1970s, southwestern Pennsylvania reached its legendary status. The region not only produced some of the finest teams in the nation but would also be the home of athletes who became college and professional legends. This era brought about the full involvement of African Americans in scholastic sport. The most recent era, linked to the decline of the steel industry, witnessed the growth of the consolidated suburban schools and the increased competition from other sections of Pennsylvania and the nation for football superiority.[13]

Scholastic football throughout Pennsylvania began in a rather disorganized and unrecognized manner. Many of the programs were generated by the students and may have received some assistance from interested parties in the community. However, the massive fan support that would be a hallmark of the game was lacking. In the 1890s attendance numbered in the hundreds at best; those watching would most likely be students or family members of the players.

Newspapers of the time did not devote a great deal of attention to even major sporting events, so high school contests were relegated to only a few lines. Scheduling was sporadic; teams often placed advertisements for games only a few days before the contest. The teams themselves did not exist from year to year, coming and going for no apparent reason. Public high schools often played prep school and even college teams. Few of the smaller or rural schools had teams during the formative years.[14]

A review of the original public school teams shows the sporadic nature of the 1890s' schedules. In 1893 Pittsburgh High School (later known as Pittsburgh Central) defeated Allegheny High School, 14-0, in what appears to be the first contest between two public schools from southwestern Pennsylvania. Pittsburgh High School was undefeated in four games that year but the other contests were with prep school and college junior-varsity teams. Pittsburgh and Allegheny met only occasionally over the next decade as both teams played most of their games against prep schools. Other than Pittsburgh High School, South High School was the only city school fielding a team in the 1800s. They began in 1898 with losses to Pittsburgh Academy and Pittsburgh High School. New Castle High School, another of the first teams in 1892, did not record another game until 1898. They won three contests and from that year have continually fielded a squad. Most of New Castle's early competition was with local college junior-varsity teams. Only two other southwestern Pennsylvania high schools supported teams prior to 1900. Both Apollo High School and Greensburg High School began playing in 1898.[15] When compared to other regions of Pennsylvania, the Pittsburgh area was slightly later in the development of high school football. Teams in the anthracite region, the southcentral section, and the southeastern sections of the state were involved in more regular scheduling and played more games in the 1890s.[16] However, any delay was quickly made up for with the explosion of the sport in the early 1900s.

Between 1900 and the founding of the WPIAL in 1906, thirty-seven additional teams were established in southwestern Pennsylvania. Allegheny County had the most with fourteen, while Westmoreland County had nine. By 1905 the sport was initiated in all southwestern Pennsylvania counties. Because of the growing number of teams, public schools increasingly scheduled games among each other, rather than with prep schools and college junior-varsity squads. Traditional and long-standing rivalries began in this formative era. Early clashes included Beaver against New Brighton in 1903, Beaver Falls–New Brighton in 1904, Monessen–Charleroi in 1905, and Rochester–Beaver and Connellsville–Greensville in 1906. The first interscholastic football conference in southwestern Pennsylvania, the Beaver Valley League, was formed in 1905. It was short-lived, disbanding after the 1909 season. Beaver and Beaver Falls each won two championships, with Beaver holding the best overall record.[17]

The growing popularity of the sport made school officials realize that some form of governance was necessary. Especially of concern were the eligibility requirements. In response, administrators from the Allegheny Preparatory School, Shadyside Academy, and the Pittsburgh City Schools formed the WPIAL in 1906. Schools joining that first year were Allegheny, Beaver Falls, Butler, Homestead, Johnstown, Pittsburgh Central, Shadyside Academy, Washington, and Wilkinsburg. In the next few years four additional Pittsburgh city schools joined the league. South came in after reestablishing football in 1911, while Peabody, Fifth Avenue, and Brushton joined after forming teams in 1911, 1912, and 1913 respectively.

For the first eight years of operation no championship was awarded. Then, in 1914, the Pittsburgh Chapter of the Syracuse University Alumni Association established the Syracuse Cup, to be presented yearly to the WPIAL school with the best overall record. The first award went to Wilkinsburg, while the following year Wilkinsburg defeated Pittsburgh Fifth Avenue in a playoff for the crown. In 1916 McKeesport, New Castle, and Pittsburgh Schenley entered into competition and Wilkinsburg won a third straight championship. Additions in 1917 were Crafton and New Brighton. Pittsburgh Central, one of the pioneer schools in southwestern Pennsylvania football, closed its doors in 1915. Although the WPIAL had a certain degree of governance over the schools and the Syracuse Cup was given to the best team, scheduling was still somewhat erratic, demonstrated by the fact that the 1917 playoff teams, Johnstown and Washington, each played only two

WPIAL foes. The 1918 nationwide influenza epidemic eliminated much of that season and no Cup was awarded.[18]

With nineteen new members coming on board in 1919 and a total membership of fifty-five by 1922, the WPIAL now included large and small schools throughout southwestern Pennsylvania.[19] Although scholastic football had grown in popularity and scope since the formation of the WPIAL, it still was not all-encompassing. Three factors, national in scope with local repercussions, would change this.

CHANGES BETWEEN THE WORLD WARS

Although statewide high school enrollment increased nearly 500 percent from 1900 to 1920, only about 40 percent of the eligible students attended in the latter year. Thus a large segment of southwestern Pennsylvania's student and fan population was excluded from scholastic sport by choice or necessity. However, with increased emphasis on compulsory secondary education, the high school student population grew by 855 percent between 1920 and 1928. Nearly 60 percent of those eligible were attending high school.[20]

The immigrant assimilation process also brought about an increased interest in high school football. By the 1920s Eastern and Southern European immigrants had been in the Pittsburgh area for over a generation. Although the ethnic culture and neighborhood were still important, American popular culture was increasingly becoming part of their lives. This was especially true for the children of immigrants. As more of them attended secondary school, they had an increased desire to participate in modern American activities in addition to functions. Compounding this were the 1920s' congressional restrictions on immigration, which diminished access to the native culture.

In addition, in the 1920s sport became an increasingly significant part of popular culture. There had been interest but the passion and adulation for teams and players became far-reaching. When America entered into the era of mass consumerism and mass media, with increased time and money, accompanied with the progress in radio and print journalism, Americans craved entertainment of all varieties. Sport figures such as Babe Ruth, Jack Dempsey, and Red Grange became national heroes.[21] While the residents of southwestern Pennsylvania's mill and mining communities followed national events, they found their local high school team more accessible and affordable. And since almost every town had its own high school team, the residents could readily identify with their local heroes and team.[22]

The popularity and community support for scholastic football in the 1920s was not just athletic in scope. It also marked the advent of a sociological shift in western Pennsylvania. Scholastic football was one of the first experiences that unified the diverse cultural and economic groups of the region. Throughout the period of industrial development, one's position on issues such as unionism and prohibition were linked to ethnicity, social class, and place of residence. For example, the majority of Poles were laborers who lived together in an ethnic neighborhood within a larger municipality. This reinforced cultural bonds and deemphasized any identification with the municipality.

When increasing numbers of second-generation Americans attended public schools, however, they looked beyond the ethnic neighborhood. The high school became a center of the larger community and the football team was its most visible representation. The movement from ethnic to municipal identification was illustrated by the increasing number of Eastern and Southern European names appearing on team rosters. Some of the greatest players of the 1920s to mid-1940s era, such as Johnny Lujack, Arnold Galiffa and George Blanda, were of Eastern and Southern European ancestry. By the 1920s crowds of over 10,000 were not uncommon at scholastic games. As sport became an integral part of American culture, and as more people from all ethnic and socioeconomic backgrounds involved themselves in this popular culture, interest in high school football grew and crossed all cultural and economic barriers.[23]

Washington High School was the only multiple winner of the Syracuse Cup during the 1920s. They captured the WPIAL championship in 1920, 1923, and 1926 and were runner-up in 1922. Oftentimes the Syracuse Cup was surrounded by controversy. Washington and Pittsburgh Fifth Avenue did not have the best records in 1920 but were selected to play for the championship based on schedule strength. In 1921 Johnstown was undefeated in the WPIAL but was denied a playoff spot because of outside losses. In protest Johnstown left the WPIAL and helped organize the Western Conference in the Allegheny Mountains. Confusion reigned for the 1924 playoff picture as six teams remained contenders in the final weeks of play. However, Jeannette, Norwin, and Braddock all had to forfeit their wins because of ineligible players. Pittsburgh Schenley was not included in the playoffs and dropped out of the WPIAL. Turtle Creek, who should have been included in the playoffs after the forfeit fiasco, was simply ignored. Eventually, New Castle was awarded their first crown. The situation prompted the *Pittsburgh Post* to write that the Syracuse Cup committee was "steeped to its neck in the most disgraceful and disgusting mess of circumstances any school affair have ever have been."

A subsequent controversy in 1926 that also included non-WPIAL losses and forfeits prompted the WPIAL to adopt a rating system developed by Ralph Gardner, a New Castle High School mathematics teacher. Also, the WPIAL abandoned the Syracuse Cup committee structure and took control of the award decision. The 1927 Syracuse Cup was the last awarded and the following year Westinghouse, the remaining Pittsburgh city school in the WPIAL, broke its affiliation.

Although the Syracuse Cup and the Pittsburgh schools were driving forces behind the early accomplishments of southwestern Pennsylvania scholastic football, neither were necessary for its continued success. With 113 members in 1929, the WPIAL had established itself as one of the premier scholastic football organizations in the country. The powerful teams and stellar athletes that carried this reputation were most often from the steel and coal towns that surrounded Pittsburgh rather than the city itself.[24] It was the combination of community-based scholastic sport and the WPIAL's unifying governance that created a basis for the achievements of southwestern Pennsylvania high school football.

Because of the wide range of enrollments among the WPIAL schools, classifications were first established in 1928. In that year Class A included the larger schools, many located in the industrial cities. Class B was comprised of the smaller schools often found in the coal-mining areas. The rapidly growing enrollments in the industrial cities prompted the WPIAL to create a Class AA for the region's twelve largest schools. In 1935 Class AA was expanded to thirty-two schools. In the pre–World War II era, New Castle was a dominant force in Class AA, winning or sharing three titles. Jeannette won or shared two AA championships in the same era. North Braddock Scott, whose enrollment figures moved the school from A to AA in 1935, was impressive in both classes. They garnered A championships in 1933 and 1934 and AA titles in 1935 and 1937. McKees Rocks won successive A titles in 1935 and 1936. Glassport was the dominant team in Class B, winning or sharing five championships in the 1930s.[25]

After their departure from the WPIAL in 1927, the Pittsburgh City League continued to hold its own championship. A year before their WPIAL departure, the league established two divisions, based upon enrollment. The winners in each division met in a playoff to decide the overall champion. Schenley won the first crown. Westinghouse was the power in the pre–World War II era, winning five titles and sharing two.[26]

The tremendous growth and power of southwestern Pennsylvania football during this pre–World War II era prompted arguments over regional superiority. Since interregional competition was uncommon, no section of Pennsylvania could lay claim to being the best. Prior to World War II, teams from southwestern Pennsylvania played sixteen games against schools from the eastern part of the state and won ten of those contests. However, eleven of those games were between Greensburg and Harrisburg Tech. Greensburg was a participant in all of the other contests with eastern teams, with the exception of New Castle's victories over Harrisburg Tech in 1924 and 1925.[27] With such a limited record it would be hard to determine comparative strength clearly. The anthracite region of northeastern Pennsylvania and the state's southcentral region also claimed the superiority of their scholastic football. Schools such as Johnstown, Kingston, Kulpmont, Mount Carmel, and Shamokin established their gridiron reputations by gaining "state championships" in the 1920s and 1930s. These champions were decided by winning the season-ending playoff between the Eastern Conference and Western Conference titlists. The Eastern Conference consisted of schools primarily from Districts 2, 4, and 11, along with some teams from District 3. The Western Conference included schools from Districts 5 and 6, along with some from District 9. While anthracite-area schools became a dominant force in these contests, the term "state champion" was obviously misleading. The lack of any competition between the WPIAL and the anthracite region preclude any real determination of statewide superiority.[28]

Despite the absence of any clear determination of scholastic power in Pennsylvania, similarities existed between southwestern Pennsylvania and other powerful football regions. The strongest teams were most often located in steel or coal-mining communities. While these communities had fairly large, rapidly growing populations, they were not among the largest cities in the state. Many of the towns had a certain degree of geographic isolation. Sometimes this meant that they were miles from another large town. However, as was more the case in southwestern Pennsylvania where large communities were relatively close, the isolation resulted from hilly terrain and waterways. Also, industrial barriers created a certain degree of isolation; the various types of mining or steel operations created a unique character in each community. These differences may not have been recognizable to an outsider, who might view every town as similar, but the residents of each community clearly viewed their own town as distinct from its neighbors. This isolation often caused the people to look inward toward the events of their own town. The high school football team became both a source of pride within the town and a representative of the community to outsiders. Powerful teams created a more impressive image and generated a greater degree of pride.

Ethnic diversity was another common element among the most powerful football towns of the pre–World War II era. English, Germans, and Scotch-Irish were the original settlers in Pennsylvania. Communities that moved from agricultural to industrial in the eighteenth century first saw large numbers of Irish, English, Welsh, Scot, and German immigrants from the 1820s to the 1870s. From the 1880s to 1923, an even greater influx of immigrants came from Eastern and Southern Europe. The regions that gained football predominance were part of this pattern. This phenomenon occurred throughout all of southwestern Pennsylvania and the anthracite region.[29]

There tends to be a correlation with industrial-based immigration and the growth and popularity of high school football. While football and other scholastic sports were popular in areas that remained either rural or German- and Anglo-based societies, the overall intensity of the community support was greater in industrial, ethnic regions like southwestern Pennsylvania and the anthracite region. The reasons for this were a complex combination of ethnicity, industrialization, and sport.

The steel and coal industries were relatively new and growing rapidly when scholastic football came of age. Consequently, many of the communities that grew in these regions were less encumbered by the traditions of the past. The massive influx of new immigrants and urban residents put their own interpretation on the traditional Protestant values of hard work and competition. Football was a new sport, had a large number of team participants, was fast moving and even violent, and focused more on team glory than on the individual. These characteristics were reflective of the new industrial areas, with their large populations, bustling and chaotic communities, and the common belief that "team" success, whether it was a corporation or a labor union, was the prime motivation. Scholastic football became more than an outlet for youthful development; it became a culture in itself. In a sense, this culture of football and the culture of southwestern Pennsylvania and other newly industrialized areas were quite compatible. When an area as populated as southwestern Pennsylvania collectively promoted a sport that was representative of their culture, the production of top teams and players was to be expected.

WORLD WAR II AND BEYOND

The Great Depression and World War II had some impact on scholastic football in southwestern Pennsylvania. Fan interest remained high during the Depression and provided a needed diversion from the crisis. Attendance did decline, as some potential spectators could not justify spending the admission price. Despite the problems, action continued. Some schools seemed unaffected by the economic crisis. Traditional powers such as Aliquippa, Butler, Glassport, New Castle, and North Braddock Scott established spring football programs in the 1930s.

World War II had a greater impact. Some schools dropped or curtailed their programs because of fuel rationing or other wartime impediments. The departure of so many young men also depleted the coaching and spectator base. Bell Township administrators attracted national media attention when they hired a woman to coach their team. New Castle continued its winning ways during the war years and Donora developed as a force in the Class AA ranks. Glassport moved to Class A and continued their success while Aspinwall took two Class

B championships during the war. Westinghouse continued as the City League power in this era.[30]

Despite the war's limitations, the era developed young men who would give southwestern Pennsylvania its great reputation in football and reflected the urban/ethnic connection of high school football. Johnny Lujack, a Connellsville product, was the first in a long line of high school stars to go on to a successful college and professional career. After graduation from Connellsville High School, Lujack matriculated to Notre Dame, where he won the Heisman Trophy in 1947. Others who played during the war years were Leon Hart of Turtle Creek, a Notre Dame Heisman winner in 1949, and Donora's Arnold Galiffa, whose play at Army earned him a spot in the College Football Hall of Fame. Pro Football Hall of Famer George Blanda, arguably the most durable player in professional football history, played for Youngwood High School during the war years.[31] As these men moved beyond the steel- and coal-town playing fields, they gained national recognition for the quality of the teams and the individuals from southwestern Pennsylvania.

Combined with the previously mentioned conditions that made football so popular in the ethnic, industrial communities, a number of factors would contribute to the increasing greatness of southwestern Pennsylvania scholastic football in the post–World War II years. The industrial towns benefited from America's economic boom as they provided steel and coal, the basic ingredients for the consumer society. Industrial workers now enjoyed a better lifestyle and encouraged their children to participate in interscholastic athletics. The war era had Americanized the children of immigrants to a point where community and school activities often took priority over the ethnic culture. Additionally, aided by the GI Bill and the need for managers, many residents gained white-collar status. Increased affluence prompted suburbanization and new school districts.

While these schools would lead the way for the overall dominance of southwestern Pennsylvania in all scholastic sports, football still reigned supreme. Not only did the steel and coal towns develop strong teams but, increasingly, so did the suburban schools. Another factor that further developed the prestige of southwestern Pennsylvania football was the entrance of another ethnic group. African Americans had migrated from the South to the Pittsburgh area by the 1920s, but it was not until the postwar era that they fully participated in scholastic athletics. During and after the war an increasing number arrived to take advantage of the higher-paying steel mill jobs. As with new arrivals in the past, the young people were anxious to participate in the popular social activities of the region. For young men, this meant athletics. African American students would make their presence known in a variety of sports in southwestern Pennsylvania, but the popularity of football would bring many to that particular athletic endeavor.[32] With regard to high school football in the years following World War II, southwestern Pennsylvania had the best of both worlds. There was enough economic vitality to support a strong commitment to the game. Simultaneously, even in the suburbs, there was still a strong connection to the ethnic/industrial culture that made the sport reflective of the region.

The post–World War II era began as Donora repeated as 1945 Class AA champion with a playoff victory over New Kensington. Dormont and Chartiers Township took the Class A and B titles respectively. Teams from the industrial cities continued to dominate the sport throughout the late 1940s and the 1950s. In Class AA New Kensington, New Castle, and Aliquippa each won two titles, while Donora won one championship outright and shared another. New Kensington went undefeated in both 1946 and 1947. They won the 1946 crown without a playoff. In 1947 they defeated Har-Brack in a playoff game played under tense circumstances. Because of the bitterness of that rivalry, New Kensington and Har-Brack agreed to suspend their Thanksgiving Day game. Ironically, the two would now meet in a season-ending match to decide the WPIAL championship. The 1947 championship was the last for New Kensington. They were undefeated in 1957, but cancellations due to the Asian flu epidemic reduced the season to seven games and they were not eligible for the title. The football fortunes of New Kensington began to fade after that 1957 season. New Castle suffered only one loss during the 1948 and 1949 seasons and gained the WPIAL crown both seasons. Although they did not win any championships in the 1950s they continued to be one of the winningest teams in the state. Aliquippa had, perhaps, the strongest teams during the 1950s. They won championships in 1952 and 1955 and lost the 1959 title game by one point to Charleroi.[33]

Braddock was the power of Class A during the 1950s. After tying Midland to share the 1954 title, they held the championship for the remainder of the decade. In the process they had a fifty-six game undefeated streak. Midland and New Canonsburg each gained outright Class A titles and shared another during the late 1940s and 1950s. In Class B Bridgeville captured championships in 1948 and 1949 and had only one losing season from 1947 to 1959. Masontown also gained two WPIAL titles, winning in 1947 and 1950. The school continued their strong football heritage during the 1950s prior to becoming part of the Albert Gallatin consolidation in 1960. In 1950, to provide an opportunity for small schools to win a WPIAL championship, the league initiated a Class C division for school with fewer than 250 students. Twelve of the twenty teams were in Greene and Washington Counties and were able to schedule the five games needed to qualify for the crown. However, the other schools were scattered throughout District 7 and had difficulty finding other Class C squads. Class C was abandoned in 1952, with McDonald winning two of the three crowns.[34]

Westinghouse dominated the Pittsburgh City League between 1945 and 1959. They won every championship except the years 1950, 1952, and 1953. Carrick was the strongest of the smaller Division II schools, winning nine divisional crowns and defeating Peabody in the 1952 playoff.[35]

A number of stellar athletes emerged from southwestern Pennsylvania in the post–World War II years. Quarterback Babe Parilli led Rochester High School to its finest seasons in the late 1940s. Dick Modzelewski anchored the Har-Brack line during the same period. Parilli and Modzelewski played college football with the University of Kentucky and the University of Maryland respectively. Both were enshrined in the College Football Hall of Fame and had successful NFL careers. Pittsburgh natives Joe Schmidt and Johnny Unitas went on to NFL stardom and the Hall of Fame. Schmidt stayed at home for college at the University of Pittsburgh and was one of the great linebackers for the Detroit Lions. At 5'10" and 138 pounds, Unitas was ignored by his dream school, Notre Dame, upon graduation from St. Justin's

High School. He went on to the University of Louisville and was drafted by the hometown Steelers. The Steelers cut him and after a stint as a construction worker and semi-pro player, he was picked up by the Baltimore Colts. The rest was history. Unitas not only became one of the greatest quarterbacks ever, but he also moved the game into the modern era with the sudden-death championship victory over the New York Giants in 1959.

Mike Ditka starred for WPIAL champions Aliquippa in the mid-1950s. He was the first southwestern Pennsylvanian to gain membership in both the College Football Hall of Fame and the Pro Football Hall of Fame. Ditka played for the University of Pittsburgh and the Chicago Bears.[36] The colorful Ditka also gained fame as a coach. He won the Super Bowl with the Bears and later directed the New Orleans Saints.

New trends in the 1960s greatly affected the future of southwestern Pennsylvania football. Post–World War II suburbanization and the baby boom brought about a shift in the region's population patterns and, consequently, new scholastic powers began to emerge. While the decline of the steel industry was still two decades away, many upwardly mobile white residents began moving to the newly developed suburbs. Pittsburgh's population dropped over 10 percent between 1950 and 1960 and 15 percent from 1960 to 1970. New Castle and New Kensington both lost approximately one-fifth of their respective populations between 1950 and 1979. Beaver Falls lost 8 percent of their residents from 1950 to 1960 and suffered a 14 percent decline in the following decade. The coal-mining regions also suffered a similar decline as Fayette and Greene Counties both had approximately 20 percent losses in the same two-decade period. Meanwhile, the suburban communities underwent a dramatic increase in residents. West Mifflin Township's population increased from 17,985 in 1950 to 27,576 in 1970, while by 1970 Bethel Township nearly tripled in size from 1950 with 33,806 residents.[37] The demographic shifts brought about realignment in the WPIAL classifications as many of the industrial and coal-town schools dropped to Class A or B while the suburban schools moved into Class AA.[38]

The consolidation of smaller school districts into regional jointures was another trend that began in the 1950s. Although the larger industrial city high schools survived, many of the smaller industrial and coal-mining towns lost their community-based schools through consolidation. Even in the growing suburbs, schools joined together in hopes of creating more efficient and productive school districts to serve the more affluent population. In the 1930s over ninety public schools from Allegheny County played football in the WPIAL. By the 1970s fewer than half that number played.[39]

Suburbanization and consolidation began to change the nature of high school sports in western Pennsylvania and other regions of the Commonwealth. Football was less likely to be played near a downtown high school within walking distance of the whole community. Increasingly, the games were played at a field adjacent to a new high school. Since the consolidations were comprised of a number of municipalities, the sport lost some of its community identification. One-time rivals were now part of the same school district. To some fans these changes were hard to accept, especially in the coal towns where the community-based high school team was no longer the pride of the community. Even if the community school remained in existence, it no longer was able to field competitive teams. However, in some of the suburbs, the expansion of the community coincided with the growth of the new high school. Consequently, a new sense of identification was established.

The athletes and teams began to change with suburbanization and consolidation. In the suburban areas many students came from more affluent families. In these wealthier districts funding supported increasingly sophisticated football programs. Weight rooms, summer football camps, and more specialized coaches improved the quality of play. Increasingly the population base of the industrial cities and, even more so, the coal towns was lower income and elderly, unable to support the type of programs being developed in the suburbs. Since the steel industry declined later than coal mining did, some of the steel communities retained strong athletic programs. However, their median income was still less than the suburbs. Thus, it was not just the increasing enrollments that shifted the balance of football power to the suburbs.[40] This trend was occurring statewide, as a movement toward suburban athletic superiority could be seen in the wealthier suburban schools.[41]

The first clear indication of the postwar growth of suburban schools was seen in 1954 when West View moved to Class AA and the industrial school district of Braddock dropped to Class A. In 1955 Baldwin, a suburban township district southeast of Pittsburgh, joined Class AA, and Greensburg suburb Hempfield made the same move the following year. Five more suburban schools, Bethel Park, Elizabeth Forward, North Allegheny, Norwin, and Shaler, followed suit in 1958. Canon-McMillan and Gateway moved to Class AA in 1959. Along with being suburban schools, many of these new Class AA teams were consolidations. Despite the growing number of suburban schools in Class AA, the industrial towns still were winning the Class WPIAL AA championships in the 1950s and early 1960s. This all changed in 1963 when West Mifflin North captured the crown with a victory over Butler. Between 1964 and 1979 (enrollment classifications were changed in 1980) suburban and newly consolidated schools won or shared thirteen Class AA and AAA titles, while schools from the industrial cities won or shared seven. (Class AA was renamed Class AAA in 1973.) The balance of power had clearly shifted. In the same period, twenty-two suburban and consolidated schools moved into Class AA and AAA, while enrollment declines forced ten industrial city schools to drop in classification.[42]

GREAT NAMES FROM WESTERN PENNSYLVANIA

The great players of the era reflected the shift in demographics as suburban and consolidated school players became as prominent as those from the industrial towns. Joe Namath, the Beaver Falls quarterback who went on to college and professional fame, was a direct product of the immigrant/industrial culture. His father migrated from Hungary and worked fifty-one years in the steel mills. Namath, a C student, saw football as a means to a better life. After Namath led coach Larry Bruno's Tigers to a 1960 WPIAL Class AA championship, he starred for coach Paul "Bear" Bryant at the University of Alabama. Namath next signed a record $427,000 contract with the New York Jets of the fledging American Football League. He made his mark on professional sports and American popular culture when he boldly predicted victory over the powerful NFL champion Baltimore Colts in 1969's Super Bowl III. The Jets victory brought about parity between the upstart AFL and the NFL, resulting in an eventual merger. Simultaneously, Namath became a Pro Football Hall of Famer and an American sports icon.[43] He was seen as a product of the tough, industrial town brand of football indigenous to southwestern Pennsylvania. Ironically, as the media began to ingrain that image into the nation's psyche, the reality was changing. Ted Kwalick, of Montour High School's WPIAL Class A 1963 and 1964 championships, like an increasing number of stars, was a product of the growing suburban schools. Kwalick went on to star at Penn State and for the San Francisco 49ers. He was inducted into the College Football Hall of Fame in 1989.[44]

Although the suburban schools were gaining power over the steel and coal towns, the 1960s and 1970s saw future NFL legends emerge from both areas. Southwestern Pennsylvania continued to produce some legendary quarterbacks during the 1960s and 1970s. Butler High School's Terry Hanratty led Notre Dame to a 1966 national championship and was Terry Bradshaw's backup for seven years with the Steelers. Joe Montana was arguably the winningest quarterback in football history. While Ringold High School never won a WPIAL crown under his leadership, he led Notre Dame to a 1977 national title and captured four Super Bowl titles for the San Francisco 49ers in the 1980s. Montana was a three-time Super Bowl Most Valuable Player (MVP) and a two-time NFL MVP. Jim Kelly came out of East Brady High School and matriculated to the University of Miami. He led the Buffalo Bills to four Super Bowl appearances and was selected for five Pro Bowl games. Pittsburgh Central Catholic made its first WPIAL playoffs under the direction of Dan Marino. Marino stayed close to home for his collegiate career at the University of Pittsburgh and became one of the great NFL signal callers with the Miami Dolphins. Marino retired in 2000 as the all-time NFL leader in touchdown passes, passing completions, and passing yardage. Marino also holds season records for touchdown passes (forty-eight) and passing yardage (5,084), both set in 1994. Running back Tony Dorsett led Hopewell Township High School to its best seasons in the early 1970s. University of Pittsburgh coach Johnny Majors prevailed over 100 other recruiters to keep Dorsett at home. Dorsett led Pitt to a 1976 national championship, winning the Heisman Trophy in the process. He later went on to star with the Dallas Cowboys. As of this writing, Dorsett and Mike Ditka were the only two southwestern Pennsylvanians to be enshrined in both the College Football Hall of Fame and the Pro Football Hall of Fame.[45]

PRESENT DAY

In the most recent era of southwestern Pennsylvania scholastic football (1980s–present), major changes affected the sport and the region. In 1980 the WPIAL was reworked as the schools were divided into four classifications of approximately the same number of schools. The playoff system was also changed in that eight teams from each division would be eligible, rather than the past practice of having the two top-rated teams.

On the positive side, the revision included more playoff participants and always settled the championships on the playing field. However, some questioned the wisdom of including teams of, perhaps, lesser quality. Also, the lengthened playoff format would infringe upon the traditional late-season rivalries. In protest of the change, Churchill, Franklin Regional, and Moon played independently of the WPIAL.[46] The revised format prepared the WPIAL for another major change in 1988. After much discussion and debate, the Pennsylvania Interscholastic Athletic Association (PIAA) finally initiated an official state championship playoff. With this the legendary superiority of southwestern Pennsylvania high school football would be put to the test. But there would be an even greater test—not only of the region's football, but one that would challenge all residents of greater Pittsburgh. The transformation of the American economy from industrial to service- and technology-based threatened to put the region in a situation similar to Detroit's Rust Belt, as hundreds of factories and thousands of workers faced an uncertain future.

The decline of heavy industry affected the Pittsburgh metropolitan area in a variety of ways. The population of the industrial communities dropped drastically. Between 1980 and 1990 Pittsburgh dropped 12.7 percent; Aliquippa, 21.8 percent; Beaver Falls, 14.7 percent; Duquesne, 15.5 percent; New Castle, 15.7 percent; and New Kensington, 10 percent. The once rapidly growing suburban communities were also feeling the effects of the economic slowdown. Bethel Park fell by 2.7 percent; West Mifflin, 9 percent; and Baldwin, 10.9 percent. Despite all of the downward trends, there were signs of hope. While Allegheny County lost residents, growth in Butler, Washington, and Westmoreland Counties gave the Pittsburgh metropolitan area an 7.9 percent population increase.[47] Also, the region was moving from an industrial to a service economy. By the 1990s nearly three times as many people worked in service industries as opposed to manufacturing. Health care and research and development were the two fastest-growing service industries.[48]

Southwestern Pennsylvania scholastic football remained a major force during the 1980s and 1990s but was increasingly challenged by other regions of the state and the nation. The 1987 North Hills squad went undefeated and captured the WPIAL Class AAAA crown. The *Pittsburgh Post-Gazette* voted the Indians the top team in Pennsylvania and *USA Today* named them number one in the nation. In 1999 WPIAL coaches selected the 1987 North Hills team the best in the region during the past twenty-five years. The Indians were indeed formidable that year. They outscored opponents 435-20 and had eleven shutouts. Even more impressive was that the twenty opposition points came against the reserve defensive squads. Eric Renkey was selected a *Parade* All-American and seven seniors played Division I and I-AA college football. Pat Carey, a fullback on the team and current North Hills defensive coordinator, stated, "I don't know if anyone will ever put together a team like that again."[49]

The advent of the PIAA state championships in 1988 saw WPIAL teams as finalists in Class AAAA, AAA, and AA. However, only Class AAAA Central Catholic was able to capture the state crown. Upper Saint Clair and North Allegheny, respectively, won the 1989 and 1990 titles, giving the WPIAL a three-year sweep in the largest enrollment category. Perry Traditional Academy, a District 8 school, unseated powerful Berwick, of the anthracite region, for the 1989 Class AAA crown. Aliquippa upheld the tradition of the industrial towns by winning the 1991 Class AA title. In 1993 the WPIAL began another "threepeat" of the Class AAAA championship with a North Hills victory. The 1994 and 1995 winners, McKeesport and Penn Hills, were considered among the finest teams in recent WPIAL history. McKeesport was undefeated in fifteen games, relying on Coach George Smith's powerful wishbone offense. Penn State–bound Brandon Short was both a defensive and offensive force for the Tigers. Penn Hills also had a 15-0 record the following season as they captured the WPIAL and PIAA titles. Coach Gordon's Indians also relied on the run with DeWayne Thompson and Victor Strader both gaining over 1,600 yards. In 1999 Pittsburgh area coaches voted McKeesport the number two team and Penn Hills tied for third in the past twenty-five years. In recent years WPIAL teams have been in the finals in 1996, 1997, and 1998 in both Class AAAA and AAA. However, they were unable to gain the crown, with two of the AAAA losses coming to Central Bucks West and two AAA defeats to Berwick. The WPIAL has had more success in the small school categories. In Class AA South Park captured the 1997 championship. Farrell won back-to-back Class A crowns in 1995 and 1996, while Rochester took the 1998 title.[50]

Since the inception of the PIAA state championships, District 7, the WPIAL, has won the most state championships, with eleven (or 25 percent) of the titles. District 2, encompassing the Wilkes-Barre and Scranton region, has been a close second with ten championships. However, if the statistics are regional in basis, southwestern Pennsylvania is second to the anthracite area, which includes sections but not all of Districts 2, 3, 4 and 11. Anthracite teams have won sixteen titles, six being held by perennial power Berwick and three by Pennsylvania's winningest team, Mount Carmel. Southwestern Pennsylvania leads in title game appearance with thirty-two, compared to twenty-two by anthracite teams. The dominance of these two regions is apparent in that only eight of the forty-four title games have been played without a Pittsburgh area or anthracite team. The dispersal of power has been relatively even with eleven different southwestern Pennsylvania schools winning the PIAA title as compared to nine in the anthracite region. Six different southwestern Pennsylvania schools won Class AAAA crowns while Berwick captured all of the anthracite region's six Class AAA titles. In Class AA Mount Carmel won three of the six anthracite PIAA titles, while different schools have won southwestern Pennsylvania's two titles. Of all southwestern Pennsylvania schools, only Class A Farrell has been able to win more than one PIAA championship. In that category four other WPIAL schools and four anthracite schools gained the crown.

Based upon the state championships and a number of other statistics, some conclusions on the relative power of Pennsylvania scholastic football can be made. While the anthracite region leads in the recent championship series, it appears that there is more of a balance of power in southwestern Pennsylvania. Since the teams in the anthracite region play in different districts, the most powerful squads sometimes do not meet until the interdistrict playoffs. With a greater number of schools in District 7, southwestern Pennsylvania teams need to peak in order to win the district championship, which could hinder them in the state playoffs.

Since teams from the two regions did not play each other prior to the PIAA playoffs, other means of comparison are needed. If one compares the top football players in the history of Pennsylvania, the southwestern region clearly has a numerical advantage. Of the "Top 100 Pennsylvanians in Football," as ranked by Paul B. Beers in 1975, thirty-eight came from the Pittsburgh area, including thirty-one from the WPIAL and seven from the city. Numerically, this rates far above the other regions—southcentral Pennsylvania with fifteen (including six Carlisle Indians); the anthracite region with thirteen; and the Philadelphia metropolitan area with nine.[51]

In the early 1970s the Pittsburgh area also ranked highest in major college recruiting. Allegheny County ranked third in the nation following Los Angeles County, California, and Cook County (Chicago), Illinois. Based upon per capita statistics the ranking becomes more impressive. Of the top twenty-five counties in per capita recruiting, five were southwestern Pennsylvania counties. Beaver was ranked second, behind Jefferson County (Steubenville), Ohio. Westmoreland, Washington, Fayette, and Allegheny ranked sixth, seventh, eighth, and eleventh respectively.[52] While it was clear that southwestern Pennsylvania developed a greater number of top-level football players, was there a greater concentration of football talent in that region? By comparing the number of football greats and major college recruits with the overall population, mixed results appear. When the population of Pittsburgh is included in the statistics, southwestern Pennsylvania becomes less impressive. For example, when considering the per capita production of top-level football stars, southwestern Pennsylvania is statistically equal to the anthracite region. However, if the Pittsburgh numbers are excluded, the WPIAL has a clear advantage over the eastern coal regions. Additionally, when Pittsburgh is included in the per capita recruiting figures, Allegheny County trails four exclusively WPIAL counties. The overall conclusion is probably not surprising to fans of southwestern Pennsylvania football. Overall, the outlying communities can boast of superiority in the sport.

Through most of the 1900s, superiority in Pennsylvania scholastic football translated to national superiority. In recent years, however, the trend has changed. Pennsylvania saw a dramatic downturn in participation and the strength of its scholastic football programs. In 1999 541 high schools fielded teams, a drop of thirty from 1979. More telling was the decline in participation. In 1979, 45,648 students played scholastic football in Pennsylvania. By 1999 the figure had fallen to 24,345, a 46.7 percent decline. This contrasts to Texas, which more than doubled its student participation from 77,037 to 159,535 in the same period. Since the mid-1970s the South has become the dominant region in high school talent. Texas, Louisiana, Georgia, and Mississippi have become the top four states in national per capita major college football player production, replacing the once dominant Pennsylvania-Ohio power base. By the mid-1980s no WPIAL county was rated in the top twenty-five in player origins.[53]

There are a number of reasons for the turnaround. As the Pittsburgh area moved from an industrial-based region to a service-based economy, the level of affluence in the suburbs rose. Gradually the ethnic/industrial football psyche began to diminish. Students became involved in new pastimes and there was a movement away from traditional sports such as football. Many high school–age students turned their attention to newly popular team and individual sports that placed more attention on participation than spectator appeal (that is, distance running, golf, soccer, tennis). In Pennsylvania, suburban schools have been a dominant force in these sports.

Another option for many, however, is to move into alternative sports that are not normally included in high school or collegiate extracurricular activities.[54] BMX racing, NASCAR racing, rollerblading, and snowboarding have become especially popular with young people. Some of these adolescents wanted to participate in sports but were "burned out" with years of involvement in adult-supervised organized athletics. Also, middle-class students of today have such a wide range of activities available that athletics no longer are held in the same esteem as in bygone days. Computers, high technology, and easy access to the automobile have lured many away from taking an interest in such sports as football.

There is also an attitudinal change among the younger generation. Many wish to seek their identity in a more individualist manner. Sadly, this has had violent repercussions in some school districts. However, for most seeking this individualist path, it simply may mean pursuing an activity that is more beneficial to oneself than to the team or the community. It can be argued that this attitude will create a generation of self-centered people who are incapable of being team players. On the other hand, America has always placed a strong emphasis on individual achievement and self-satisfaction.

Simultaneously, integration in the Southern high schools advanced the already strong football passions in that region. Lower-income African Americans viewed the sport in much the same manner as the children of immigrants saw football a generation before. It was a way to demonstrate membership in the "American" culture and, perhaps for a fortunate few, a means of socioeconomic mobility. Also, comparatively, the South lagged behind the Northeast in professional sports and other forms of entertainment that were accessible and affordable to most young people. This resulted in an overemphasis upon high school sports. The relatively higher population growth of the Sun Belt South over the Northeast provides for a greater pool of talented athletes. What has made the South the hotbed of high school football in recent years is strikingly similar to what made southwestern Pennsylvania dominant a half century before. In both regions there was rapid growth but still an underclass eager to demonstrate their growing involvement in the social structure. Southwestern Pennsylvania may still produce top-flight gridiron stars, but the evidence is clear that there has been decline.[55]

While the decline in overall prominence of southwestern Pennsylvania scholastic football may be disconcerting to longtime supporters, the sociological and demographic patterns explain why it is not surprising. However, it is not necessarily an unhealthy trend. The negative and even deadly consequences of some recent youth undertakings have caused the media to question the very nature of modern adolescent activities. However, for most young people, disinterest in such traditional sports as football has few negative consequences. Many of the new pursuits enhance physical fitness and build character and camaraderie. The athletic skills of such events as rollerblading and snowboarding are different, but no less demanding, than those of the traditional sports. Additionally, many of the alternative sports can be enjoyed without the encumbrance of adults. This is not to say that some type of adult supervision is unnecessary, but young people need to spend time interacting with each other in order to develop social skills. In the past, play and sport served that purpose. However, in recent years there has been an increasing trend toward adult control of play and sport, taking away a vital adolescent learning experience. Consequently, young men should not be chastised for lacking interest in scholastic football, but they should be channeled into activities that have a positive outcome. Whether adults enjoy that activity should not be the criterion for judgment.[56]

After over a century of history, what has been the impact of high school football upon southwestern Pennsylvania? As with most sociological phenomenon, there have been both positive and negative effects. The sport has brought the region a great deal of national attention as to the development of high quality athletes. However, this legendary status was often mixed with less-than-complimentary and, at times exaggerated, commentary on the grim, gritty environment that produced these players. Many articles on the origins of Pittsburgh area football players included mention of dirty coal towns or soot-encased steel communities. High school football did bring ethnically and economically diverse communities together. It was often the first activity where people of different cultural and financial backgrounds found common ground as they rallied around the home team. But at the same time these communities became rather insulated from each other. The rivalries between small cities, boroughs, and townships would preclude cooperation when the region needed to come together during periods of economic decline. Football served as a means of assimilation for the children and grandchildren of the Eastern and Southern Europeans and Southern African Americans. If one looks at the list of football greats, a high percentage came from these cultural backgrounds and they were but a small number of the young players and fans who saw football as a means to assimilation. However, since most of the mills and mines in the Pittsburgh area have closed, this phenomenon has ceased. With the demise of the ethnic/industrial era and the diminished glorification of football, a large pool of potential football players are swayed toward other activities. Thus, the glory days of high school football may be on the wane. Ironically, the recent service- and technology-based economic growth and the much-improved national image of the Pittsburgh region have been, in part, responsible for the decreased importance of high school football.

Despite any negative consequences, scholastic football was an integral part of the development in southwestern Pennsylvania and other mill and mine regions. The sport reflected the character of these regions while providing a much-needed diversion from the hard work and long hours. Football was an important factor in assimilating the children of European immigrants and Southern blacks to a new culture. The high school team took them beyond their ethnic culture and helped them deal with the diverse nature of American life. As a result residents moved from an ethnocentric mind-set to greater focus on community life. Undoubtedly, sport was often emphasized over education in the process. However, football and other sports often brought residents into the educational milieu. Interest in the high school team led to concern about the school system. In consideration of these factors, scholastic football was invaluable to the region. If the glory days have passed, southwestern Pennsylvania can take pride in its storied history. But history means change and the changes may offer even more and better opportunities to the young people of southwestern Pennsylvania.

Paul J. Zbiek is associate professor of history at King's College in Wilkes-Barre, Pennsylvania, and the coauthor of *The Jews of Wilkes-Barre: 150 Years in the Luzerne Valley*.

11

ART ROONEY AND THE PITTSBURGH STEELERS

ROB RUCK

WITH ART ROONEY, Pittsburghers always knew what came first. "Money has never been my god—never," Rooney responded in 1970 to a question about moving the team. "I've had tremendous offers. Back in the early 1950s, I could have moved to Baltimore, and then later, to Buffalo, Atlanta, New Orleans, Cincinnati. The propositions they made were fantastic." Other owners might have leapt at the chance, but not Rooney. "If you didn't have ties," Rooney reasoned, "if you didn't care for your city and its people, if you were just looking for wealth, you could have picked up and gone. But that's not you, not if you care for your city. And I believe Pittsburgh is a great city. I believe if we win, we'll do as good as we would in probably any of those other towns."[1]

And they did.

The most beloved man in the city's sporting history, Art Rooney embodied the evolution of Pittsburgh sport from its emergence on the sandlots early this century to its ascendance as the City of Champions in the 1970s. His team became a more enduring symbol for the city than the steel it once made. No other institution in Pittsburgh's past has so effectively united its disparate people across racial, ethnic, class, and geographic boundaries. Nor has any made so many feel so good about themselves and their city. But Rooney was revered as much for who he was as for the Steelers' winning ways. Pittsburgh knew Rooney as a hardworking, hard-playing guy from a tough part of town who never quit on a friend, a slightly devilish yet deeply devout family man with a shock of white hair, thick black-rimmed glasses, and an ever-present cigar, usually jammed firmly into the corner of his mouth.

In the somewhat mythic but still essentially accurate saga Pittsburghers have woven out of the strands of Art Rooney's life, sport is a product of hardworking people and tight-knit communities. On the sandlots, Pittsburgh created a sporting world in its own image. At its best, this sporting world nurtured a pantheon of native sons—Honus Wagner, Josh Gibson, Billy Conn, Johnny Unitas, and Dan Marino—who transcended their sport. Three homegrown teams, the Homestead Grays, the Pittsburgh Crawfords, and the Pittsburgh Steelers, attained legendary status while scores of other sandlot clubs—the McKees Rocks Rangers, the Garfield Eagles, and the Bloomfield Rams—left their mark on opponents' bodies and their own neighborhoods' psyches. Though they often struggled, sacrificed, and lost, these sporting paladins persevered and in the end triumphed—to the greater glory of themselves, their neighborhoods, and their city. As rugged and diverse as the city itself, these athletes and teams came to represent Pittsburgh to the world and just as importantly to Pittsburghers themselves. After a while, the Steelers were not just Rooney's team, but Pittsburgh's team.

By the later years of his life, when the team he created had won acclaim as football's "best team ever," Art Rooney had become a larger-than-life hero. Almost forgotten by then was the long accepted wisdom that Rooney was, as Myron Cope called him in 1970, "professional football's champion loser." The Steelers were once the league's doormats, consistent losers in the 1930s and '40s, mediocre at best in the 1950s and '60s. "Same old Steelers," Pittsburghers sighed in resignation and despair. The public knew three things about us in those days, Art Rooney Jr. said bluntly. "They knew we were Rooneys, they knew we were dumb, and they knew we were cheap."[2]

Roy Blount once described Art Rooney as a cross between the comic strip character Jiggs and Cambria County's Charles Bronson, a coal miner's son who won fame as a rough-hewn actor. Rooney was known about town as "the Chief." His twin sons started calling him that because they thought Art resembled the actor who played Perry White, the *Daily Planet*'s editor, on *Superman*. Art did not have Clark Kent to send on assignment, but he could get Big Daddy Lipscomb, Mean Joe Greene, and Terry Bradshaw to do his bidding. His athletic and promotional talents, as well as his ability to pick winners at the track, gave rise to legend. And when the Steelers won acclaim as sport's most glorious franchise of the 1970s, Art was hailed not only as their owner but as Pittsburgh's patriarch of sport. Despite the celebrity, Rooney remained an accessible, unpretentious guy in the city where he had lived all but a few of his 87 years. A bit of a rogue, a poker-playing, cigar-smoking raconteur who rarely missed morning Mass, and the easiest touch in town, Rooney displayed the constancy and loyalty that characterize Pittsburgh at its best.[3]

Like Pittsburgh, Art Rooney was a product of the immigrants who worked in the region's mines and mills. By the turn of the century, their labor made the city the globe's industrial epicenter; Rooney helped make it Titletown, USA.

Pittsburgh attracted overlapping streams of migrants throughout the nineteenth and early twentieth centuries. They came first from England, Scotland, and Wales, then Ireland and Germany, and finally from Eastern, Central, and Southern Europe and deep in the American South. These sojourners and their offspring turned the city from a manufacturing center of 78,000 on the eve of the Civil War to a roaring industrial metropolis of over 450,000 by 1900. Pittsburgh's population climbed even further, to about 670,000 in 1930. These men and women made the coal, steel, and other products that fueled the nation's growth. Though Pittsburgh's working people often spoke a different language and practiced a different religion than those laboring alongside them, they shared two experiences—a life defined by hard work and recreation that revolved around sport.[4]

The Rooney clan came to the United States during the nineteenth-century exodus from a famine-stricken Ireland. Art's mother's family came from Rosscommon in 1849 and produced coal miners while his father's, from Newry, provided the iron and steel industry with puddlers and rollers. His father, Dan, was born in Old Tradiger, Wales, where his father worked for a while before arriving in Pittsburgh when he was about seven or eight years old. Both Dan and his father belonged to the Amalgamated Association of Iron, Steel Workers and the Rooney children were brought up on stories of the Homestead Strike of 1892.

Dan Rooney left Pittsburgh for Coulter, a small coal-mining town on the Youghiogheny River and his wife's hometown, sometime after the union's defeat at Homestead. Arthur Joseph Rooney, Dan and Margaret's first child, was born there on January 27, 1901. The men on Margaret's side of the family worked in the mines and Art frequently vacationed with her relatives in the Buena Vista and Boston coal patches when he was a boy. Dan, who had once worked in the mills, ran Coulter's only hotel.[5]

The Rooney family left Coulter not long after Art's birth, living in a few other coal towns until they settled on the north shore of the Allegheny River, directly across from Pittsburgh's central business district. In Pittsburgh, Dan owned Rooney's Café and Bar, known for its nickel beers, free lunches, and the sporting and political set that congregated there. Rooney's Café and Bar was in the part of the North Side known as "the Ward." Dan, his wife, three daughters, and six sons lived in rooms atop the saloon on General Robinson Street. A number of honky-tonk gambling parlors, breweries, and sporting houses were nearby. So was Exposition Park, home to the Pirates until 1909, when Barney Dreyfuss, frustrated by the spring floods that frequently left his ballpark a quagmire and hoping to attract a more genteel audience, built Forbes Field in Oakland. Exposition Park remained behind, home grounds to the Federal League's Pittsburgh franchise in 1914 and 1915 and a score of neighborhood teams. High waters remained a problem, too, until after World War II. "In those days, before flood controls, if you spit in the Allegheny River, the flood came up," Art recollected. "It wasn't anything unusual for us to leave for school by going out a second-floor window in a skiff."[6]

Pittsburgh's skilled working classes in the decades after the Civil War exerted greater power over their workplaces, local politics, and the town's cultural life than they would during any other epoch in the city's history. The Rooneys were at home in that assertive working-class milieu.

The Ward, Rooney conceded, "had a bad reputation as a rough and tumble working-class section, but it had wonderful people." Arriving in the neighborhood as a young boy, Art stayed there the rest of his life. The Irish and their descendants set the tone, with newer immigrants from Italy and Poland, as well as African Americans, gradually moving in. One boarding house, Art's son Dan remembered, was called the League of Nations because its residents came from so many different countries. Gaelic was spoken in many homes and Irish wakes often went on for three days. "The people were poor," Art Rooney explained, "and probably the only time a lot of them ever had a ride in an automobile was going to the cemetery when someone died." Once there, the mourners scattered to visit their own departed. "Then you would hear them hollering the *caoine,* which is the old Irish cry. It was fantastic. . . . You would hear them hollering the *caoine* all over the graveyard."

Though immersed in an Irish American neighborhood, Rooney was well exposed to Pittsburgh's ethnic mix. "From the time I was a kid, and my family was that way, I just never knew of any difference in what you were." The kids' teams, Rooney remembered, were usually mixed by race. When he and his wife, the former Kathleen McNulty, bought a large Victorian house on North Lincoln Avenue in the Ward in 1931, they stayed in it for the rest of their lives, even while the area's racial balance shifted.[7]

The neighborhood possessed what Rooney described as a terrific union consciousness. "I remember a guy in the Ward who 'did the buck' on the railroad," he told Myron Cope. "It means he was a scab." Unable to endure the hostile reception of his neighbors, the man left town, only to return as a carnival fighter. "As soon as we heard about him coming back, we got ahold of Squawker Mullen. Squawker was a national amateur champion—just a little fellow, maybe 110 pounds, but, boy, could Squawker fight!" When an out-of-shape Mullen began to lose the fight, Art's brother Dan reached over the ropes and hit the fellow, socking "him like you would nail a bird in midair." Before long, carnival hands were fighting the boys from the Ward in a free-for-all that brought the tent down.[8]

The six Rooney brothers were baptized both in the Catholic Church and the sporting fraternity. The latter came on the Ward's sandlots and in its gyms, where they displayed a competitive zeal and athletic prowess that carried them through sport's changing seasons. "You went on the playground when the sun came up, and you didn't leave till the sun went down," Art later related.[9]

Art never held a regular job in his life. He went to work at a steel mill once, but didn't last for long. After a few hours on the job the men took their morning break. "I just left and didn't even go back for my pay," Rooney explained. "I could see right away that there must be some easier way to make a living."

All of the Rooneys were capable of "putting up their dukes" if called upon. That was part of growing up in the Ward. "We were from Northern Ireland," Rooney once explained. "They called us yellow bellies. Even tho' we went to the same parochial school we had plenty of fights with those other Irishmen." The Rooneys always had boxing gloves, a resident remarked years later to writer Roy McHugh, "and boy, could they fight, and boy, could they punch." Brother Vincent fought professionally under the name of Duke York, and Dan Jr. had a reputation as a brawler that even his later ordination into the priesthood could not erase. He once chased Homestead Grays' pitcher Smokey Joe Williams off the field after the Hall of Fame hurler beaned him. During their summers barnstorming as baseball players, Art and Dan picked up a few dollars by going into the ring against carnival fighters. "That was made to order for Dan and me," Art remembered, "because we could lick all those carnival guys. I mean, what kind of fighters would a carnival have?" A fighter who lasted a round was paid $5. "But whenever Dan went in there, I don't think the carny guy ever lasted a round."[10]

The Rooney boys refined their skills at the St. Peter's Lyceum, a neighborhood boxing center run by the parish. "In those days," Art noted, "each neighborhood had a boxing team." The St. Peter's squad, which included several professional fighters, trained in the big gymnasium under the school. The boxing team drew upon the Ward's youth, white and black, but was augmented by boys from other parts of town. Rooney, a rugged welterweight, won the 1918 American Athletic Union championship. Two years later, he lost in the final round, this time as a representative from Georgetown University where he was studying.

Art made the U.S. Olympic squad at 135 pounds in 1920, but he decided not to go to Antwerp for the games and turned pro instead.

Sammy Mosberg, whom he beat in the trials, replaced Art on the team and won the gold medal. In a post-Olympic fight, Rooney beat Mosberg again. "I had a few fights but I didn't care for it that much. I was in Milwaukee and was going to leave from there to Australia for a fight but I decided I better stay home in America." Always more of a hometown boy than a globetrotter, Art hung up the gloves with few regrets.[11]

In later years Art returned to boxing as a promoter. He and Barney McGinley, a Braddock bookmaker who became a part owner of the Steelers, formed the Rooney-McGinley Boxing Club. During the 1930s, Rooney-McGinley promoted weekly cards at Hickey Park in Millvale and Duquesne Gardens in Oakland. Pittsburgh grew a rich crop of talent for them to harvest, including Billy Conn, Sammy Angott, the Zivic brothers, and Charles Burley. They put Pittsburgh on boxing's map. "[Until] Rooney and McGinley appeared on the local fight horizon," *Courier* sportswriter Wendell Smith claimed in 1939, "the boxing industry here was running on 'hot air' and the dividends were more than poor. But when they stepped in the picture, boxing took an upturn."[12]

Rooney-McGinley's biggest night came during the summer of 1951, when they staged a heavyweight championship bout at Forbes Field. Following Joe Louis's retirement in 1949, Ezzard Charles and Jersey Joe Walcott fought for the vacated title. Charles decisioned his Camden, New Jersey, foe to win the title and outpointed him in a rematch. Their third fight, held in Pittsburgh, was a different story. Walcott, a 6-1 underdog, KO'ed Charles with a left hook in the seventh round. The gate, almost a quarter of a million dollars, set a local record.[13]

By the early 1920s Art's days as a fighter were over, but he was just coming into his prime as a baseball player. Art had learned the game at Exposition Park and the Phipps Playground across the street. When he was only fifteen, he suited up for games against the Homestead Grays, the Kansas City Monarchs, and the House of David, a barnstorming club from a religious commune in Benton, Michigan, whose players were known for their long beards. Art's first and favorite team was the Phipps AA, a top semi-pro outfit. Later clubs included the Pittsburgh Collegians, the North Side Civics, the North Side Board of Trade, and a half-dozen other semi-pro and sandlot teams who were happy to put the talented young ballplayer in the lineup. With his brother Dan, he often went on the road for weeks, even months at a time, playing for semi-pro clubs as they barnstormed through the tri-state area and New York during the summer.[14]

Art played baseball through the 1920s, either for a sandlot, semi-pro, or minor league club, usually with Dan as his teammate. In 1925 Art played center field and Dan caught for Wheeling in the Middle Atlantic League's inaugural season. The brothers tore up the circuit, which produced scores of major leaguers. Art finished second in batting and led the league in runs scored, hits, games played, and stolen bases. Dan finished third in batting and was the league's leader in doubles. Their feats, however, were not enough for Wheeling, which finished near the bottom of the league. The Yankees tried to sign Dan for a reputed $5,000, an enormous sum at the time, but another calling pulled him toward the seminary instead. Art signed with the Chicago Cubs, but after one minor league road trip he realized that he didn't have a major league arm. He signed with the Boston Red Sox a few years later but never reported. Art reasoned that he could make more money playing for semi-pro clubs and avoid the grueling, merry-go-round life of a minor leaguer. He played baseball, he reckoned, until 1930.[15]

But Art was more than a player. He managed and promoted the game, too. "From the time I was a kid, I was the manager of teams, running things, selling tickets. Kids don't have the opportunity to organize that I had then," he explained. Sometimes he and his players even made a small sum for their efforts. But money was not the driving force behind sandlot ball.

In the off-season, the Rooneys turned to football. Dan played at Duquesne University, and then St. Bonaventure, before entering the priesthood and serving for seven years on a mission in China. Aided by a $5,000 donation from light-heavyweight champ Billy Conn, Dan, now Father Silas Rooney, OFM, built a church and a school there. He returned to St. Bonaventure as its athletic director. Art played football, too, but twice declined Knute Rockne's invitation to play in South Bend. Rooney headed instead to the Indiana State Normal School (now Indiana University of Pennsylvania), where he played football and baseball, then moved on to Georgetown, where he boxed and played baseball, and finally to Duquesne, where he played football. At Duquesne Dan joined him in the backfield during the 1923 and 1924 seasons. Art graduated Duquesne's School of Business in 1924; he did his postgraduate work on the city's sandlots.[16]

Rooney's place in football history evolved not so much from playing the game as from promoting it. Even as a youngster playing pickup ball in the Ward, Art was usually the de facto organizer, setting the matches and getting his comrades together for practice and play. And as professional football developed during the 1920s, Rooney's role grew accordingly.

The first professional football game, according to the National Football League, was played between the Pittsburgh Athletic Club and the Allegheny Athletic Association in 1892 at Recreation Park in Allegheny City. But college football was vastly more popular than the pro game during the first half of the century. It drew more fans, attracted more attention, and compensated its players better than what passed for professional teams. "The pro game then," according to Rooney, "wasn't even a hop, skip, and a jump from semi-pro ball, maybe just a hop." Based in towns throughout Pennsylvania, Ohio, Indiana, and Illinois, semi-pro and erstwhile pro football was played by working-class men before working-class fans. But the success of college ball created a deep pool of players eager to continue to play and fans who wanted to see them perform. In response, the American Professional Football Association, the forerunner to the NFL, formed in 1920. Pittsburgh, however, did not enter the league until 1933.[17]

For the first third of the century the differences between sandlot, semi-pro, and professional football were relatively small. Players circulated among these levels, suiting up for the highest bidder. So did college players, who routinely took to the field for professional and semi-pro teams under assumed names. Given the inability of the early pro leagues to dominate the market, independent semi-pro clubs flourished. Art Rooney formed one of these teams in the Ward in the early 1920s.[18]

"I was no more than twenty-two," Rooney recalled, "when I started up a team called the Hope-Harvey. I owned it and coached it and in the important games played halfback."[19] Rooney named his team for Harvey, the neighborhood doctor who tended to the players' injuries, and Hope, the Ward's firehouse, which the team used as a dressing room. The sixteen to twenty players on the team passed the hat at games and occasionally charged admission. They usually covered expenses; sometimes the players divided a little that was left over.

The Hope-Harveys took on other local sandlot and semi-pro clubs and hosted visiting pro teams. "I remember we played the Canton Bulldogs and Jim Thorpe in Pittsburgh once," Rooney said. "I tried a field goal but it was blocked. Thorpe picked it up and ran for a touchdown, and as I recall, they beat us, 6-0." Being able to hold the Bulldogs and the renowned Thorpe to a narrow victory underscores the close level of play between professional and semi-professional football in the 1920s. The game, Rooney noted, claimed little sophistication. "Strictly shoving and pushing."

For $75 Rooney recruited Duquesne University football coach Joe Bach for a game against West View. "Early in the first quarter," Rooney later explained, "we blocked a punt and naturally that started a brawl. After a while, the crowd got into the spirit of the thing and poured onto the field. So instead of a fight, we had a riot." Bach, realizing that the game was over, left. "The next day, I sent someone to Joe's house to pay him his $75. Bach refused to take it, until my guy told him, 'Go ahead. The Hope-Harveys haven't finished a game yet!'"[20]

After Rooney quit playing and focused his attention on coaching and promoting the team, the Hope-Harveys climbed to the upper ranks of the region's burgeoning semi-pro circuit. The team began to draw its players, mostly working-class men in their twenties and thirties who held jobs during the day and practiced at night, from beyond the Ward. But a core of local players remained with the squad throughout the 1920s as Rooney upgraded the team. Several had played ball in college, including his younger brother Jim, and a number of All-Americans.

The Hope-Harveys eventually became the Pittsburgh Steelers, but they went through several name changes along the way. By the late 1920s the club was called the Majestic Radios, for the North Side radio manufacturer that sponsored the team to promote its products and win neighborhood goodwill. One of the top independent teams in the region, the Majestics featured Harp Vaughan, Mose Kelsch, Jim Levey, and Jim Rooney in the backfield. Kelsch had grown up on the still heavily German Troy Hill; the 154-pound Levey, who played shortstop for the St. Louis Browns in the 1930s, came from East Liberty. Jim

Rooney was the youngest brother. The foursome had enough talent to start for some pro clubs.

After learning the game in the Ward, Jim Rooney played for Allegheny High School and Bellefonte Academy before heading to the University of Pittsburgh, where he played halfback and quarterback and handled kicking duties for Dr. John "Jock" Sutherland, who had succeeded the legendary Glenn "Pop" Warner as head coach in 1923. A soccer-playing native of Scotland who came to Pitt to study dentistry in 1914, Sutherland had starred for several of Pitt's national championship teams. Under Sutherland, Pitt won five more national titles and went to four Rose Bowls. In Jim Rooney's senior year Pitt finished the regular season undefeated and was accorded national honors by some selectors despite a crushing loss to underdog USC in the Rose Bowl on New Year's Day, 1930.[21]

On the train returning from the Rose Bowl, North Side Republican Party leader James O'Donnell asked Jim Rooney if he wanted to enter the state legislature. "I didn't think much of it," Rooney recounted fifty years later, "but he gave me the job." Given the one-party nature of Pittsburgh politics in the 1920s, where registered Republicans outnumbered Democrats over thirty to one in 1929, the party's selection of Rooney as the nominee was tantamount to election. Art, a former ward chairman himself, changed the team's name to the J. P. Rooneys to boost his brother's career.[22]

Jim Rooney, who had picked up a few dollars on the side by playing semi-pro football on Sundays under an assumed name while still at Pitt, kept playing football while a state representative, distinguishing himself more on the field than in the legislature. The 6'2", 210-pound back passed, ran, and kicked the J. P. Rooneys to the top of the region's gridirons, and he would have led his brother's team into the NFL in 1933 if not for a car wreck on the eve of Pittsburgh's entrance into the National Football League. Two people died in the crash on a mountain road near Bedford. Jim survived, but he was hospitalized for eight months and never played football again.

Art Rooney's team was good enough to play professional football, but Pennsylvania's sabbatarian legislation (known as the "Blue Laws") limited professional sports on Sundays. That proscription was little bother for semi-pro promoters, who could bribe constables to ignore their games, but it kept NFL teams out of Pittsburgh and Philadelphia. Playing on Saturdays, meanwhile, was out of the question for a pro team in Pittsburgh because powerhouses Pitt, Carnegie Tech, and Duquesne were far more popular.

But when the state's Blue Laws changed to make Sunday play possible in 1933, Rooney was ready. Well connected politically and aware of the prospective legislation, he had already purchased an NFL franchise for $2,500 and arranged a schedule for the 1933 season. He relinquished coaching duties and hired former Washington and Jefferson star Forrest "Jap" Douds as player-coach. "Between you and me," his brother Jim confided decades later, "he was no coach." Rooney also renamed the J. P. Rooneys the Pittsburgh Pirates.

The Pirates fielded mostly native sons or former Pitt, Duquesne, and Carnegie Tech players, but their working-class crowds of 3,000–5,000 a game in 1933 were far smaller than the 30,000 fans Pitt sometimes attracted to a game. The eighteen players on the roster made about $100–$125 a game. Victorious in their first game, a 17-0 win over Cincinnati, the Pirates finished the year with a 3-6-2 record. Losing seasons became the norm, and the Pirates went a decade before putting together a winning season in 1942. By then they had been renamed the Steelers. During World War II the Steelers and the Philadelphia Eagles combined squads for the 1943 season, playing as the Steagles. The following year the Steelers merged with the Chicago Cardinals to become the Card-Pitts. They lost all ten games they played that season.

In 1940 Rooney sold the Steelers to Alexis Thompson, who had inherited a fortune made in cosmetics. Within a week he bought a partial interest in the Philadelphia Eagles, owned by his friend and later NFL commissioner Bert Bell. Thompson, however, was unhappy in Pittsburgh and eager to move the Steelers. Rooney, regretting his sale of the club, then talked Thompson and Bell into exchanging franchises and players. Rooney remained a minority owner of the Steelers until 1946, when he regained majority control of the club.[23]

That season Jock Sutherland took over coaching the team. The following year the Steelers made the playoffs for the first time ever. But Sutherland died suddenly after the season and the Steelers did not return to postseason play until 1962.

Though Rooney maintained the team's offices, first in the Fort Pitt Hotel and then the Roosevelt Hotel, football was not always his primary focus. He left personnel decisions to the coaches, and the Steelers developed a reputation as one of the league's worst teams. "On most teams," Rooney admitted, "the coach worries about where the players are at night. On our team, the players had to worry about the coach." Abby Mendelson, who wrote the team's official history, remarked that Rooney seemed "to run the club out of a little book he kept in his jacket pocket, held together with rubber bands." Though the NFL has become the envy of professional sport for its lucrative revenue stream, Rooney's Steelers were a break-even or marginal-loss operation during the 1930s and '40s. Family members said the club turned a profit only once during its first twenty years. To Rooney the season was successful if at its end he had enough money to field a team the next year. His earnings as a fight promoter and handicapper were often what kept the club afloat. "In those days," he said, "nobody got wealthy in sports. You had two thrills. One came Sunday, trying to win the game. The next came Monday, trying to make the payroll."[24]

Though Pittsburgh was much more of a baseball than football town, Rooney persevered. "I thought it would become just as much of a football town because of the people of western Pennsylvania," he reasoned. "The people here are coal miners, steelworkers. They work hard, and football would fit in just as well as baseball." But in the 1930s, as Rooney struggled to keep the team solvent, he often played what would have been his home games in other cities, including New Orleans, Louisville, Johnstown, and Youngstown, in order to boost the gate.[25]

When the Steelers emerged as the best team of the 1970s and continued to win during the 1980s and 1990s, they were hailed as a model football operation. Their earlier personnel decisions, on the other hand, were often laughable. They traded their top pick in the 1939 draft to the Chicago Bears, who selected future Hall of Fame quarterback Sid Luckman. In return, the club picked up Edgar "Eggs" Manske, who lasted just one season. Before the 1955 season they cut Johnny Unitas, who had grown up on Mount Washington and played ball at St. Justin's High School, despite Dan Rooney's protests. Dan had competed against Unitas while quarterbacking North Catholic High School to a city championship, and he knew just how good the quarterback was. The Steelers passed on Jim Brown in the college draft and sat Jack Kemp and Len Dawson on the bench before trading them.[26]

Rooney, respected by his peers for his ability to place the NFL's interests ahead of any one franchise's, was offered the job of league commissioner in 1960 when Bert Bell died. He turned it down and was instrumental in putting Pete Rozelle in the commissioner's office instead when the owners deadlocked. In later years Rooney pushed more conservative owners to recognize the NFL Players Association and to open its television rights to open bidding among the networks.[27]

Perhaps the best football decision Art ever made was to allow his eldest son, Dan, to take over the Steelers. "Art tended to rule with his heart," former player Jerry Nuzum explained. "The boys tend to rule with their heads." Dan, who hired Chuck Noll as head coach, led the club as it reached football's promised land. Like his father, Dan Rooney became one of the most well-regarded owners in the league, both by players and other owners.

Although Art never pushed his sons to join in his endeavors, each of them did. Sport was too much a part of their world to ignore. The Rooney home, not far from what became the site for Three Rivers Stadium, had the largest yard in the neighborhood and was the place where all their friends gathered to play ball. Art even knocked down a garage to expand the playing area and flooded half of it during the winter to make a hockey rink. His five sons worked for the Steelers, other NFL teams, or in the family's racing concerns. Art Jr. became the Steelers' scouting director. Tim, Pat, and John worked in horse-racing.[28]

Art Rooney never moved from the North Side, and after his death his son Dan returned to the family home. During the 1990s Dan began grooming his son, Art Rooney II, to take over the club, insuring a third generation of Rooney ownership.

If, as Franz Kafka wrote, suffering brings enlightenment, then Rooney surely must have become professional football's most insightful owner during his first four decades with the team. The standard interpretation of the Steelers' difficulties was that Art failed to concentrate fully on football. Rooney admitted as much himself. "Although I understood the football business as well as anybody in the league, I didn't pay the attention to the business that some of the other owners gave it. I was out of town a great deal of the time, at the racetracks. With me, the racetrack was a big business. And generally I'd have a head coach who was like me—he'd like the races." No one, however, ever questioned Rooney's acumen at the track.[29]

Art Rooney became one of horseracing's top handicappers in the epoch before the advent of parimutuel betting. "I bet on horses from the time I was young," Art confessed. "The first time I went to the races I didn't know any more about horses than most people." He soon overcame that liability, learning the industry from the bottom up and cultivating friendships with grooms, riders, and trainers who often tipped Art to how the horses were running.[30]

His expertise at picking winners became legendary after "Rooney's Ride," two days spent at two New York racetracks in 1936. Accompanied by former Pittsburgh light-heavyweight Buck Crouse, Art arrived at the Empire City track in New York City with $300. By day's end he was up $21,000. Before heading back to Pittsburgh, Art went to Joseph Madden's saloon for dinner. Madden, a well-known member of New York's sporting life, talked Art into delaying his return and heading instead to the track at Saratoga the next day. There Rooney's streak continued. He bet $8,000 on an 8 to 1 entry named Quel Jeu and won in a photo finish. In the fifth race he bet $10,000 on another 8 to 1 horse. "In that entry," Madden recounted, "the four horses came out of the fog and hit the finish line in a heap—it looked like a dead heat for all four nags. As I had a few clams on this event, I nearly died waiting for the picture to come down. But Artie lit a cigar, got out of the crowd and went to the men's room, and when I brought him the good news there, he was telling the . . . groom the difference between the single wingback and Warner's double-wing."[31]

Rooney knew when to quit. He returned for a third day at the track and placed a bet with bookmaker Tim Mara, founder of the New York Giants football team, in the first race. When Rooney's horse was disqualified he said, "I think it's time to go home," and left. Rooney never revealed how much he won that day—estimates range from $250,000 to $750,000. Whatever the sum, it vastly exceeded the worth of the football team. Upon returning to Pittsburgh, he told his wife Kathleen, "We don't have to worry about money again."[32]

Art began buying ownership stakes in several tracks in the 1940s and bred racehorses at Shamrock Farms in Maryland. The Ruanaidh Company (Gaelic for Rooney) owned and later sold the Green Mountain Park in Vermont, Randall Park in Cleveland, and Liberty Bell Park in Philadelphia. It retains interests in New York's Yonkers Raceway and the Palm Beach Kennel Club.[33]

Art Rooney's reputation was built on more than sport. He was regarded as someone who would invariably help a person in need, whether that meant paying for a funeral or taking a hungry man into his home and feeding him. His children routinely brought friends over who stayed for days or weeks at a time.

Part of his generosity dovetailed with his involvement in local politics. "Coming from the Ward," Rooney revealed, "you knew politics from the day you were able to speak." Art first learned about them in his mother's kitchen and his father's saloon, where the Ward's Republican leaders often gathered. Until FDR and the New Deal swept through the region in the early 1930s, the Republican Party dominated Pittsburgh politics. Irish Americans were especially active. Rooney later promoted sporting events as political fundraisers, registered voters as a district committeeman, and while still in his twenties, took over as the 22nd ward's chairman.[34]

"In those days," Rooney explained, "ward politicians were entirely different from ward politicians today. They lived in the neighborhood and for them and everybody else, everything was in the neighborhood." Being involved in politics then, he asserted, meant helping people. "When I was a ward leader, when you moved into the ward, we got to know you." Rooney remained loyal to the men and the party with whom he first cast his lot.[35]

"One thing you never do," Rooney argued, "is change parties, religions, or wives." He stayed a Republican even though most of the local party became Democrats during the 1930s. He was even persuaded to run for the registrar of wills in an election year when a Republican stood virtually no chance against a Democratic Party headed by Franklin Roosevelt. David Lawrence, a long-time friend and Pittsburgh's Democratic Party leader, accompanied Rooney to campaign appearances. Art had been a batboy for Lawrence's ballclubs and the two developed a lifelong friendship that transcended party affiliation.

Lawrence, who later served as Pittsburgh's mayor and Pennsylvania's governor, remarked, "Art is a true-blue guy who will be with you when you die." At rallies Rooney admitted to the voters that he knew nothing about the registrar of wills, not even where its offices were located. "But," he pledged, "if I'm elected, I promise to put someone in the job who does know what he's doing." He lost.[36]

Rooney's personal largess knew no color line and his reputation in black Pittsburgh was no less celebrated than among whites. Joe "Showboat" Ware, a talented and versatile athlete during the 1920s, echoed the sentiments of many in the black community when he described Rooney as a Robin Hood. "He was exceptional. He did things that were unreal. Like if a kid needed an operation and they wanted money on the barrelhead, he paid for it. He took care of people when they were hungry. He got them firewood and coal. . . . He never missed out." In a reference to Art's brother Dan, the priest, Ware testified, "You might well say that he [Art] was the black sheep, but he was as good as those who wore the cloak. Art took care of people and he's one of the best I ever met."[37]

During the depression, Rooney promoted at least two boxing cards a month in the huge schoolyard at St. Peter's Church and turned the proceeds over to the St. Vincent DePaul Society for poor relief. He regularly scheduled at least one football game a year whose proceeds went to a charity or a social cause. The diocese, the Shriners, Greek Relief, and a canteen run for servicemen during World War II were among the beneficiaries. When Lowell Perry, the University of Michigan All-American, was seriously hurt during the 1956 Steelers' season, Art took care of his medical expenses, got him a job doing radio commentary, and paid his way through law school. He routinely helped former players make the transition from pro ball to work and stood by those, like Ernie Holmes, who found themselves in trouble. Holmes, who lived on the edge, once shot at a state trooper in a helicopter. In 1983, after Gabe Rivera, the Steelers' top pick in the draft, was nearly killed in a crash that left him paralyzed from the waist down, Art escorted Rivera's mother to breakfast and Mass each morning before joining her at Gabe's bedside in the intensive care unit. While Rooney was loathe to discuss his generosity, there was no shortage of Pittsburghers willing to document his good works. Magistrate Baldy Regan, a classmate of Art Jr., credited Rooney for getting him hired as a county detective. "All the kids on the North Side knew if they could just get to Mr. Rooney, they'd have a shot in life. You knew he would help."[38]

Though professional sport was largely segregated during the first half of the century, Rooney was well connected to his opposite numbers in the black community. He was an intimate of Cumberland Posey Jr. and Gus Greenlee, the owners, respectively, of the Homestead Grays and the Pittsburgh Crawfords. "Cum Posey and I were close," Rooney recalled. "He was older than I was . . . but we became close friends when he was at Duquesne and I was at Duquesne's grade school." They played against each other frequently on the sandlots, Rooney explained, because when a white team played the Grays they sought the best available athletes—including Art and Dan Rooney—in order to stand a chance. Rooney also promoted black boxers, including several of Greenlee's fighters, and booked his basketball team, the Rooneymen, against teams sponsored by Posey and his Homestead Grays co-owner, Rufus "Sonnyman" Jackson.[39]

His friendship with Posey went further than the ballfield. Art lent Posey money when the Grays were short of funds. "I was able to help him," Rooney conceded, "but there is no question that if I needed help and he could afford it, he would have helped me. . . . The same with Gus Greenlee. We were close." Once Rooney and Posey had ballclubs barnstorming through West Virginia. "We were just a swing ahead of them and one of their automobiles didn't show for a game. Cum called me on the phone and said, 'I need a player.' . . . So I sent him a kid, a red-headed Irish fellow. He called me back on the phone and said, 'Didn't you have something darker?'" Another time, Rooney shared a book about racism that he found compelling with Posey. He was an honorary pallbearer at his friend's funeral.[40]

Rooney's friendship with Gus Greenlee grew out of their mutual political loyalty to James Coyne, Allegheny County Republican boss during the 1920s. Art encouraged Greenlee, a powerful numbers baron on the Hill, to get more involved in sport. Greenlee returned from his first road trip with the Pittsburgh Crawfords and told Rooney that he hadn't done him any favors urging him to sponsor a ballclub. In a game in a Southern town, the Crawfords had a runner on second base. A man with a shotgun in one hand and a megaphone in the other shouted from the sideline, "Hey, nigger! You take one step off that bag and I will blow your head off." Greenlee, on at least one occasion, turned to Rooney for financial help, while Rooney's football teams practiced at Greenlee Field on the Hill, the first local facility with lights. Art was also a regular at Greenlee's Hill District nightspot, the Crawford Grill. "The Hill was a tremendous place," Rooney recalled fondly. Art socialized at Greenlee's Frankstown Avenue home and attended his friend's funeral.[41]

He attended hundreds of funerals, and even more wakes, sometimes three or four a night in later years. Art seemed to know just about everyone and Pittsburghers felt a personal connection to him even if none existed. He was as comfortable in the company of priests as he was with those from the city's tenderloin.

Rooney, who had an African American on his first NFL team, also hired black employees in the front office. The Hope-Harveys took to the field with Rudy Cole, a black player from the North Side, while the J. P. Rooneys signed African American tackle Ray Kemp after he graduated Duquesne University. Kemp, who had grown up in nearby Cecil playing both football and soccer, worked days as a doorman at the old Pittsburgher Hotel, practiced in the evenings, and played for Rooney's team on Sundays in 1932. He was still on the team when the Rooneys became the NFL's Pittsburgh Pirates in 1933. But that was his only year on the team.[42]

Thirteen African Americans played in the APFA or its successor, the NFL, between 1920 and 1933. But in 1933, Kemp and Chicago Cardinal star Joe Lillard were the only two still playing. Following that season, in what Arthur Ashe described as a "gentlemen's agreement" by the owners, the NFL quietly eliminated black players from their game. The league remained segregated until after World War II.[43]

Only a handful of African Americans played for the Steelers in the 1950s and '60s. Their Super Bowl squads, however, were split almost evenly between white and black players. The Steelers drafted African Americans from football powerhouses, but they also became one of the first teams to discover the enormously talented but largely overlooked players at the smaller black colleges. Bill Nunn Jr. became a Steeler scout in 1967 and later assumed greater duties for the team. When he had written for the *Pittsburgh Courier,* the city's black weekly,

Nunn annually selected a Black College All-American Team. His exceptional contacts with black schools helped the Steelers draft or sign as free agents a score of gifted players, including Mel Blount, Joe Gilliam, Ernie Holmes, Donnie Shell, and John Stallworth.[44]

Winning the Super Bowl might have been tantamount to an apotheosis for Rooney, who hated losing so much that no one in the family dared talk about the Steelers with him for days following a defeat. But after the Steelers won their second Super Bowl, Rooney underscored his concern about how much sport had changed in his lifetime. "It's lost its romance," he stated. "It's all big business now."[45] Sport might have lost its romance, but Pittsburgh will never stop loving Art Rooney.

If Rooney's sandlot club from the city's North Side ultimately won the hearts and minds of the people of the entire region and a following around the world, it was not only because his team won a then-unprecedented four Super Bowls. It was because Rooney was so much a product of the city and its sense of ethics. Rooney never strayed far from his roots, reflecting Pittsburgh's shot-and-a-beer ambience as well as its focus on family, work, and religion. In his eulogy at St. Peter's Church, the Most Reverend Vincent M. Leonard said that Rooney was "the friend of politicians, of thugs and thieves, of people good and evil, and the three qualities he possessed that left the most lasting impression were his humility, his courage, and his charity." In the years ahead, as in years past, Art Rooney and his Steelers will remain at the center of the sporting story that Pittsburghers like best to tell about themselves and their city.[46]

NOTES

1 • BETWEEN THE WHALE AND DEATH

1. Stefan Lorant, *Pittsburgh: The Story of an American City* (Garden City, N.Y.: Doubleday, 1964), 322–27.
2. Chet Smith, *Pittsburgh and Western Pennsylvania Sports Hall of Fame* (Pittsburgh: Wolfson Publishing, 1969), 64.
3. For Greb and Tunney, see Gene Tunney, *Arms For Living* (New York: Wilfred Funk, 1941), 190–94.
4. Quoted in interview with Billy Conn, in Peter Heller, *"In This Corner . . .!" Forty World Champions Tell Their Stories* (New York: Simon and Schuster, 1973), 224–25.
5. Joseph Page, "The Fine Art of Dirty Fighting," *Boxing Illustrated and Wrestling News,* November 1959, 28.
6. *Pittsburgh Post Gazette,* December 29, 1936.
7. Heller, *"In This Corner . . . !"* 223, 241.
8. *Pittsburgh Post-Gazette,* October 4, 1940.
9. Heller, *"In This Corner . . . !"* 243–44; *Pittsburgh Post-Gazette,* October 5, 1940.
10. Heller, *"In This Corner . . . !"* 216–17.
11. Ibid., 246–47.

3 • REFLECTIONS ON THE PRE-RENAISSANCE STEELERS

1. *Life* 59 (Dec. 24, 1965): 78–79; *National Geographic* 127 (March 1965): 342–71; *Saturday Review* 48 (May 22, 1965): 46–47.
2. *Sports Illustrated,* Sept. 13, 1965, 41–42, 69–70.
3. Cited in David Neft and Richard Cohen, eds., *The Sports Encyclopedia: Pro Football: The Modern Era, 1960–1989,* 8th ed. (New York: St. Martin's, 1989), 86.
4. *Sports Illustrated,* Jan. 11, 1999, 84.
5. Ibid.

4 • PITTSBURGH POISON

1. Lowell Reidenbaugh, *Take Me out to the Ballpark,* 2nd ed., rev. (St. Louis: Sporting News Publishing, 1987), 221.
2. Philip J. Lowry, *Green Cathedrals: The Ultimate Celebration of All 271 Major League and Negro League Ballparks Past and Present,* rev. ed. (Reading, Mass.: Addison-Wesley,

1992), 217–19; Munsey and Suppas, 1996–99, "Forbes Field, Pittsburgh, Pennsylvania," in Ballparks, available on-line: http://www.ballparks.com/baseball/national/forbes.htm (June 6, 1999).

3. Traynor, quoted in Lowell Reidenbaugh, *Cooperstown: Baseball's Hall of Fame: Where the Legends Live Forever,* rev. ed. (New York: Gramercy Books, 1999), 317. The nickname story is recounted in many sources. See Frederick G. Lieb, *The Pittsburgh Pirates* (New York: Putnam's, 1948), 229, and Donald Honig, *A Donald Honig Reader* (New York: Simon and Schuster, 1988), 483–84. Heights and weights of players are a common feature of printed and on-line baseball encyclopedias, as well as baseball cards. I have used *The Baseball Encyclopedia: The Complete and Official Record of Major League Baseball,* 9th ed., rev. (New York: Macmillan, 1993). This book is commonly referred to as the Macmillan Encyclopedia, which is how I will refer to it hereafter.

4. Hubbell, quoted in Abby Mendelson, "Here Comes That Big Poison!" in Pirateball.com: Official Web Site of the Pittsburgh Pirates, available on-line: http://www.pirateball.com/glorydays/features/WANERBROTHERS.html (June 7, 1999); "Uncle" Wilbert Robinson, quoted in Reidenbaugh, *Cooperstown,* 318. Lloyd Waner, a .316 lifetime hitter, certainly wasn't an easy out, but he comes up short by comparison with a brother who hit .333 lifetime with power. Practically anybody would.

5. Bob Broeg, "Booze, Plus Hits . . . Paul Waner's Specialties," *Sporting News,* March 28, 1970, clipping in the Baseball National Hall of Fame and Museum, Cooperstown, N.Y. (hereafter cited as HOF); Macmillan Encyclopedia, 1588.

6. "Lloyd Waner," in Total Baseball On-Line, available on-line: http://www.totalbaseball.com/player/w/wanel101/wanel101.html (June 7, 1999); Macmillan Encyclopedia, 599, 611–12, 829–30, 840–41; Hubbell, quoted in an untitled article by Bob Broeg in the *St. Louis Post-Dispatch,* July 27, 1982, clipping in HOF. Joe, Dominic, and Vince DiMaggio in the 1930s, '40s, and early '50s; Felipe, Jesus, and Matty Alou in the 1960s and '70s; and Ed, Frank, Jim, Joe, and Tom Delahanty, whose careers spanned the years 1888 to 1915. The comparison with the Aarons is whimsical, of course, because Tommie was a bit player for seven years while his brother Hank, the career home-run leader, also amassed a number of other lifetime records. He's third on the all-time hit list, ninth in doubles, second in runs scored, and first in runs batted in.

7. Herman, quoted in Mendelson, "Here Comes That Big Poison."

8. Willam Curran, *Big Sticks: The Phenomenal Decade of Ruth, Gehrig, Cobb, and Hornsby* (New York: Harper Perennial, 1991), 213; Macmillan Encyclopedia, 229–76.

9. "Records and Lists," in Pirateball.Com: Official Web Site of the Pittsburgh Pirates, available on-line: http://www.pirateball.com/glorydays/recordsGAMESBATTING.html (June 7, 1999). There is a separate URL for each record, e.g. ". . . /glorydays/recordsATBATS.html," ". . . /glorydays/recordsHITS.html," and so on. Craig Carter, ed., *The Complete Baseball Record Book, 1987* (St. Louis: Sporting News Publishing, 1987), 215–16.

10. Bill James, *The Bill James Historical Baseball Abstract* (New York: Villard Books, 1986). James, high priest of modern baseball statistics, virtually single-handedly established sabermetrics, which he defines as "a coined word, the first part honoring the SABR (Society for American Baseball Research), the second part indicating measurement. Sabermetrics is the mathematical and statistical analysis of baseball records." Bill James, *The Bill James Baseball Abstract, 1982* (New York: Ballantine Books, 1982), 3. See also John Thorn and Pete Palmer, *The Hidden Game of Baseball: A Revolutionary Approach to Baseball and Its Statistics,* rev. ed. (Garden City, N.Y.: Dolphin Books, 1985). Michael J. Schell, *Baseball's All-Time Best Hitters: How Statistics Can Level the Playing Field* (Princeton: Princeton University Press, 1999), is a provocative new look at hitting in which modern players supplant many of the perennial names on lists of all-time great teams.

11. Statistical charts in the author's possession. I used the "Bill James Electronic Baseball Encyclopedia," © 1995 Miller Associates, Inc., software program to work up the figures. Total chances and successful chances are modern sabermetric statistics that attempt to measure the value of the defense more precisely. Sabermetrics is single-minded in its insistence that *runs* are all that really matter in baseball, because runs are what determines who wins and who loses. So all meaningful statistics will measure aspects of the game in relation to runs: hitting and running in terms of runs produced; pitching and defense in terms of runs prevented. In defensive statistics, the number of total and successful chances tend to correlate with the range of the fielder, the amount of ground he can cover. The greater the range, the greater the likelihood of more successful chances, that is, plays that produce an out and therefore contribute to the prevention of runs by the opponent.

12. Traynor, quoted in Jim Laughlin, letter to Thomas E. Schott, Sept. 8, 1988. The table below compares Speaker and Waner's defensive statistics, figured as a 154-game seasonal average, a good example of the kind of analysis that sabermetrics can produce. The table shows that Lloyd Waner achieved twenty-four more putouts per season in center field than did Speaker, a significant amount. And the reason for it was his slightly greater range (the possibility of more successful chances per game) and surer hands (fewer errors).

Comparison of Defensive Statistics—
Tris Speaker and Lloyd Waner (154-Game Seasonal Average)

	Speaker	*Waner*	*Variance*	*Percentage*
Years	17.53	11.81	5.72	48
Games	154	154	0	0
Total chances	426	432	–6	–1
Successful chances	413	424	–11	–3
Putouts	388	412	–24	–6
Assists	26	13	13	100
Errors	13	7	5	72
Double plays	8	3	5	199
Fielding average	.970	.983	–.013	–1
Total chances per game	2.77	2.80	–.04	–1
Successful chances per game	2.68	2.76	–.07	–3

It should be noted that Thorn and Palmer gauge fielding excellence by a so-called *linear weight measure* called Fielding Runs. Without going too far down in the weeds with this, linear weights express a player's batting, running, pitching, and fielding abilities in terms of *runs contributed* or *prevented.* It is expressed as a single number—which can be positive, zero, or negative. This number equals the runs contributed or prevented beyond what a league-average player would contribute or prevent during that year. This average is defined as a baseline of zero. For example, in 1926, Paul Waner had a league-leading thirty-eight batting runs. This is the number of runs he produced by his hitting above what the average player in the league produced in 1926. That same year he also contributed seven fielding runs, that is, his defense in the field prevented seven runs above what the average outfield prevented in 1926. Both of the Waner brothers have positive fielding run numbers for their careers, and a quick look at the records in *Total Baseball* shows clearly how age took a toll on their fielding abilities. See John Thorn and Pete Palmer, *Total Baseball* (New York: Warner Books, 1989), 686, 1527.

13. Statistical chart in author's possession. Lloyd Waner is far down the list of outfielders when it comes to career fielding runs, however. The top man in this category is Speaker (248), followed by Ashburn (227), Max Carey (202), Mays (184), and Roberto

Clemente (173). By contrast, Paul Waner has forty career fielding runs and Lloyd has seventy-eight. See "Total Baseball On-line: Fielding (new)," available on-line: http://www.totalbaseball.com/ (Aug. 13, 1999).

14. "Harrah's Heritage," available on-line: http://www.harrah.net/heritage.html (June 13, 1999).

15. Honig, *Honig Reader,* 480; Broeg, "Booze, Plus Hits."

16. Unidentified newspaper clipping, dated Dec. 19 [1926?] in HOF.

17. Honig, *Honig Reader,* 481–82; Reidenbaugh, *Cooperstown,* 317.

18. Unidentified newspaper clipping, in HOF (n.d.).

19. Honig, *Honig Reader,* 483.

20. "Baseball Quotes" in Baseball Almanac, available on-line: http://baseball-almanac.com/quowane.html (June 7, 1999).

21. Ibid.

22. Unidentified newspaper clipping, in HOF (n.d.).

23. Ibid.

24. Honig, *Honig Reader,* 58.

25. Lawrence S. Ritter, *The Glory of Their Times: The Story of the Early Days of Baseball Told by the Men Who Played It* (New York: Macmillan, 1966), 288; Carter, ed., *Complete Baseball Record Book,* 146. Paul went six-for-six in his rookie year on August 26, 1926. The only other Pirates to accomplish this feat were Jacob Stenzel in 1896, Ginger Beaumont in 1899, Dick Groat in 1960, and Wally Backman in 1990.

26. Abby Mendelson, "Little Poison, Big Poison," World Series Section, n.d. [1970s], article in HOF.

27. Jim Laughlin, letter to Thomas E. Schott, Sept. 17, 1988.

28. Daniel Okrent and Steve Wulf, *Baseball Anecdotes* (New York: Oxford University Press, 1989), 126, 127.

29. Ibid., 127.

30. Howard H. Grossklos, letter to Thomas E. Schott, Nov. 12, 1988.

31. Unidentified newspaper clipping, in HOF (n.d.).

32. Ritter, *Glory of Their Times,* 279.

33. Stan Windhorn, "P. G. and His Pint," *Key West Citizen,* July 1, 1975, clipping in HOF. Paul also knew how to play the saxophone and fooled around with it occasionally; Lloyd admitted to being able to carry a tune on the violin.

34. Ritter, *Glory of Their Times,* 279.

35. Ibid., 280.

36. Ibid., 280–83.

37. Ibid., 283; minor league record in Craig Carter, ed., *Daguerreotypes,* 8th ed. (St. Louis: Sporting News Publishing, 1990), 299.

38. Ray Berres, letter to Thomas E. Schott, Nov. 19, 1988; "Lloyd Waner," in Total Baseball On-Line.

39. Carter, ed., *Daguerreotypes,* 298.

40. Ritter, *Glory of Their Times,* 284; Macmillan Encyclopedia, 240, 2412. The story of the Pittsburgh outfield in 1927 is an interesting one. Besides the Hall of Fame Waners and Barnhart, the team also had another player eventually enshrined in Cooperstown, the regular centerfielder Kiki Cuyler, already an established star and hero of the 1925 World Series which Pittsburgh had won in seven games. About midseason Cuyler ran afoul of Manager Donie Bush. Cuyler, already furious at being moved from third to second in the batting order, had just experienced a hitless game. He exploded. "To hell with winning," he raged. "I didn't get a hit and that's what counts." Bush promptly benched him, promising that he would never play another game for the Pirates as long as he was manager. Kiki didn't. In the face of loud fan protest and "We Want Cuyler"

banners all over Forbes Field, Bush never relented. Cuyler didn't even so much as pinch hit for the remaining sixty-nine games of the season. And he sat out the entire World Series, too. His presence in the lineup against the Olympian Yankees might not have mattered. But considering that Pittsburgh won the 1927 pennant on the final day of the season by a scant 1½ games over St. Louis, the break between the two men might have easily cost the pennant. Owner Barney Dreyfuss quietly traded Cuyler at the end of the season to Chicago for a couple of utility players, Pete Scott and Sparky Adams. The Cubs got one of the greatest bargains in the history of the game. Reidenbaugh, *Baseball's Hall of Fame,* 76. It's inconceivable, of course, that such a thing could happen today in today's money-driven game. Far more likely that the manager would get fired for ruffling the sensibilities of the star.

41. Thorn and Palmer, *Total Baseball,* 83; Lieb, *Pittsburgh Pirates,* passim.

42. Other outstanding players that came over to the Pirates were Deacon Phillippe, Chief Zimmer, Claude Ritchey, and Tommy Leach.

43. "Pirates Team History" in Pirateball.com: Official Web Site of the Pittsburgh Pirates, available on-line: http://www.pirateball.com/glorydays/features/WANERBROTHERS.html, http://www.pirateball.com/glorydays/history.html (June 7, 1999); Lieb, *Pittsburgh Pirates,* 41–47; Thorn and Palmer, *Total Baseball,* 83.

44. In 1995 the Cleveland Indians finished 30 games ahead of the Kansas City Royals in the American League Central Division. But the season was only 144 games long instead of the regulation 162.

45. Lieb, *Pittsburgh Pirates,* 99–110.

46. Ibid., 128–29; see also G. H. Fleming, *The Unforgettable Season: The Most Exciting and Calamitous Pennant Race of All Time* (New York: Holt, Rinehart, and Winston, 1981). In one of the many uncanny coincidences in baseball history, the only pennant race ever decided by a closer percentage occurred that very same year in the American League where Detroit bested second-place Cleveland by .004 percentage points.

47. Lieb, *Pittsburgh Pirates,* 135–56; David S. Neft, Richard M. Cohen, and Michael L. Neft, *The Sports Encyclopedia: Baseball,* 19th ed. (New York: St. Martin Griffin, 1999), 44.

48. Lieb, *Pittsburgh Pirates,* 216–18.

49. The single time the Bucs won the pennant during that time was in 1927. Technically, that team had five future Hall of Famers on it: the Waners, Traynor, Cuyler, and a twenty-year-old second-string shortstop named Joe Cronin. But both Cuyler and Cronin spent more than half the season on the bench. Four future Hall of Famers were Pirate regulars in 1926 (Traynor, Paul Waner, Cuyler, and outfielder Max Carey, with Cronin as a rookie who played in only thirty-three games). In 1928 and 1929 Traynor and the Waners played every day, but HOF pitcher Burleigh Grimes was a member of the pitching staff. Future HOF shortstop Arky Vaughan came on board in 1932. Outfielder Freddy Lindstrom brought the number to five HOF regulars in 1933 and 1934, but Grimes was back as pitcher in this latter year also, and Waite Hoyt, another HOF pitcher, was a Pirate from 1933 to 1937. See Neft, Cohen, and Neft, eds., *Sports Encyclopedia: Baseball,* 150–82.

50. Ibid., 154; Thorn and Palmer, eds., *Total Baseball,* 500. Lloyd Waner finished sixth in the balloting for MVP in 1927.

51. David Bauer, ed., "Sports Illustrated Presents Baseball's 20 Greatest Teams of All Time," 1991, 13; Howard Siner, *Sweet Seasons: Baseball's Top Teams Since 1920* (New York: Pharos Books, 1988), 6–7; Macmillan Encyclopedia, 234. As late as September 5, the two sluggers were tied in home runs, but Ruth hit three homers the next day and another thirteen over the next three weeks.

52. Siner, *Sweet Seasons,* 7.

53. Neft, Cohen, and Neft, eds., *Sports Encyclopedia: Baseball,* 123, 152; Siner, *Sweet Seasons,* 8.

54. Both quotes from unidentified, undated newspaper clippings in HOF; Morris Eckhouse and Carl Mastrocola, *This Date in Pittsburgh Pirates History* (New York: Stein and Day, 1980), 240–41.

55. David S. Neft and Richard M. Cohen, *The World Series: Complete Play-by-Play of Every Game, 1903–1989 Compiled by the Authors of the Sports Encyclopedia: Baseball* (New York: St. Martin's Press, 1990), 123; Ritter, *Glory of Their Times,* 288.

56. Ritter, *Glory of Their Times,* 289. Gabby Hartnett's dinger, the "homer in the gloaming," is one of the most famous in baseball history. It happened on September 28, 1938, in the bottom of the ninth at Wrigley Field in Chicago. The Cubs had gradually pulled even with the Pirates during the month and the pennant hung in the balance. With the score tied at 5, the Cub catcher poked a pitch from Mace Brown into the left-field bleachers. Brown had been one strike away from getting the out, after which the umpires would have had to call the game because of darkness.

57. Ritter, *Glory of Their Times,* 291; Carter, ed., *Daguerreotypes*, 298–99.

58. Honig, *Honig Reader,* 489.

6 • LET'S GO BUCS!

1. Quoted in Bob Smizik, *The Pittsburgh Pirates: An Illustrated History* (New York: Walker and Company, 1990), 82.

2. Quoted, along with the story of the incident, in ibid., 130.

3. Quoted in John McCollister, *The Bucs: The Story of the Pittsburgh Pirates* (Lenexa, Kans.: Addax Publishing Group, 1998), 181.

4. Smizik, *Pittsburgh Pirates,* 132.

5. See Richard F. Peterson, "Growing Up with Clemente," *Crab Orchard Review* (Spring/Summer 1999), 228-43.

6. A. Bartlett Giamatti, *Take Time for Paradise* (New York: Summit Books, 1989), 103.

7. Pittsburgh Pirates 1991 Highlight Video (Major League Productions, 1991).

8. Ron Cook, "Leyland's Epilogue," *Pittsburgh Post-Gazette,* September 26, 1996.

9. Robert Dvorchak, "Cordova Zeroes In," Special Section, "A Summer in the Sun," *Pittsburgh Post-Gazette,* October 21, 1997.

10. Steve Novotney, *27 Outs: The Story of the 1997 Pittsburgh Pirates* (*Pirate Report*, Ogden Newspapers, Inc., 1998), 13.

11. Paul Meyer, "High Fives for Ramirez and Pirates," *Pittsburgh Post-Gazette,* June 4, 1998.

12. Bob Walk, KDKA radio broadcast, June 3, 1998.

13. Meyer, *Pittsburgh Post-Gazette,* June 4, 1998.

14. Paul Meyer, "Trying to Regroup without 'The Kid,'" *Pittsburgh Post-Gazette,* July 6, 1999.

15. I was stunned and saddened on March 21, 2000, on hearing the first allegations against Al Martin, by then a San Diego Padre, of domestic abuse and possible bigamy. The allegations seemed so difficult to absorb, so incongruous with the Al Martin the public knew—with his role in Pittsburgh as a team leader, his dignity and apparent probity, and, yes, his sweetness. But this is a baseball essay. Martin's private life is beyond its purview, and would in fact require an essay in itself, one that an outsider is not qualified to write.

7 • AN UNFORGETTABLE TEAM THAT PITTSBURGH FORGOT

1. *Variety,* Nov. 7, 1979, 18; *New York Times,* Nov. 6, 1979, sec. 3, p. 10; *Washington Post,* Nov. 14, 1979, sec. B, p. 13.

2. Terry Pluto, "Red, White and Blue: The ABA," in *The Official NBA Basketball Encyclopedia,* ed. Alex Sachare, 2nd ed. (New York: Villiard Books, 1994), 180.

3. *New York Times,* April 4, 1967, 51, and Feb. 3, 1967, 22.

4. *Sports Illustrated,* Feb. 13, 1967, 56.

5. Ibid., Oct. 23, 1967, 47.

6. Ibid.; *New York Times,* Nov. 26, 1967, sec. 5, p. 3.

7. For a further discussion of early professional basketball, see Todd Gould, *Pioneers of the Hardwood: Indiana and the Birth of Professional Basketball* (Bloomington: Indiana University Press, 1998); Peter C. Bjarkman, *The Encyclopedia of Pro Basketball Team Histories* (New York: Carroll and Graf, 1994); Robert W. Peterson, *Cages to Jumpshots: Pro Basketball's Early Years* (New York: Oxford University Press, 1990); Robert D. Bole and Alfred C. Lawrence, *From Peachbaskets to Slam Dunks* (Canaan, N.H.: B and L Publishers, 1987); and Joseph Kane, *Famous First Years* (New York: H. N. Wilson, 1964).

8. *Pittsburgh Post-Gazette,* Oct. 24, 1967, 30.

9. Terry Pluto, *Loose Balls: The Short, Wild Life of the American Basketball Association* (New York: Simon and Schuster, 1990), 80.

10. Vince Cazzetta, phone interview with author, Jan. 10, 2000 (hereafter referred to as Cazzetta interview).

11. *Pittsburgh Post-Gazette,* Oct. 24, 1967, 30.

12. Ibid., Oct. 6, 1967, 27.

13. *Sports Illustrated,* Oct. 23, 1967, 47.

14. *Pittsburgh Post-Gazette,* Oct. 6, 1967, 24; Oct. 27, 1967, 30; *Pittsburgh Press,* Oct. 22, 1967, sec. 4, p. 7; *Sports Illustrated,* Oct. 23, 1967, 47; *Ebony,* January 1968, 72.

15. Cazzetta interview; *Pittsburgh Post-Gazette,* Sept. 20, 1967, 38.

16. David Wolf, *Foul! The Connie Hawkins Story* (New York: Holt, Rinehart, and Winston, 1972), 164.

17. *Sports Illustrated,* Oct. 28, 1963, 30.

18. Ibid., Nov. 15, 1999, 22.

19. Robert Slater, *Great Jews in Sport* (Middle Village, N.Y.: Jonathan David Publishers, 1983, 1992), 122; *Sports Illustrated,* Nov. 15, 1999, 22.

20. Wolf, *Foul!* 167.

21. *Pittsburgh Post-Gazette,* Dec. 21, 1967, 25; *Pittsburgh Press,* Dec. 3, 1967, sec. 4, p. 2.

22. Garry Davidson, *Breaking the Game Wide Open* (New York: Atheneum, 1974), 42, 43.

23. Pluto, *Loose Balls* (subsequent references appear as page numbers in the text).

24. Charlie Williams, phone interview with author, Jan. 12, 2000 (hereafter Williams interview).

25. *Pittsburgh Post-Gazette,* Jan. 17, 1968, 49.

26. Ibid., Oct. 26, 1967, 32.

27. Wolf, *Foul!* 161.

28. *Pittsburgh New Courier* (national edition), Nov. 18, 1967, 14.

29. *Pittsburgh Post-Gazette,* Nov. 8, 1967, 28.

30. Ibid., Nov. 30, 1967, 28, 38; Dec. 2, 1967, 13.

31. Ibid., Dec. 8, 1967, 32; Dec. 15, 1967, 26; Dec. 18, 1967, 37; Dec. 20, 1967, 26; Dec. 22, 1967, 19; Dec. 28, 1967, 22.

32. Ibid., Feb. 22, 1968, 22.

33. Ibid., Oct. 26, 1967, 32.

34. *Pittsburgh Press,* March 26, 1968, 36.

35. *1970 Census of Population and Housing for Pittsburgh, Pennsylvania, No. 162* (Washington, D.C.: U.S. Government Printing Office, 1972). Figures for the Lower Hill District were compiled by combining census tracts 303, 304, 501, 503. For unemployment rates, the percent of families living below the poverty level, and the percent of blacks, see pages 4 and 5, 100 and 101, and 148 and 149 respectively. The middle class areas used to compare unemployment rates were Spring Hill, Duquesne Heights, Beechview, Brookline, and Shadyside. For information on Banksville, Stanton Heights, and Squirrel Hill, consult tracts 2010, 1005, and 1402, 1403, and 1404 respectively. Census information on Lawrenceville may be found on pages 7, 103, and 151.

36. *Pittsburgh Press,* April 7, 1968, 1, 6; *Pittsburgh Post-Gazette,* April 9, 1968, 1.

37. *New York Times,* April 8, 1968, 31; Williams interview.

38. *Pittsburgh Post-Gazette,* April 9, 1968, 8; *Pittsburgh Press,* April 11, 1968, 20.

39. *Pittsburgh Post-Gazette,* April 20, 1968, 7; *Pittsburgh Press,* May 3, 1968, 35.

40. *Pittsburgh Post-Gazette,* April 25, 1968, 35.

41. *Pittsburgh Press,* April 27, 1968, 7; *Pittsburgh Post-Gazette,* April 27, 1968, 15.

42. Wolf, *Foul!,* 177.

43. *Pittsburgh Post-Gazette,* April 29, 1968, 30.

44. Ibid.; *New Orleans Times-Picayune,* April 29, 1968, sec. 2, p. 9.

45. *Pittsburgh Post-Gazette,* April 30, 1968, 21.

46. Cazzetta interview; *Pittsburgh Post-Gazette,* April 30, 1968, 21.

47. *The First ABA Championship,* videotape (Promark Sports Associates, 1997); *Pittsburgh Press,* May 2, 1968, 41.

48. *Pittsburgh Post-Gazette,* May 3, 1968, 33; May 4, 1968, 10.

49. Pluto, *Loose Balls,* 83.

50. Wolf, *Foul!* 180.

51. *Sporting News,* May 18, 1968, 42.

52. Pluto, *Loose Balls,* 83.

53. *Pittsburgh Press,* May 5, 1968, sec. 4, p. 1.

54. *Pittsburgh Post-Gazette,* May 6, 1968, 30; May 9, 1968, 41; *Pittsburgh Press,* May 9, 1968, 43; *Sporting News,* May 18, 1968, 42; *Pittsburgh Post-Gazette,* June 11, 1968, 22.

55. *Sporting News,* Dec. 14, 1968, 27.

56. Pluto, *Loose Balls,* 101.

57. *New York Times,* August 23, 1969, 22.

58. *Life,* June 27, 1969, 67.

9 • BASEBALL IN THE AGE OF DISCO

1. *The Bulletin,* Aug. 13, 1979, Willie Stargell Files, 1962–79, Giamatti Research Center (hereafter GRC), Cooperstown, N.Y.

2. Lawrence W. Levine, *Black Culture and Black Consciousness* (New York: Oxford University Press, 1977).

3. Rob Ruck, *Sandlot Seasons: Sport in Black Pittsburgh* (Urbana: University of Illinois Press, 1987); Jules Tygiel, *Baseball's Great Experiment: Jackie Robinson and His Legacy* (New York: Oxford University Press, 1983).

4. David Halberstam, *October 1964* (New York: Villard, 1994); Nelson George, *Elevating the Game* (New York: HarperCollins, 1992); Thomas Hauser, *Muhammad Ali* (New York: Touchstone, 1991); Elliott J. Gorn, ed., *Muhammad Ali: The People's Champ* (Urbana: University of Illinois Press, 1995).

5. John A. Parrish, "Lemons in the Sun," *Playing Around: The Million-Dollar Infield Goes to Florida* (Boston: Little, Brown, 1974), 101; Ron Fimrite, "Baseball 1979," *Sports*

Illustrated, April 9, 1979; Bob Adelman and Susan Hall, *Out of Left Field: Willie Stargell and the Pittsburgh Pirates* (New York: Two Contents Publishing Group, 1976), 9–10.

6. On black film, see Daniel Leab, *From Sambo to Superspade: The Black Experience in American Films* (Boston: Houghton Mifflin, 1985) and Donald Bogle, *Toms, Coons, Mulattoes, Mammies, and Bucks* (New York: Viking Press, 1973). On black music, see Michael Haralambos, *Right On: From Blues to Soul in Black America* (London: Drake, 1975), and Nelson George, *Where Did Our Love Go? The Rise and Fall of the Motown Sound* (New York: St. Martin's Press, 1985).

7. Roberto Clemente Files, 1960–69, GRC; Donald Hall with Dock Ellis, *Dock Ellis in the Country of Baseball* (New York: Simon and Schuster, 1989), 211.

8. Bruce Markusen, *Roberto Clemente: The Great One* (Champaign, Ill.: Sports Publishing, 1998), 221–25.

9. Ibid., 266; Roger Angell, "The Sporting Scene: Some Pirates and Lesser Men," *New Yorker,* Nov. 6, 1971.

10. Roberto Clemente Files, 1970–72, GRC; Bill Nunn Jr., "Change of Pace," *Pittsburgh Courier,* Oct. 30, 1971; Markusen, *Roberto Clemente,* 278.

11. Roberto Clemente Files, 1960–69, GRC; C. R. Ways, "Pirates' Clemente: He's Finally Arrived," *Sunday Herald Traveler,* April 9, 1972, Roberto Clemente Files, 1970–72, GRC; Pat Jordan, "Clemente and Oliva: Same Ends, Different Means," *Sport,* Aug. 1970.

12. *New York Times,* Oct. 18, 1972; Jess Peters, "Mr. Do It Yourself of the Pittsburgh Pirates," *Black Sports,* November 1972.

13. Roy Blount Jr., "Another Keel Haul in the East," *Sports Illustrated,* July 14, 1975; Robert Clemente File, Accident, GRC.

14. William Leggett, "Four Murderers in a Row," *Sports Illustrated,* July 3, 1972; Ways, "Pirates' Clemente"; Ron Fimrite, "A Half of Loafing Now Undone," *Sports Illustrated,* Sept. 9, 1974; "Stennett Gets 7 Hits as Pirates Win, 22-0," *New York Times,* Sept. 17, 1975.

15. Charley Feeney, "Playing Games," *Pittsburgh Post-Gazette,* Aug. 7, 1975.

16. Pat Jordan, "Three Rivers, Two Strikes," *Sports Illustrated,* July 8, 1974; Adelman and Hall, *Out of Left Field,* 151; Charley Feeney, "Playing Games"; Charley Feeney, "Mammoth HR Shots Are Stargell's Badge," *Sporting News,* Aug. 11, 1979.

17. Willie Stargell and Tom Bird, *Willie Stargell: An Autobiography* (New York: Harper and Row, 1984), 136; Leonard Koppett, "Pirates Open Their New Park, But Reds Celebrate 3-2 Victory," *New York Times,* July 17, 1970; Phil Musick, "Promos Give Boost to Bucs Attendance," *Pittsburgh Post-Gazette,* June 25, 1979; *Sporting News,* Oct. 30, 1971, Pittsburgh Pirates Team File, GRC.

18. Stargell and Bird, *Willie Stargell,* 136; Mike Downey, *Chicago Sun Times,* Aug. 8, 1979; John McCollister, *The Bucs: The Story of the Pittsburgh Pirates* (Lenexa, Kans.: Addax Publishing Group, 1998) 197.

19. Roy Blount Jr., "No Disgruntlements Round Here," *Sports Illustrated,* Aug. 10, 1970; Hall, *Dock Ellis,* 264; Adelman and Hall, *Out of Left Field,* 53–56.

20. Bruce Markusen, "Integration's Team: The 1971 World Champion Pittsburgh Pirates," unpublished manuscript; "The All-Blacks," *Sports Illustrated,* Sept. 13, 1971.

21. Hall, *Dock Ellis,* 188.

22. Roy Blount, "On the Lam with the Three Rivers Gang," *Sports Illustrated,* Aug. 2, 1971; Roy Blount, "A Loudmouth and His Loud Bat," *Sports Illustrated,* April 9, 1979; Arthur Daley, "The Nice Guy Who Finished First," *New York Times,* Dec. 2, 1971; Ron Fimrite, "Two Champs from the City of Champions," *Sports Illustrated,* Dec. 24, 1979.

23. Adelman and Hall, *Out of Left Field,* 21; Stargell and Bird, *Willie Stargell,* 65; Hall, *Dock Ellis,* 123.

24. Adelman and Hall, *Out of Left Field,* 91, 45.
25. Ibid., 145, 226.
26. Ibid., 147, 183.
27. Ibid., 19, 11, 52.
28. Ibid., 53, 112, 186.
29. Charley Feeney, "Bashful Bucco Al Oliver," *Sporting News,* Jan. 3, 1972.
30. Roy Blount Jr., "Now Playing Right: Manny Sanguillen," *Sports Illustrated,* March 19, 1973; Ron Fimrite, "Two Catchers Cut from Royal Cloth," *Sports Illustrated,* June 26, 1972.
31. *Black Sports,* Oct. 1972, Manny Sanguillen File, GRC; Dennis Morabito, UPI report, Jan. 11, 1973, Manny Sanguillen file, GRC; "Manny's Task," *Newsweek,* April 2, 1973.
32. Hall, *Dock Ellis,* 209.
33. Ibid., 161–63, 316–17.
34. Ibid., 22–23; Adelman and Hall, *Out of Left Field,* 187–91, 94.
35. Hall, *Dock Ellis,* 144, 186–187, 202–6, 215–16, 31–37; "Personalities: Ellis vs. Guard," *New York Times,* July 10, 1972, 41.
36. Ibid., 183.
37. Ibid., 174–78; Blount, "On the Lam with the Three Rivers Gang."
38. Hall, *Dock Ellis,* 26–27; *Pittsburgh Courier,* Aug. 28, 1971.
39. Hall, *Dock Ellis,* 270, 282–92; Blount, "Another Keel Haul in the East."
40. "Dock Ellis Suspended by Pirates," *New York Times,* Aug. 17, 1975; Hall, *Dock Ellis,* 297, 299.
41. Hall, *Dock Ellis,* 292–95, 300–306; "Pirates Lift Suspension of Ellis," *New York Times,* Aug. 31, 1975.
42. McCollister, *The Bucs,* 193; Larry Keith, "Now They're Burying the Opposition," *Sports Illustrated,* Sept. 11, 1978.
43. Blount, "A Loudmouth and His Loud Bat."
44. Ibid., 44; Keith, "Now They're Burying the Opposition," 31; Vito Stellino, "Sports Super Agent: He Makes Millionaires," *Pittsburgh Post-Gazette,* June 11, 1979.
45. Charley Feeney, "Unruly Fan Has Bucs Up in Arms," *Pittsburgh Post-Gazette,* June 25, 1979; Stargell and Bird, *Willie Stargell,* 190–91; McCollister, *The Bucs,* 189, 199.
46. "Sugar Bear, Formerly Gentle Ben," *Newsweek,* Aug. 2, 1971; Anthony Cotton, "Fine, Like Good Wine," *Sports Illustrated,* Aug. 20, 1979; "Willie's Dilemma," *Newsweek,* July 23, 1973; Jordan, "Three Rivers, Two Strikes."
47. Stargell and Bird, *Willie Stargell,* 130; Leon Altman, "A Special Man and His Special Way with the Game," *New York Times,* Oct. 21, 1979; Lacy J. Banks, "Big Man, Big Bat, Big Heart," *Ebony,* Oct. 1971; Howie Evans, "Stargell Takes Another Roundtrip," *Black Sports,* Aug. 1971; Roy Blount, "This Big Man Is the Cool Man," *Sports Illustrated,* Oct. 5, 1970.
48. Banks, "Big Man, Big Bat, Big Heart"; Blount, "This Big Man Is The Cool Man"; "Jess Sports Chest," *Pittsburgh Courier,* 2 Oct. 1971; Bill Nunn Jr., "Change of Pace," *Pittsburgh Courier,* Aug. 28, 1971; Willie Stargell Files, 1962–79, GRC.
49. Cotton, "Fine, Like Good Wine"; Stargell and Bird, *Willie Stargell,* 204–6; Pittsburgh Pirates press release, Willie Stargell Files, 1962–79, GRC.
50. Roger Angell, "The Sporting Scene," *New Yorker,* Nov. 26, 1979; Joseph Durso, "Pirates, Basking in Sweep of Reds, Await Bigger Test," *New York Times,* Oct. 7, 1979; "The Full-Tilt Boogie Buccaneers," *Time,* Oct. 15, 1979.
51. Joseph Durso, "Imposing Pirates Make Their Run," *New York Times,* Sept. 9, 1979; Dave Anderson, "Pops Hit One for the Family," *New York Times,* Oct. 18, 1979; E. M. Swift, "Flying into the Series," *Sports Illustrated,* Oct. 15, 1979.

52. Pete Axthelm, "Swingin' in the Rain," *Newsweek,* Oct. 22, 1979; Phil Musick, "Has Kuhn Fooled Mother Nature?" *Pittsburgh Post-Gazette,* Oct. 12, 1979; Hal Quinn, "The Boys of Shiver," *Macleans,* Oct. 22, 1979.

53. Ron Fimrite, "A Series of Ups and Downs," *Sports Illustrated,* Oct. 22, 1979; "Pops Go the Pirates," *Time,* Oct. 29, 1979.

54. "Pops Go the Pirates"; Murray Chase, "Pirates Take Series with 4-1 Triumph," *New York Times,* Oct. 18, 1979.

55. Bob Nold, "Transfigured," *Akron Beacon Journal,* Oct. 14, 1979; Phil Musick, "Stargell Takes Spot next to Mom and Flag," *Pittsburgh Post-Gazette,* Oct. 6, 1979; Leon Antman, "A Special Man and His Special Way with His Game," *New York Times,* Oct. 21, 1979; "Pops Won It for Bucs," *Macleans,* Oct. 29, 1979; Fimrite, "Two Champs from the City of Champions"; "Smithsonian Gets Stargell's Uniform," *Pittsburgh Courier,* Nov. 10, 1979; Mark Goodman, "Willie Stargell," *Family Weekly,* April 6, 1980.

56. "MVP Stargell Recalls Calif Projects Roots," *Pittsburgh Courier,* Oct. 27, 1979; Charles V. Feeney, "He's Low Key but High Caliber," MYBBWS Scorebook 1979, Willie Stargell File, 1962–79, GRC.

57. Roger Angell, "The Sporting Scene: Wilver's Way," *New Yorker,* Nov. 26, 1979.

10 • COAL, STEEL, AND GRIDIRON

1. Paul B. Beers, *Profiles in Pennsylvania Sports: Athletic Heroes and Exploits from Past and Present in the Commonwealth Where Sports Are Almost Everyone's Passion* (Harrisburg, Pa.: Stackpole Books, 1975), 40.

2. Ibid.

3. For a good overview of industrial growth and ethnicity in Pittsburgh, see John Bodnar, *Lives on Their Own: Blacks, Italians, and Poles in Pittsburgh, 1900–1960* (Urbana: University of Illinois Press, 1982).

4. Roger B. Saylor, *Scholastic Football in Southwestern Pennsylvania, 1892–1982* (Enola, Pa.: Roger B. Saylor, 1983), 1. Saylor wrote books covering the development of high school football in each region of the state. A statistician, he presents meticulous research on each school and conference. Although the books are indispensable for any research on the subject, they are limited in interpretation or anecdotal information.

5. Beers, *Profiles in Pennsylvania Sports,* 26–32, 40–61.

6. Bill Steigerwald, "Pittsburgh," in *The 1999 World Book Year Book* (Chicago: World Book, 1999), 315, 316.

7. See Bodnar, *Lives on Their Own.*

8. James Mulhern, *A History of Secondary Education in Pennsylvania* (Philadelphia: self-published, 1933), 439–75, 501–4, 510, 516.

9. Ibid., 513–16; see also Bodnar, *Lives on Their Own,* chap. 9.

10. Peter Levine, *American Sport: A Documentary History* (Englewood Cliffs, N.J.: Prentice-Hall, 1988), 53, 54; Steven A. Riess, "Sport and the Redefinition of Middle Class Masculinity in Victorian America," in *American Sport History: Recent Approaches and Perspectives,* ed. S. W. Pope (Urbana: University of Illinois Press, 1997), 188–98.

11. See Bodnar, *Lives on Their Own.*

12. Saylor, *Scholastic Football in Southwestern Pennsylvania,* 1, 105, 152, 162, 163.

13. Ibid., 1, 165–76; Beers, *Profiles in Pennsylvania Sports,* 40–61.

14. Saylor, *Scholastic Football in Southwestern Pennsylvania,* 1, 165 (indications of the loose structure can also be gathered by reading the accounts of the formative years regarding each individual high school).

15. Ibid., 1, 61, 105, 129, 152, 153, 160.

16. Paul J. Zbiek, "The Importance of High School Football in the Wyoming Valley,"

in *The History of Northeastern Pennsylvania: The Last 100 Years* (Nanticoke, Pa.: Luzerne County Community College, 1989).

17. Saylor, *Scholastic Football in Southwestern Pennsylvania,* 1, 5, 6, 53, 54, 55, 65, 77, 78, 84, 93, 94, 100–102, 108, 109, 124, 125, 160, 161, 182. Because of its rural location, most schools in Greene County did not initiate football until the 1920s, although Waynesburg played games sporadically between 1905 and 1916.

18. Ibid., 165.

19. Ibid.

20. Mulhern, *Secondary Schools,* 445, 446, 516, 517.

21. Roderick Nash, "Sports Heroes of the 1920s," in *Major Problems in American Sports History,* ed. Steven A. Riess (Boston: Houghton Mifflin, 1997), 324–29.

22. Beers, *Profiles in Pennsylvania Sports,* 20–39.

23. Ibid., 20–39, 45–49.

24. Saylor, *Scholastic Football in Southwestern Pennsylvania,* 165–69.

25. Ibid., 167, 168, 177.

26. Ibid., 217, 218.

27. Ibid., 220.

28. Zbiek, "Importance of High School Football."

29. See Bodnar, *Lives on Their Own;* and Donald L. Miller and Richard E. Sharpless, *The Kingdom of Coal: Work, Enterprise, and Ethnic Communities in the Mine Fields* (Philadelphia: University of Pennsylvania Press, 1985), for a good overview of the ethnic and community structure in the respective areas.

30. Saylor, *Scholastic Football in Southwestern Pennsylvania,* 106, 107, 168, 169, 177, 217.

31. Ibid., 45, 90, 119, 130, http://www.collegefootball.org, Arnold Galiffa, Leon Hart, Johnny Lujack; http://www.profootballhof.com, George Blanda; Beers, *Profiles in Pennsylvania Sports,* 88–92.

32. See Bodnar, *Lives on Their Own.*

33. Saylor, *Scholastic Football in Southwestern Pennsylvania,* 67, 106, 136, 137.

34. Ibid., 23, 87, 169, 170.

35. Ibid., 18.

36. Beers, *Profiles in Pennsylvania Sports,* 88–92; www.collegefootball.org, Mike Ditka, Dick Modzelewski, Babe Parilli; www.profootballhof.com, Mike Ditka, Johnny Unitas; http://www.cmgww.com/football/unitas/jubio/html.

37. U.S. Bureau of the Census, Pennsylvania, 17th (1950), 18th (1960), 19th (1970), 20th (1980), 21st (1990).

38. Saylor, *Scholastic Football in Southwestern Pennsylvania,* 170–73.

39. Ibid., 2, 11–46.

40. Ibid.

41. Paul J. Zbiek, "A Town and Its Team: High School Basketball and Community Development and Decline in Nanticoke Pennsylvania," North American Society for Sport History (NASSH) Conference, May 1993.

42. Saylor, *Scholastic Football in Southwestern Pennsylvania,* 170–78.

43. Beers, *Profiles in Pennsylvania Sports,* 40–49; http://www.profootballhof.com, Joe Namath.

44. Saylor, *Scholastic Football in Southwestern Pennsylvania,* 28; www.collegefootball.org, Ted Kwalick.

45. http://users.penn.com1967Egmb/skannon.htm; http://infoplease.com/ipsa/A0109347, A0109430, A0109463.

46. Saylor, *Scholastic Football in Southwestern Pennsylvania,* 175.

47. 20th Census (1980), 21st Census (1990).

48. *1999 World Book Year Book,* 514, 515.

49. http://www.pitt-gazette.com/sports_headlines/199909hsteams7.asp, Nov. 11, 1999, pp. 1–5.

50. Ibid.; http://piaa.orgsprtscntr/sprtscntr.html.

51. Beers, *Profiles in Pennsylvania Sports,* 88–92.

52. John F. Rooney, *A Geography of American Sport: From Cabin Creek to Anaheim* (Reading, Mass.: Addison-Wesley, 1974), 123, 133.

53. Mark Kram, "Passing on the Option," *Philadelphia Daily News,* Nov. 5, 1999, 150–52; John F. Rooney Jr. and Richard Pillsbury, *Atlas of American Sport* (New York: Macmillan, 1992), 64–67.

54. http://piaa.orgsprtscntr/sprtscntr.html.

55. Rooney and Pillsbury, *Atlas of American Sport,* 23, 26.

56. Lansdale Shaffmaster, professor of social science (early childhood education), interview with author, Keystone College, November 1987.

11 • ART ROONEY AND THE PITTSBURGH STEELERS

1. Myron Cope, *The Game That Was* (New York: World Publishing, 1970), 138.

2. Ibid., 122; *Pittsburgh Press,* Aug. 25, 1988.

3. Roy Blount Jr., *About Three Bricks Shy of a Load* (Boston: Little, Brown, 1974), 53.

4. Francis Couvares, *The Remaking of Pittsburgh: Class and Culture in an Industrializing City, 1877–1919* (Albany, N.Y.: SUNY Press, 1984), 32, 81. The numbers for Pittsburgh's population include the inhabitants of Allegheny City, a separate entity until 1907.

5. Coulter is often referred to as Coulters or Coultersville.

6. Couvares, *Remaking of Pittsburgh,* 159. Three Rivers Stadium was built in 1970 on a footprint that included part of the old Exposition Park; Deborah Weisberg, "An Irishman Named Rooney," *Pittsburgher* (Oct. 1977): 48.

7. Arthur J. Rooney, interview with author, July 30, 1980, Pittsburgh, Pa.; Rob Ruck, "Sandlot Seasons: Sport in Black Pittsburgh," Ph.D. thesis, University of Pittsburgh, 1983, 394–96; Sean Connolly, "The Rooney Touch," *Pittsburgh Magazine,* Sept. 1975, 37; Cope, *The Game That Was,* 124.

8. Cope, *The Game That Was,* 126.

9. Art Rooney interview.

10. Robert Markus, Tribune Press Service clip in *Steeler Notes,* n.d.

11. Roy McHugh, "Ever-Tough Dan Rooney a Hard-to-Beat Priest," *Pittsburgh Press,* Jan. 11, 1981, 2; Cope, *The Game That Was,* 125; Dave Anderson, "For Rooneys, a Funeral and a Wedding," *New York Times,* Jan. 18, 1981; Roy McHugh, *Pittsburgh Press,* Aug. 25, 1988.

12. *Pittsburgh Courier,* Aug. 19, 1939, 15.

13. Ruck, "Sandlot Seasons," 415–16.

14. Cope, *The Game That Was,* 125

15. Robert Obojski, *Bush League: A History of American Minor League Baseball* (New York: Macmillan, 1975), 272; Art Rooney interview; Charles F. Kramer, ed., *25th Anniversary Middle Atlantic League, 1925–1949* (n.d.).

16. Carl Hughes, "Father Dan Rooney Learned His Sports in District," *Pittsburgh Press,* July 18, 1948; Joseph F. Rishel, *The Spirit That Gives Life: The History of Duquesne University, 1876–1996* (Pittsburgh: Duquesne University Press, 1997), 211; Gary Tuma, "Steelers' Rooney in Retrospect," *Pittsburgh Post-Gazette,* Aug. 26, 1988.

17. *Pittsburgh Post-Gazette,* Dec. 25, 1982, 37; The Allegheny Athletic Association team paid William "Pudge" Heffelfinger $500 to play for them in what the NFL records as the first commercial transaction.

18. Bill Nack says in a *Newsday* column on Jan. 5, 1975, that the Hope-Harveys were founded in 1916. Most other accounts suggest a later date.

19. Cope, *The Game That Was,* 127.

20. Ibid., 127; Don Kowett, *The Rich Who Own Sports* (New York: Random House, 1977), 33.

21. National champions were chosen by a variety of publications and football authorities during these years. Pitt was a unanimous choice as the national champion in 1915 and 1916. It shared honors in the other seasons. *1998 Pitt Football Media Guide* (Pittsburgh: Geyer Printing, 1998), 134–41, 153–57, 164.

22. James P. Rooney, interview with author, March 30, 1982, Pittsburgh, Pa.

23. Roy McHugh, *Pittsburgh Press,* Aug. 25, 1988.

24. Dan Rooney Jr., "Mr. Rooney," a WPXI television special, Oct. 8, 1982; Rooney interview, *Pittsburgh Press,* July 19, 1981, D-2; Abby Mendelson, *The Pittsburgh Steelers: The Official Team History* (Dallas: Taylor Publishing, 1996), 22, 25; Ruck, "Sandlot Seasons," 392–93; Robert Dvorchak, "The Home Game," *Pittsburgh Post-Gazette,* April 7, 1999; Tuma, "Steelers' Rooney in Retrospect."

25. Bob Labriola, *Steeler News,* August 1988.

26. Mendelson, *Pittsburgh Steelers,* 22, 25; Ruck, "Sandlot Seasons," 392–93.

27. *Pittsburgh Press,* Aug. 26, 1988.

28. Weisberg, "An Irishman Named Rooney," 48.

29. Cope, *The Game That Was,* 130.

30. Kowett, *The Rich Who Own Sports,* 36; Parimutuel betting recomputes the odds to reflect the changing amounts bet on horses in a given race. The track and the state take a percentage of the amount bet and winners split the remainder. Prior to the partimutuel system, betting was done with a bookmaker at the track, a betting parlor, or on the phone. Once a bet was down, the odds did not change even if more money was subsequently placed on that horse. Nor did the state or the track take a cut of the action.

31. John Lardner, *It Beats Working* (Philadelphia: Lippincott, 1947), 58–59.

32. Weisberg, "An Irishman Named Rooney," 51; Dave Anderson, column in the *New York Times,* Jan. 18, 1981. Different accounts of Rooney's ride cite different amounts bet; Gannett News Service, Aug. 27, 1988.

33. Mendelson, *Pittsburgh Steelers,* 11.

34. Quoted in Cope, *The Game That Was,* 134; *Bulletin Index,* June 9, 1938.

35. Art Rooney interview.

36. Kowett, *The Rich Who Own Sports,* 32; Weisberg, "An Irishman Named Rooney," 50; Art Rooney interview.

37. Joe Ware, interview with author, June 23, 1980.

38. Weisberg, "An Irishman Named Rooney," 53; Blount, *About Three Bricks Shy of a Load,* 38; Ron Cook, "Chief among Us," *Pittsburgh Press,* Aug. 25, 1988; *Steeler News,* n.d.

39. Art Rooney interview; *Pittsburgh Courier,* Jan. 18, 1941, 17.

40. Ruck, "Sandlot Seasons," 427–28, 430–33.

41. Art Rooney interview.

42. Ray Kemp, interview with author, July 17, 1981, Pittsburgh, Pa.

43. Arthur R. Ashe Jr., *A Hard Road to Glory: A History of the African-American Athlete, 1919–1945* (New York: Warner Books, 1988), 106–9.

44. Mendelson, *Pittsburgh Steelers,* 26.

45. Weisberg, "An Irishman Named Rooney," 51.

46. *Pittsburgh Post-Gazette,* Aug. 28, 1988.

INDEX

INDEX

INDEX